Tender Moments
DIARY OF A FIRST-TIME MOTHER

To you own very tender moments . . .

Barbara Jenkins

Aug 17, '90

Tender Moments
DIARY OF A FIRST-TIME MOTHER

Vivianne Winters

Illustrations by Rose Margaret Braiden

Pacific Coast Publishers

Requests for permission to make copies of any part of this work should be mailed to: Pacific Coast Publishers, 710 Silver Spur Road Suite 126, Rolling Hills Estates, CA 90274-3695 U.S.A.

Published by:

Pacific Coast Publishers
710 Silver Spur Road Suite 126
Rolling Hills Estates, CA 90274-3695 U.S.A.

Library of Congress Cataloging in Publication Data
Winters, Vivianne
    Tender Moments: Diary of a First-time Mother
    Bibliography
    Includes section on Secrets of Successful Journaling
1. Infants—California—Los Angeles—Case studies. 2. Mothers and
daughters—California—Los Angeles—Case studies. 3.
Parenting—Psychological aspects—Case studies. 4.
Mothers—Psychology—Case studies. I. Title.
 HQ774.W89   1990   306.8'742   90-26469
ISBN 1-878374-35-4 Softcover

Printed in The United States of America

Dedication

As children, consumed with the fascination of the discovery of life, we loved our parents unconditionally. Yet, we never truly appreciate our parents until we become parents ourselves.

This book is dedicated to the unending love and commitment of parents to their children, and the ever-increasing discovery of children being more intelligent and more sensitive than we tend to give them credit.

Disclaimer

This book is intended to entertain and enlighten. Every effort has been made to make this book as complete and accurate as possible. However, there may be mistakes both typographical and in content. The author and Pacific Coast Publishers shall have neither liability for, nor responsibility to, any person or entity with respect to any loss or damage caused, or alleged to be caused directly or indirectly by the information contained in this book.

The people and events in this book are real. The names of those people who are not immediate relatives have been changed to preserve their privacy.

Preface

Being pregnant is a deeply emotional and moving experience. But having a baby is most definitely a life-altering experience. It is consuming and intimidating as well as incredible.

The first thing new mothers-to-be do is read—everything they can. They want to learn about how to take care of a baby, what to do in every instance, how to feed them, how to talk to them, how to raise them—everything about their life. Although women have been giving birth since the beginning of time, mothers still have no idea what to expect when their first born arrives.

In addition to talking to other mothers, I looked for a book that would provide the kind of information I needed. I needed to read about a baby's behaviors and activities from the moment of birth as well as the emotions and feelings of the mother. I wanted to know what to expect so I would know how to act and what to do in a specific situation. The book I sought also needed to tell me how a woman, in her words, balanced all the roles—wife, daughter, friend, career woman—in her life.

Alas, as far as I knew, this special kind of book did not exist. So for all future mothers, I decided this book needed to be written. With as much objectivity and subjectivity as I could muster, I put my pen to paper and wrote this book—a first-time mother's journal of her baby's first year.

I have tried to capture the events, the feelings, the interactions among my friends and family, and how my life has changed because of the miracle of the birth of my first child, Tiffany. I made it a mission to write as often as I could, to record every incident, good or bad, how I balanced (at least tried to) all of my responsibilities and my feelings about all of it.

I feel that new mothers and mothers-to-be need this information as a helpful guide to raising a baby, as confirmation that they are doing the right thing, and validation of their feelings. I hope that this insightful, factual and humorous book will be as much help to other new mothers as it was for me to write it.

Introduction

This book was originally written for my daughter, Tiffany— the gift of a "memory" of her early years, a time in her life of which she will have little, if any, recall; and a gift to be given to her in her adult life. Tiffany's first year of life was spent on a tree-studded parcel of land in a rural community of northern California, in a house that her father and I built ourselves. The entries at the end of this published portion of Tiffany's early life (the first thirteen months) are noticeably quite short. I had been hospitalized for meningitis during Tiffany's thirteenth month, and after release from the hospital was still very ill.

Vivianne Winters

July

I am in complete awe and amazement. After seventeen long "overdue" days and thirty-six hours of labor, I finally heard you cry. My glorious baby girl was here—alive and well!

As I said, you were seventeen days past your due date when your Daddy and I arrived at Hilltop Hospital at 8:00 am yesterday morning, prepared for Dr. Smith, my obstetrician-gynecologist, to induce labor. We worked through thirty-six hours of labor, but you refused to be born. We finally had to "help" you out—by cesarean surgery. I had waited and labored a very long time and the only thing I wanted or thought about was to hold you in my arms.

I was so excited and relieved when I finally heard you cry and saw your arms and legs jutting out at the world. I knew that my baby had finally been born. While I was in awe of the miracle of your birth, everyone else seemed only to be in awe of your size. Dr. Smith was amazed at how large you were.

"My gosh, Vivianne, no wonder you couldn't deliver this baby. She's a big girl."

"A girl!" My mind raced through thoughts of having a little girl, girls' names, dresses, ruffled panties, different colored baby nylons to match her dresses, hair ribbons, she couldn't have her own phone until . . . she couldn't date until . . . My mind came back to the operating room as I heard Dr. Smith calling my name.

9

"Vivianne? Vivianne? Are you with us?"

"Yes," I answered, "I'm with you. I was just daydreaming about having a little girl."

"This baby is bigger than I thought she'd be, I'd guess nine and one-half pounds."

Daddy said, "I'll bet she's ten and one-half pounds."

The surgical nurse guessed, "Nine pounds."

I didn't guess or really care at that moment about how much you weighed. I was more interested in getting to touch you and hold you. All I wanted was to feel your firm and alive little self in my arms. I wish I could have seen you up-close immediately after you were born, but the surgical nurse took you over to the corner of the operating room to a portable covered newborn bassinet. You were only about ten feet away, but it seemed farther. The nurse had to dry you off, wrap you up to warm you, and suction the mucous from your mouth and nose. The nurse then evaluated your color, heart rate, breathing, reflex response and muscle tone. These were all part of a newborn evaluation called the Apgar score.

The pale, bland green walls of the operating room, lined with cabinets full of surgical supplies and wheeled table trays for surgical instruments, seemed cold and foreboding as I waited for your Apgar checks to be completed. Only then would I be able to get a closer look at you.

It had only been a couple of minutes, but it seemed forever, before the nurse finally brought you over to me. However, I had to be content with a close look, a kiss, and to feel your soft skin against my cheek, because both of my arms were secured to the operating table. They had started shaking at the beginning of the surgery and had to be secured, so I couldn't wrap my arms around you.

I didn't really feel like your Mom until I had that kiss, and more than a one-second; look at your precious little self. You were soft, plump, and beautiful. I'm so thankful that you looked healthy.

That's all I ever wanted, for you to be healthy. But, you're beautiful, too. I mean, truly beautiful. My parents, your Grandma Ani-Poo and Popie, were afraid you might look like a little shriveled up being, a little "red raisin," as my father put it. You're not a little "red raisin." You're soft, pink, and round, though I'm sure I'd think you were beautiful even if you did look like a little red raisin.

The nurses prepared to take you up to the nursery where you would have your first complete newborn exam. Since your Pediatrician, Dr. Kelley, was off call this weekend, his associate, Dr. Williams, would perform your first exam.

The nurses prepared to transfer you to the nursery and your Daddy left the operating room to get the camera he had left outside earlier. He took your first picture from outside the operating room, looking into the clear portable bassinet as the nurses took you up to the nursery. You were ten minutes old. Daddy also took a couple of pictures of me through the operating room window as Dr. Smith finished my surgery. Daddy then followed you up to the nursery and watched as Dr. Williams examined you. Even though I knew I would see you again and hold you as soon as I could, I felt cheated by not having had more contact before you were taken away from me. I missed you already. Your Daddy would be with you until I could see you again.

The fatigue, and pain of labor are already lost in the back of my mind. I'm tired, but so eager to hold you. I want to see you, and to see that you have two arms, two hands, two legs and feet, all of your fingers, all of your toes—that everything is where it is supposed to be.

I had wanted so much to have a "natural" childbirth, or as close to one free of medication and intervention, as safely possible. I worked very hard to prevent unnecessary interventions. Dr. Smith worked right along with me. He knew how important it was to me. Each intervention that had to be introduced was done only when necessary, not out of convenience. We ended up needing almost every intervention, unfortunately; but it was truly needed. I passionately wanted to avoid having a cesarean, but there we were—mid-cesarean as you first greeted the world.

One good thing about the cesarean was it gave Daddy a chance to be the star. He was the first to hold you, the first to get a real good look at you—a privilege I feel should have been mine; but, Dads rarely get a chance to be in the spotlight in this process.

I had worried about your Dad feeling left out at this point in the delivery and beyond, as we planned to breast-feed. A number of the books I had read on pregnancy, childbirth and early life with an infant at home, said that Dads felt left out from the point of birth unless Moms did what they could to prevent it. This was said to be especially true when the infant was breast-fed, as the father didn't get to share in the feeding of his baby (unless or until the mother began to express breast-milk into a container so that the father and/or others could share in feeding the baby).

Well your Dad certainly wasn't feeling left out. He was the star—the first parent you really saw after you were born, a special bonus for him. I said that Daddy was the first parent that you saw, yes saw, to the best of your newborn abilities. (We requested that Dr. Smith use erythromycin ointment in your eyes at birth instead of silver nitrate. A baby's eyes are treated at birth to protect against infection that may have been present in the mother's vagina during birth. Silver nitrate has been used routinely for years, but causes the eyes to swell shut, some alternative antibiotic compounds such as erythromycin ointment have proven just as effective and allow the baby to see at birth.)

As Dr. Smith completed his "needle-work," the surgical nurse called the nursery to find out how much you weighed. Ten pounds nine and one-half ounces! Wow! Daddy gets the prize for the closest guess. He thought you were ten and one-half pounds. No wonder labor was so long. You and God knew we weren't going to fit a size ten and one-half baby through a size eight opening. You just had to wait for the rest of us to realize and accept it.

At 9:15 pm my surgery was finished. It was off to the recovery room for an hour of observation as my anesthesia wore off. I had been given an epidural block, which blocks all of your sensation from mid-chest level to the tip of your toes. The big plus of that type of anesthesia was that it allowed me to stay completely awake, alert and aware of everything that happened.

Daddy came down to the recovery room to see how I was doing and to tell me how you were. Frank, my recovery room nurse let your Dad come in to talk with me. Visitors aren't allowed in the recovery room, but Frank used to work with me in the coronary care unit. He stretched the rules as a personal favor, and we appreciated that. It was nice to have friends to take care of me during this exciting, yet stressful time.

Daddy and Frank wheeled me up to my room "a la gurney". I had a bed next to the window in one of the few rooms in this hospital with a spectacular view. We could see the night lights of downtown Redding from our hilltop perch. There were definite advantages to having a baby at the hospital where you work.

We had only been there a few moments before Jennifer, one of the nurses from the Nursery, came in and asked me if I wanted to see you.

Of course I do! **Finally!**

Jennifer came back with you, wrapped in a soft flannel blanket and wearing a pink stocking hat. You were so beautiful! So pink. I couldn't believe how much I loved you already. How wonderful it was to hold you. You weren't crying then. You were warm, smiling and sleepy.

It was so nice to be together. Just the three of us, enjoying the fact that you were there and so healthy.

As I put you to my breast to feed for the first time, I wondered if you would accept it. You latched on and started right in with your late dinner. Your suckling efforts lasted only a couple of minutes before you fell asleep, but you knew exactly what to do. I'm glad somebody on this team knows what to do.

July 22

This morning I woke up as a Mom! It's 7:00 am and a beautiful, clear, sunny day. It's hard to believe that I am really a mother, that I have a baby, and that from this point forward I am a parent. I wish I felt stronger right now so that I could get out of this bed and walk, or should I say waddle, down the hall to see you in the nursery. But I'm not supposed to get out of bed until this afternoon. My blood pressure dropped down a bit too far when my nurse helped me get out of bed to waddle into the bathroom a few minutes ago. The dropping blood pressure means that my "blood volume" is low. In other words, my body was too dry, from the loss of blood and fluids during labor and surgery. The plan is to soak up this IV bottle with the pitocin in it, then one more large bottle of IV fluid without the pitocin. The pitocin helps the uterus to contract more rapidly after delivery, which stops the after-delivery bleeding and draining faster. I'm also massaging my abdomen at regular intervals to further speed up the contraction. After my body has absorbed the two bottles of IV fluids my nurse will recheck my blood pressure when I get up. If my blood pressure doesn't drop too much at that time, I would then be clear for "take-off" to head down the hall to the nursery.

As I lie here feeling sorry for myself (because I can't walk down to the nursery to see you) I suddenly realized that no one has brought you to me since the first time I held you last night. I called for Gretchen, my nurse, and asked if she would bring you to me. Gretchen said you couldn't come to my room because they had to start an IV on you during the night and that you were taken to the intensive care nursery right after our first visit.

I was upset that I wasn't told during the night. I asked Gretchen why you had to have an IV and be transferred into intensive care. She told me it was due to your blood sugar being too low, that you were in no real danger—the IV and the transfer were done just to be safe.

My heart sank. I thought something else might have happened to you and they weren't telling me. I felt so helpless. I asked how soon Dr. Williams would be in this morning. Gretchen said he's usually in before 8:30 am. I would wait until a few minutes before 9:00 am. If he doesn't come in by the time his office hours start I will phone him.

This surprise announcement of your transfer to the intensive care nursery scares me. I do have to admit that, from the moment I realized I was pregnant, I have been scared by any little out of the ordinary occurrence that involved your well-being, or any threat to it. I feel very anxious and helpless right now. I can't move very well yet. I can't walk far enough to see you, and you can't come to see me. I'm afraid of what might be happening with you. I feel like you've been stolen from me before I even get to know you and tell you how much I already Love you. I wish I could hold you **now**. I will hold you this afternoon, one way or another.

Dr. Williams arrived at 7:45 am. He had already seen you and spoken to Gretchen, and knew that I was upset. He explained that large babies often have difficulty keeping their feedings down for the first day or two. That alone wasn't much of a problem; but that, along with your initial blood sugar test being low and continuing to run low, made your condition a bit more precarious. He had you transferred to the intensive care nursery and started an IV. As the IV and the transfer into the intensive care nursery were precautionary measures, he waited until after I had the opportunity to spend some time with my brand new baby. Transferring you into intensive care essentially made you off-limits to me, until I could walk down to see you, since you couldn't be brought to my room.

I felt a lot better after talking with Dr. Williams, but not completely relieved. I will feel less anxious once I can go to the intensive care nursery and see you for myself. My anxiety has eased enough for me to start thinking about something besides how upset I am.

I finished what I could eat of my breakfast at a little after 8:00 am and began looking at the "girls'" name chart I made when I was pregnant. I made a chart for "boys" and one for "girls." They were each about the size of a tabloid magazine. On them were listed in large, easy-to-read letters ten to twenty of the names your Dad and I were most interested in. I had decided that having these charts would make it easier for us to narrow down our lists together. This way we could both study the lists at the same time, say the names over and over and eliminate the ones we decided against, until we had narrowed it down to one.

We had looked at our chart of girls' names for quite a while last night, but it's so much easier to zero in on the best names now that I have seen you. As I was looking over our girls' names your Dad called to say he would be coming in soon. When he arrives we can work on selecting a name for you.

Daddy arrived and we looked at names again. We had two favorite first names—Tiffany and Carissa, but we haven't been able to decide on a middle name that we liked. We just can't decide which first name, or middle name we should choose for you. After deciding on it, against it, and saying it a number of times—we decided on Tiffany Carissa. It fits you beautifully. A beautiful and unique name for a beautiful and unique little lady.

4:30 pm: What a long day. I passed the blood pressure test—finally, so my nurse is taking my IV out.

She said I can take a shower now. The shower is down the hall, past the Nursery. I want to see you and **hold** you, but I don't have the energy to come and stay with you and take a shower. I'm too light-headed and noodle-kneed. The choice is obvious; I want to see you. I hope you don't mind a sticky Mommy.

I put on my robe and proceeded to waddle down the hallway toward the nursery. My whole body was weak and very sore. I could feel muscles aching that I didn't know I had. I certainly wasn't in danger of breaking any speed limits on my little trek down the hall. As I walked up to the window of the intensive care nursery, I could see you inside lying on an elevated platform with clear plastic sides. Above you was an infra-red light for warmth. You wore only a diaper and a pink stocking hat, in addition to the three cardiac monitoring electrodes and a temperature sensor taped to your body. I was so very sorry that you had to be in there.

I was only moments away from holding you, my sweet little girl.

Your nurse helped me into a rocking chair. It had a very low seat. I needed help balancing myself as I lowered my aching muscles. There was nothing the least bit graceful about my movements. I must have looked like a wind-up toy whose "wind" had almost run out.

Your nurse then disconnected you from the heart monitor and the temperature sensor, wrapped you in a soft flannel blanket, and placed you in my arms. How wonderful it was to get to hold you again. I had waited so long. Our close encounters, up to this point, have been too few and far between.

17

Once you were handed to me I could see the IV in your little hand. The needle, the tubing, the tape all looked so large, so out of proportion to your tiny hand. According to your nurse, if the blood sugar tests they have been taking every two hours stayed within normal range, as they had for the last three times, they would remove the IV and transfer you to the regular nursery. "Keep up the good work, sweet Tiffany."

Not only did I get to hold you, but I was able to feed your formula to you. You were on formula for a while, since I hadn't been able to produce any breast-milk with the electric breast pump yet.

Once I had been able to spend some time with you there, I no longer felt the near-paranoia that I had experienced this morning when I was first told of your transfer into intensive care. I was no longer worried that something else was wrong. Yours really is a small problem, thank goodness!

As I sat there in the intensive care nursery holding you, seeing the other little dears that were there with severe problems, with more of an uncertain outcome, I was a bit ashamed of my reactions to your situation. I was so thankful that you were healthy. You really are very sturdy and very healthy. You just need a boost to get you through your first days.

All I ever wanted was for you to be healthy. The fact that you are so beautiful and precious is a delightful bonus. I Love you, sweet Tiffany. I don't know if you will ever know how much **I love you** or how happy I am that you are here with us at last.

The nurses have been very patient with my questions, concerns and my profound slowness in feeding you. Your nurse told me that feeding you slowly would keep you from gagging and coughing up your feeding. If you recall, Dr. Williams said that large babies have difficulty keeping their feedings down. Now I have seen for myself exactly what he was talking about. I understand why he wanted you in intensive care.

You kept down less than half the amount of the feeding

that you had taken in. I started feeding you even slower, but I was feeding you too slow at that point. Your nurse asked me to go a little faster so you wouldn't lose interest and fall asleep because of the slow pace.

I didn't do a very good job of going faster. It was so hard to watch you cough and gag on your feeding. I fed you a little, you gagged, then coughed. I fed you a little more, you gagged, then coughed. I started to cry. It was so frightening and agonizing. I kept at it, but it was incredibly stressful to watch you go through such trauma just to eat. Your nurse was very patient and very supportive of me, and that was greatly appreciated.

5:30 pm: Your Daddy arrived as we neared the end of your feeding. I was so happy to have held you, fed you, and stayed with you so long, but I was also very upset at seeing just how hard it was for you to eat.

I'll be glad when your first two days of life are completed. I hope by then you'll be able to eat more easily. It must be horrible to be hungry and have to experience so much trauma, just to get the food you need. Poor baby.

After we finished feeding you I had to get back to my room. I had been with you for a little over an hour and my knees and arms had been shaking almost half of that time. I wasn't supposed to be up that long. Oh well, maybe no one else noticed.

At 7:30 pm Daddy went back to spend some time holding you. I wouldn't let him hold you when we were in there together during your feeding. Heck, I had waited so long before I could waddle down there to finally spend some time with you, I wasn't about to let anybody else hold you during that very special time.

When Daddy arrived at the intensive care nursery your nurse sent him back to my room to ask me if I wanted to feed you again as it was time—an offer I couldn't refuse. Maybe somebody around here has some "knee starch" I could use.

8:30 pm: we did a little better with your feeding this time. I wasn't as profoundly slow as I was at the last feeding. You stayed interested in your feeding and kept down a little over half of it. I wasn't as selfish this time either. I shared the feeding with your father.

When I was back in bed, after the feeding, I almost fell asleep. I was exhausted. I didn't have any more strength. I knew I would have to decline going down to the nursery for your next feeding. Daddy said he would stay so that he could feed and hold you. He certainly loves his sweet little girl.

It's just after midnight. Your Daddy came to tell me that you did well with your 11:00 pm feeding, that your blood sugar was still behaving itself and your IV was out. If you can keep up the good work your IV will stay out, and you will be able to get into the regular nursery. Then we can feed, visit and cuddle in my room, and with a bit more privacy! Keep up the good work, Tiffany. I'm sure that you can do it.

July 23

11:30 am: Dr. Williams told me that he transferred you into the regular nursery!

No sooner had he left my room with the news than your nurse came in to ask me if I was ready for my baby.

Absolutely!

After you arrived I couldn't get you to nurse. You kept hitting at my nipple, but you wouldn't take it into your mouth You started to cry, then scream. I felt frightened and very inadequate. I had no idea what was wrong. I was certain that you knew what to do—you had taken to breast-feeding so well at our first effort. Almost in tears, I called for a nurse.

Jackie, one of the nurses from the nursery, came to help me. She identified the problem as nipple confusion. The long easy-flowing bottle nipple you had been eating from while in the intensive care nursery had made it easy for you to draw the milk out; you didn't have to work for it. With breast-feeding the nipple doesn't go into your mouth as deeply, or flow as easily. You had to work harder to get the milk. You were rebelling against that short nipple and the extra work.

Jackie told me this wouldn't be easy to correct. It would take a lot of time working with you, even fighting, with your indifference at struggling with that less generous source of food to get through this problem. I understood, by your uncontrollable crying, that you were frustrated and hungry.

Jackie showed me a trick to stop your crying and frustration.

She told me to get your attention, to distract you from your troubles, by talking loudly to you as I raised you up and down a bit in my arms, while holding you about a foot in front of my face.

It worked. I would have been totally lost without Jackie's help.

I'm so frustrated. I feel like my joy at being a mother is equalled by my frustration and anger that almost everything I had hoped and planned for has not happened. Almost everything I had worked to prevent during your birth happened. The Pitocin, the rupture of the membranes, the internal fetal monitor, medication, and then to top it all off, delivery by cesarean. Then you ended up in intensive care! Now to think that I might not be able to breast-feed you! We have already had to concede to so many things—we can't lose this too. We will work this out. I want to breast-feed you. I want you to have the benefits of starting out with human milk.

We worked very hard at the next feeding. It was incredibly stressful on both of us; but you did finally take about half of a full feeding, judging by the amount of time that you suckled contentedly. That may not sound like much, but it was quite an accomplishment. Now that you have managed to get some nourishment at a breast-feeding, hopefully next time it won't be as stressful to attain the same or better results.

Shortly after we had finished the feeding, your nurse came to take you back to the nursery, so that we could both recuperate from our ordeal. As the nurse carried you away, my lunch arrived.

After lunch I walked down the hall to the nursery—the regular nursery. It was wonderful to see you there and not in intensive care hooked up to the cardiac monitor and the temperature sensor. You're such a big baby that you completely filled your clear plastic bassinet. The other babies had enough room around them in the bassinet to have their toys sitting on the bottom of it beside them, where they could look at them. You filled it so, that the two small stuffed toys that were in there with you had to be put on top of your legs and were leaning against the sides of the bassinet.

4:00 pm: I walked down the hall to the nursery again; I loved seeing you there. I know that Dr. Williams said that your feeding problem was common in large babies and that it and the low blood sugar problem should clear up in a day or so; but it was seeing you in the regular nursery that reassured me that we would be going home together and soon.

July 24

2:30 am: We just finished a long and intermittently successful feeding. The end result was, I believe, great. I was assured that you were satisfied with the feeding, that you had taken in enough breast-milk, because you fell quietly asleep as you suckled. I felt that we had gained some ground in combatting your nipple confusion throughout the last twenty-four hours. I hope we can develop this into a positive trend, that this won't prove to be an isolated success.

There is a war going on in my brain today. I want to ask Dr. Smith to let me stay in the hospital another day because I'm afraid to go home. At the same time, I'm afraid to ask him, since there is no real reason for me to stay. Technically, I feel in good enough shape to go home. I'm just afraid to. I can't put my finger on the fear exactly. It's completely emotional, nothing is really wrong with me.

I believe part of the problem is I'm not positive that Dr. Kelley, your regular Pediatrician who is just back from vacation, will discharge you today. You have done well for the twenty-four hours that you have been out of intensive care. I can't think of any reason that Dr. Kelley wouldn't discharge you. I'm just not positive that he will, and I don't want to leave this hospital without you. The rest of the fear is vague. I don't feel as though there is any reason for me to stay here, yet I'm very uncomfortable about going home. Maybe I'm afraid of my lack of knowledge about babies, about being responsible for my new child. Maybe I'm just overwhelmed. I just don't feel comfortable about going home today.

Maybe every first Mom feels this way. I don't know what to say to Dr. Smith when he comes in. I doubt that he would send me home if I'm not ready or if I'm afraid that you won't be discharged until tomorrow.

As I was still debating whether to ask Dr. Smith for another day in the hospital, he came into my room. After talking with me he asked me if I wanted to go home today.

"You haven't said so exactly, but I think I hear that you need to stay another day. So instead of leaving an order for discharge conditional upon Tiffany's discharge, I'll have my associate, Dr. Craig, evaluate you for discharge tomorrow." (Dr. Smith starts a three week vacation tomorrow.)

Overwhelmed with a feeling of relief, I mumbled, "Thank you, Dr. Smith."

As the night lights of Redding begin to stand out against the night-time sky, I'm feeling very good about having spent this day in the hospital. I feel like it was an extra day to gain confidence. This extra day was put to very good use. I feel that today's breast-feedings gave me more confidence in how to work with you, and how to handle your nipple confusion.

We will keep at it. We will continue to breast-feed. We will not give in to bottle feeding. (Can you hear the emphaticism in my words?)

Throughout the day I have also become better at transferring you into different positions—laying you across my shoulder, cradling you in my arm, lying you on your tummy, lying you on your side with a little bolster pillow behind you. I'm not good at it yet, just better. Better than terrible, but I'm making progress. Practice makes perfect.

To many people becoming better at transferring a baby into different positions may sound silly, but I have only minimal experience with babies. I didn't have any brothers or sisters to practice on. I had done some "babysitting" during junior high and high school, but none of my charges were infants, let alone newborns. My experience in handling babies was limited to a few days working in a hospital nursery during my nurse's training.

Being female does not endow you with an in-born proficiency for handling babies. (Is there, per chance, a special male friend reading this with you? If so, do you hear me young sir? When

it's brand new to we ladies, we are just as scared and feel just as inept as you do. It's important that you realize that.)

As I experience feeling more confident, more comfortable with handling you and feeding you today, I believe that lack of confidence is really what made me afraid of going home. It may also have been the physical drain of thirty-six hours of labor followed by surgery, the new "Mom-ness", or both; but my confidence has been slow in coming.

It's about 7:30 pm now, and am I ready for us to get out of here and go home. I hope Dr. Jeffreys will come by before we leave tomorrow. He's the plastic surgeon that your Pediatrician, Dr. Kelley, referred us to. I want to meet him and get his feelings on your little "angel tag" (the loose tag of skin on your right cheek). I want to know when he feels it can be removed.

The wee hours: You and all of your "roomies" in the nursery are having a particularly fussy evening, for whatever reason. The nurses can't figure it out. It isn't a full moon, and it isn't a north-wind (local superstition). No one knows why, but all of the babies are in an uproar. I wonder if you are all predicting an earthquake!?!

The nurses were having a hard time with a room full of totally upset, screaming newborns. So you and I spent a lot of time together, as did the other Moms and their babes. For us, it was a chance to make up for some of the time we weren't able to be together during that first twenty-four hours.

Jennifer, your night nurse, brought you in to me every hour and a half. A couple of times it was only an hour and fifteen minutes apart. At least that's what Jennifer said. I wasn't watching the clock.

July 25

Today we will go home, a new family. Outside it is clear, sunny, and hot—a beautiful day to start a new life at home.

I'm so glad we stayed here yesterday. It gave me more time to gain expertise in handling and feeding you, combating the nipple confusion you experienced, not to mention the fact that I wasn't sure you'd be able to go home with me. The uncertainty of whether you could go home with me, if I was discharged yesterday, was a real strain on my heart.

Dr. Jeffreys just left. He said he felt that we should wait until after your newborn period (the first three weeks), and you are in a period of stable weight gain before subjecting you to the mini-surgery of removing the angel tag on your cheek.

Dr. Craig is here: he just announced that he has written our discharge, our "walking orders."

I will call Daddy to let him know that he can come to take his new little family home. Then I'll call Grandma Ani-Poo and Popie. The other day Grandma Ani-Poo said she would bring flowers from her garden for all of the nurses, the day I was discharged from the hospital, and that they would also help us get settled in at home.

11:00 am: Grandma Ani-Poo and Popie arrived with two buckets full of flowers for the nurses. The nurses have all been wonderful. From the beginning of labor, right up to our discharge, they have been very caring, compassionate and patient ladies! I know I required a lot of patience during the last twelve hours of my rather long labor and also when you went through that first day of nipple confusion.

11:30 am: Daddy arrived and was ready to take his new family home. He and Popie took everything down to the car while I changed into some real, non-hospital clothes. When we were ready to leave the hospital for home, Grandma Ani-Poo and Popie left for lunch. They would meet us at the house to help us move in and get settled after we had a chance to take our new baby home, just the two of us, without an audience.

The next step was getting you ready. You should have seen us, trying to dress you in your homecoming clothes! Four hands trying to dress a tiny baby in tiny clothes. You weren't terribly impressed with our fumbling efforts.

The situation was pretty funny. Especially when we tried to put my father's crocheted lace baby cap on you. It was just too small for your substantial little self. It barely reached down to your ears! Undoubtedly, my father didn't weigh over 10 pounds when he was born.

Once we finally finished dressing you, you decided that maybe the whole thing wasn't worth it. You started to cry. It was about 12:30 pm and you could have been hungry. I tried to plan your previous feeding so that you wouldn't be hungry at this time, but those things seldom work out.

You were still crying as our nurse, Leslie, escorted us to the business office, via wheelchair, where we had to sign some papers before leaving. You cried so loudly and so continuously, that the office clerk, who had misplaced our paperwork, let us go without finding the papers. She told us she would mail out anything that needed to be signed.

Once we arrived at the car and finished wrestling your infant carseat into the correct position, it was time to feed you, or to try to feed you. I pulled out a bottle of the dextrose (sugar) and water solution I had brought from the hospital nursery— just in case. I didn't want to use it, since feeding you from a bottle now could make your switch to breast-feeding just that

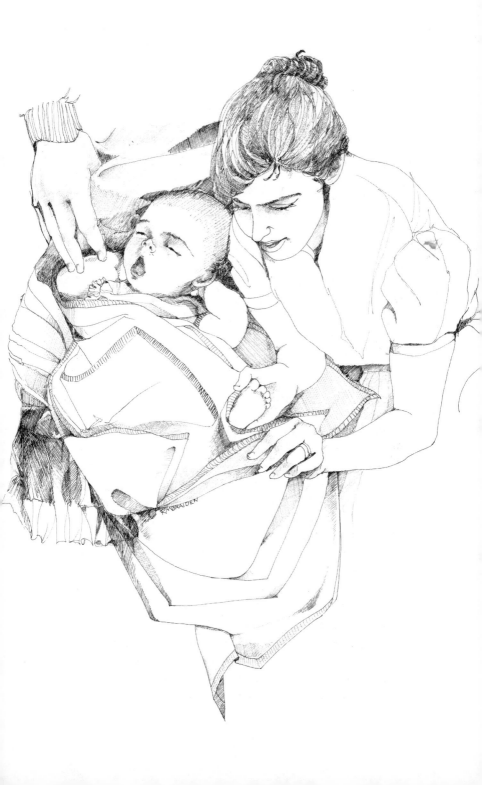

much harder, but you were hungry and I wasn't prepared to breast-feed you in public just yet. As I said, I didn't want to use the bottle, but at that point I was glad I had it. I let you "eat" from it as we pulled out of the parking lot and headed down the hill from the hospital toward home. As soon as the car started moving you quieted down and quickly fell asleep.

You slept all the way home, a twenty-two mile drive from the hospital in town to our home in the rural countryside. You slept until we rolled to a stop in our gravel driveway. We parked in the shade of the large oak tree near the kitchen door. Once the car stopped you started to cry again.

Your first visitors came bounding toward the car. They were our dogs Teaki and Libra. Teaki is a beautiful female golden retriever. Libra, one of the puppies from Teaki's litter last summer, is a willowy small-framed female black labrador. Libra is a remarkably gentle creature whose fluid, graceful movements are a pleasure to watch.

I hadn't seen the "puppies," as we call them, for five days, the length of my stay at the hospital. They were very eager to greet me, but your crying confused and upset them. They didn't know what to think about the strange, distressed sound of your cries coming from the back-seat of the car. Libra was intrigued and a bit overwhelmed at the same time. Teaki was very concerned about the source of the distressed cry. She strained to see into your carseat, but couldn't see beyond the coverlet we had used to prop you up in the seat.

Your distress needed to be tended to, but that would have to wait for a few minutes. The puppies and I had always been very close. I couldn't be away from them for five days and come home with a new "creature" (a possible replacement in their eyes) and walk past them with you in my arms. If they became too active, they would have to be shooed off and we couldn't do that to them without giving them some "lovies" first and a planned introduction to this new member of the family. The potential for jealousy in this situation was too great. I wanted their first experience with you to be positive—a sharing experience, not a closed "don't-bother-me-now" experience. On the other hand, I couldn't have them weaving and jumping around as I tried to walk to the house with you, and possibly get knocked down by their excited activity of wanting to find out what that noisey, wailing, little "puppy-like" thing was. So your Daddy and I played with the puppies for a few minutes before we took you out of the car.

You cried as you waited alone in the shade, in your carseat. Poor Tiffi, I'm sure you couldn't have possibly understood why you were left there for, what to you, must have seemed an eternity.

Sometimes it is hard to choose the **right** "mother" action, and the right "wife" action, the right "woman" action, the right "responsible pet-owner" action. Living multiple roles, as everyone does, causes conflicts. As you add new roles, especially significant roles such as that of a parent, the number and frequency of conflicts increase, which means there must be compromise between the roles. Today's difficult decision of whether to let you cry for three or five minutes as we tried to do the right thing by the puppies, and for your upcoming relationship with them was only the beginning. There is fear and anxiety—"Will I always—mostly—ever—make the best decisions?" I will do the very best I can.

After playing with the puppies a few minutes I crawled into the backseat of our little car, and pulled you out of your carseat. I held you, rocked with you, and sang to you until your tiny frazzled nerves were soothed. Then we crawled out of the car to introduce you to the puppies.

I was afraid to hold you down near my waist to let the puppies see you, in case they wanted to lick you. My waist level is about their eye level. I invited them to look at you while holding you at breast level. That way they had to stand on their hind legs to see you. I figured they wouldn't be as likely to lick your face if they had to concentrate on their balance at the same time.

The puppies behaved themselves beautifully. Each stood

on their hind legs to look at you. They were fascinated by you and your new-baby smell. They took turns peering at you. They each balanced themselves, without using me as a support, for long periods of time. This wasn't surprising for Libra; she is very agile. But I was impressed at how long Teaki maintained her balance. She is a young dog, but is a bit overweight. You cried periodically during the introductions, but you didn't seem frightened. We praised the puppies for their terrific behavior.

Once inside the house, I looked for our kitty, Mildieu, without whom our family introductions wouldn't have been complete. We found Mildieu sitting in a spot of sunlight on the carpet in the family room. She looked at you with reserved interest, befitting of feline aristocracy. But when we sat down right next to her, she became intrigued. She curiously, but gently, sniffed at your face and hands as she scanned your entire self with her eyes. As we dismissed ourselves from her company, she decided to follow us, but only after a short, yet appropriate, period of disinterest in what we might be doing next.

After introducing you to Mildieu, I took you directly to your nursery. I couldn't wait to show it to you. I had made your diaperstacker, your crib bumpers, your quilt and your curtains myself, out of a soft material with wide pastel-shaded rainbow stripes, where each pastel color blended softly into the next shade. I had shopped long and hard for the "perfect" fabric for your nursery. I was very proud of how lovely it was, and so eager to show it to you. I suppose that was sort of silly, as you weren't the least bit interested. What you were interested in was lunch which was overdue at that point. Grandma Ani-Poo and Popie arrived just as you started to breast-feed. Popie helped Daddy unload the car.

Grandma Ani-Poo brought what I needed into the nursery as you feasted fervently. A successful breast-feeding! What a victory! Success at home, without help from hospital personnel. We will be able to continue to breast-feed you. I'm certain of it.

By early evening it had started to cool outside. We were pretty much settled into the house. During the afternoon Grandma Ani-Poo had fixed a casserole for Daddy and me for dinner. After Grandma Ani-Poo put the casserole into the oven, she and Popie left for home so we could spend our first evening at home together, just the three of us. Daddy and I appreciated that a lot. Soon afterward Daddy had to leave to make some phone calls at a neighbor's house. For some unknown reason, our phone just stopped working. It was just Tiffany and Mommy at home alone. This was the first time we had ever been completely alone. Holding your beautiful soft, yet sturdy, little body made me cry.

I'm so incredibly happy that you are here, here where I can hold you in my arms. Sometimes it's hard for me to believe that you're real. I still find it hard to believe that the hospital sent you home with unknowledgeable me and trusts me to take proper care of you, and give you the support and direction that you need to grow and flourish. I can promise you that your Daddy and I will do our very best, but the prospect still scares me.

We know virtually nothing about little ones, although we now own approximately twenty books on newborn and infant care, parenting tips, "identify-that-rash" manuals, and assorted child-rearing books, not to mention the pregnancy and childbirth books. I've read through all of them at least once. The books on newborn and infant care I've read three to four times.

I know that reading all of these books won't make me a good mother or an insightful parent, but when you consider the fact that I know nothing, I couldn't help but learn something about babies and mothering by studying them.

Today marked the first time for your Daddy and I to each change your diaper. It was amazing that when we were in the hospital you just never needed a change during the times you were with us, your nurses had done all of your diaper changes. I didn't even realize that until I changed your diaper this morning. Our first diaper change on our own baby seemed such an awesome concept, but I'm sure that we will each have twenty-five or so changes to our credit within a week.

July 26

Good morning, sweet Tiffany, this is the first time that you greeted a new day, a beautiful and sunny day in your own home. You are still here. You're not a dream. You are real, my baby girl. Sometimes when I hold you and look at you, it's as though I'm holding and looking at myself, as though you aren't Tiffany, but a little Vivianne, a little version of me, a piece of me. It's very strange, but I can't always separate from you. I can't always see you as an individual person and not some type of ethereal extension of myself. But you are not me. You are Tiffany. My daughter. Your own person. I'm in awe of your very existence. I will have to work on internalizing that—to identify that you are a person, separate from myself.

There weren't any nurses to come and take you back to the nursery so that I could sleep in a little this morning. I was up feeding you much of the night. In both my reading and my talks with Dr. Smith, I learned that if you decide to breast-feed you need to understand that the baby will eat approximately every two to three hours instead of every three to four hours, as a formula-fed baby would; and that it could be as often as every hour and a half.

What the books and the Doctors don't tell you is that the time of that frequency starts at the end of the feeding. If it takes thirty minutes to burp you and get you settled and asleep before I can go back to bed or back to whatever, I must subtract that time from the amount of time until the next feeding. The point being that the opportunity for rest between feedings isn't as long as it sounds. Every two to three hours becomes every one and one-half to two and one-half hours—sometimes every one to two hours. That thirty or so minute difference may not sound like much but added up through the night; night after night, that's going to amount to something—exhaustion. I will have to learn to rest during the day when I have the chance. I guess I'm looking for a little sympathy. But in lieu of that, I'll just bathe myself in the sheer joy of having you here.

Today we credit you with your first smile! We felt sure you smiled when you were still in the hospital. We didn't make it official earlier, since the nurses were in agreement that it was only "gas" at this age.

But today, you definitely smiled at me when I drew my finger down the center of your forehead, off of your nose like a little ski jump, and dotted you on the chin. You did it twice! And that's only part of it. I told your Daddy about the news. A few hours later, Daddy was walking around the house with you on his shoulder, trying to get you to fall asleep. He took you into the master bedroom and showed you one of the paintings on the wall. While you were contemplating the picture, Daddy did the very same thing on your face that I'd done earlier. You smiled for him, too. I consider that scientific proof of a real smile, not just a lot of hot air.

New babies certainly are a lot of work. There are seven or more diaper changes each day, and that's only the beginning. The only method a baby has of communicating her needs is to cry. When your baby cries, at least at the beginning of your parenting experience, you start checking for possible sources of the problem, one by one—a process of elimination. The order of elimination varies from person to person, and may vary from incident to incident. One possibility is a dirty diaper, so you check the diaper for "deposits." This is a real favorite with parents and others. It is the first or second thing people will try in their repertoire. It is funny, because the baby really couldn't care less about diaper deposits, unless the contents of a wet diaper is causing her to be too cold. Then you try feeding the baby, try burping baby, soothing baby, walking with baby on your shoulder, singing to baby, playing with baby. You just keep trying things until you identify and solve the problem. Or if you aren't able to identify the problem—then you realize you really have a problem. Where do you go from here? You start over, try something else, feel incompetent, or cry; it all depends upon how refreshed or how exhausted you are at the time. For those of us whose knowledge of infant care comes from reading only, rather than experience, we spend more time fumbling and fretting than we do producing results.

July 28

As we held and talked to you while sitting on the sundeck this morning, you amazed us by bringing your fist to your face to hold your pacifier against your mouth. Purposeful movements at age seven days? You are such a smart little critter. How could you be doing things like that at such an early age? I'm so amazed and happy that you are here and healthy. There are times that I just cry when I hold you. I am in complete awe of you.

July 29

This morning I wanted to find out how much you weighed. I stepped onto the bathroom scale to weigh myself. You were sitting in your infant seat on the floor. Then I picked you up and stepped back onto the scale. I weighed twelve pounds more when I was holding you—so your weight, by subtraction, is about twelve pounds. We must get a baby scale to be more accurate about your weight. Ounces are important, half-ounces are important! (Notice how I cleverly did not tell you how much I weighed?)

It's early evening and we have just finished your dinner "in rotation." Rotation being, Tiffany eats as dinner cooks, and Mommy sets the table. Tiffany is full and content. Daddy and I sit down to eat and Tiffany starts to cry. Mommy gets up and soothes Tiffany while Daddy finishes his meal. Then Daddy soothes Tiffany while Mommy finishes her meal. Once everyone has eaten, Tiffany is happy again. The true reason why babies start to cry or fuss when Mom and Dad sit down to eat is, so far, an insoluble curiosity and point of frustration to we new parents.

During your after-dinner diaper change I noticed a small amount of bleeding at the base of your umbilical cord stump. That makes the second time today that we've noticed some bleeding. At the first incident, earlier today, I had deemed that you should wear "designer" diapers—custom cut to allow extra room around your stump. Tonight, we ended up leaving your diaper off altogether, to prevent it from chafing against your stump during the night. I put two lap pads in your crib hammock, put a cloth diaper on you and pinned it down at your thigh level and swaddled you expecting to change the diaper and lap pads each time you "piddled" or "pookied" (our baby language word for a bowel movement.) I was just too worried about your cord to be comfortable with you wearing a diaper, even a cut down diaper tonight.

Have you ever wondered where people come up with the
"pet words" they use when talking to babies. I've come up with
a couple myself, but I couldn't guess where they came from;
they just found their way into my mind somehow.

If someone wanted to collect the information, they might
compile *Baby Bylines- A Dictionary for Friends of People with
Babies.* The entries would look something like:

Bottle: "bah-bah"; "bott-bott";
Bowel movement: "boo-boo"; "pookie"; "poo-poo"; "poty";
Dirty: "dir-dirs"
Milk: "mikkie"; "moo"
Urinate: "tee-tee"; "tinkle"; "wee-wee."

Often even the most reserved of women and the surliest
of men will convert to a conversation of "babyese" (baby talk)
when talking to a baby—particularly their own baby.

July 30

Your umbilical cord stump is better this morning, no
redness or bleeding, so we have you wearing your "designer"
diapers again. One more crisis solved, at least temporarily.
Now let's go outside and enjoy the beautiful summer day.

After spending some time at the park, at the mall and
visiting with friends, we headed for home. Your Daddy and I
relaxed with you in the family room and enjoyed the air- conditioning on this hot afternoon. We delighted in watching your activities. We put your pacifier in your mouth and noticed that
you reached to hold it a different way than your usual. You
hooked your first three fingers behind the plate of the pacifier
and pushed it toward your face, holding it with both hands. In
the past you brought your whole fist to the plate of the pacifier,
to hold it against your face. Your Dad and I smiled at each
other, bubbling with exclamations of what a bright baby you

were. Imagine using your fingers at the ripe old age of nine days. Next, you'll be playing the piano!

Isn't it amazing how parents speculate on their children's possible future accomplishments. It isn't surprising that we would speculate about them, but how we speculate and always toward the apex of that particular endeavor. Not that our child may become an attorney, or even a judge, but a Supreme Court Justice; not become just a dancer, but a prima ballerina; and not just develop the ability to play the piano, but that they will "play" Carnegie Hall.

July 31

Today you went through your baby exercises for the first time. The purpose of the exercises is to relax your tight little muscles; tight from being wadded up in a little ball inside of me for so many months. The exercises involve gently moving your fingers, wrists, elbows, shoulders, feet, knees, hips, etc. through their range of motion. They will decrease the residual muscle tension sooner than would happen otherwise on their own. And pave the way for you to move through new baby accomplishments as soon as you are ready.

You allowed me to move you through the exercises, but I wouldn't say you enjoyed them. You didn't fuss or protest verbally, but you were very stiff, and reluctant to move. Of course, what should I expect from a first "work-out?" You didn't understand what I was doing and resisted many of the motions. There was confusion in your expression as I continued to take your arms and legs through the exercise motions that you resisted. I hope you will come to enjoy these exercises soon.

August

August 1

As you, Mildieu and I sit here on the couch, I'm running the events of the day through my mind. It pretty much amounted to cleaning the house, when I could—one task at a time, throughout the day. I just realized that you went a long time between feedings today before asking for a refill. It's so rare for you to take a "real" nap, of any duration, during the day, that I just busied myself using the time to catch up on undone chores. I should have noticed and awakened you earlier from your nap, to increase the number of feedings you had today. Please, excuse me.

August 2

We just finished your first "light-of-day" feeding. I played with you on my lap, pinching up your lips, your cheeks—making silly faces with your sweet round little face, and interjecting "duck" sounds and other silly and nonsense noises. We were having a good time just being silly. During our play you broke out in a hearty and unmistakable "aha-ha-aha," launched with an enormous smile. I had imagined that when I first heard you laugh, it would be very small and high-pitched, a squeaky little noise. I was totally amazed when I heard a deep, laughing sound coming from such a little person. Your laugh is beautiful and captivating.

You flowed with me today as I took your arms and legs through the motions of your baby exercises. You seem to enjoy them now instead of just tolerating them. The radio was on. With the music in the background, the fluid-like quality of our movements gave me the illusion that I was dancing with you. You grinned and smiled through most of "the dance."

You ate more often today, and don't seem to be any the worse for yesterday's fewer feedings. Good!

August 3

It's mid-morning and already very hot. I'm certain it will get to be over one hundred degrees today. Reluctantly, I had you wearing just a t-shirt, pastel of course, with your diaper, instead of the drawstring sleeper with mitted cuffs. I say reluctantly, because I've noticed your nails are starting to grow past that little ridge of flesh at the end of your finger.The obvious solution would be to cut your fingernails instead of worrying about mitted cuffs, but I'm afraid to cut your nails out of fear I will cut you. You spend most of the time with your hand drawn into a fist, and resist or withdraw your fingers from any attempted manipulation beyond just allowing you to grasp my finger. I'm afraid that you will wiggle or twist at the wrong time, and I might end up cutting the tips of one, or more, of your fingers. What a horrible, chilling thought! Good grief, another new parent crisis. I've got to work on this. I can't keep you wearing mitted cuffed sleeves or mittens over your hands for the rest of your life.

Your umbilical cord stump fell off! Hurray! That in itself reduces my nervous tension level by about thirty percent. I no longer have to custom cut diapers for it or worry about tension across it that might cause it to bleed and possibly become infected. What a relief.

Should I worry about you not repeating a new action? I worry about everything else, why not that? It has been four days since you first held your pacifier with your fingers. I haven't seen you do that again. It's back to the "whole fist" trick. Everything you do, and everything you don't do is significant, or potentially significant. I don't always know which is which. First-time mothers—in a constant state of fret over something.

August 4

I'm psyched up for trying to cut your fingernails today. Wish us luck, and me a steady hand.

It's done. Your nails are trimmed. Far from a professional job. But they are trimmed, and you still have all of your fingers. You did start out with nine, didn't you!?!

August 5

This was your first day without custom-cut diapers. Your "newly-debuted" belly button was healing. I am pleased to announce that your little belly button is an "inny," as opposed to being an "outy." I was hoping that you would have an inny. Innys are so much better looking, especially for girls.

Maybe I shouldn't expose myself to possible untold embarrassment but what the heck? During my pregnancy, I asked

Dr. Smith if I could specify that I wanted my baby to have an inny-type belly button? He told me, as he giggled, that ninety-plus percent of the people do have innys, but that you can't specify your preference. What you get is what you get. Well, as far as I was concerned, it was worth asking. I wanted to know.

I gave you your first tub bath today in the little sink-insert tub. You screamed bloody murder the entire time. Grandma Ani-Poo and Popie watched, listened and tried to help. They stopped watching about half-way through, thinking that the size of your audience had an influence on your feelings about the bath. I had covered you with the little gown I'd taken off of you before your bath, thinking you might be crying because you didn't like being totally undressed. It didn't seem to make one bit of difference. You continued to scream until you felt hot and your skin color went from red to purple.

You did survive the bath. So did I, despite the fact I felt "lower than a lizard's lungs" for putting you through such an ordeal. I felt part of your protesting was due to my inept technique. Dare I tell you that you went "pookie" in the bath water and that Grandma Ani-Poo changed it mid-way? I would never have been able to give you a decent bath alone. Of course, I rather doubt whether having a decent bath would have mattered to anyone but me.

By the time you read this, bathing will, no doubt, will be one of your favorite pastimes, and you'll find this whole episode hard to believe.

After such physical and emotional exertion on your part, everyone theorized that you would fall into an exhausted sleep once you finally realized that the world wasn't coming to an end. You, however, had other ideas. You never did sleep much this evening or any other night. You were eating almost every two hours. You gulped your "Mother's milk" and spit up a fair amount of each feeding. You also had non-stop hiccups at each feeding.

August 6

My gosh you're growing—already! I noticed before that your hair was getting longer in the back, now it's getting longer in the front, too. Your fingernail beds are definitely longer. Your nails, especially your thumb-nails, keep growing. As you slept , in my arms, I was distressed; distressed that I haven't yet been able to catch you in the right state of consciousness, and have both hands free to cut your nails again. I must work on that one!

August 7

I'm sitting here watching the Olympics, with you asleep in my lap. I'm sure that you're dreaming; you made some "o-o-o-o-oh" sounds and "grunts," and laughed once. All the time you were moving—one hand, one foot, an arm or a leg—as though you were doing something in your dream. How can such a little creature dream!?! What little baby things could you be dreaming about? Soft blankets, warm hugs, loving smiles? What do babies dream about?

Lately I've noticed that your hands, arms and particularly your legs, have been more relaxed. I believe this was in response to your baby exercises. Recently you've spent more time with your arms stretched out, your hands relaxed, and your legs in greater degrees of extension. I'm pleased that you responded so well to your exercises.

Speaking of pleased, I am currently very pleased and

impressed with myself. I finally cut all of your fingernails at the same time! For me that is an accomplishment!

August 9

Throughout the mid-morning, you were awake and happy, watching and enjoying everything and everyone. Then you fell asleep. At 5:30 pm you were still asleep. If you aren't more active and awake some of the night, I'll be worried about you and want to check it out with Dr. Kelley in the morning.

August 10

This morning I stopped worrying about you since you had fussed a couple of times during the night. Dr. Kelley was spared one call from an over-reactive new Mom. Today you were back to your usual, occasionally fussy, sometimes sleepy, self. A relief for me.

Tomorrow will be your first Doctor's appointment. You need to have another bath before your appointment. I hope Daddy can help us with your bath this afternoon. He hasn't been in on that yet. I want him to watch me give you a bath first so he can see for himself that you scream bloody murder. I don't want him to try to give you a bath by himself and think that you're only screaming because he's giving you the bath and think that you're quiet and cooperative when Mom does it.

The day was almost over by the time we put you to bed. We weren't able to give you a bath today. It just didn't work out. Looks like I'll be giving you one alone tomorrow. That should prove very interesting. Grandma Ani-Poo and Popie were here for the others. I always ended up needing them to do something. I know I can do it by myself without waterlogging you, but I'll miss having the back-up. Isn't it remarkable that something like bathing an infant alone should send me into such a tizzy.

August 11

I was out of bed early; 6:30 am, to ensure getting everything done in time for your Doctor's appointment, I hope. Today was the day for your "five-mile check-up," and it's a twenty-two mile drive to the Doctor's office. Daddy ended up having to work today so he couldn't go with us. I'm not yet able to drive. Dr. Smith said not to drive for the first three weeks after my surgery. Our neighbor Arlene will take us into town when it's time.

Before we could go to town, we had to get you washed up. That's right, it was time for Mom to bathe you "solo."

I could hardly believe it. I completed your bath without flooding half of the kitchen counter-top or causing small waterfalls over the edge of the counter. You didn't even cry or scream. You even seemed to enjoy part of it. Bless your little heart, I'm truly amazed! I wonder if this is the beginning of a trend or just an accident? Time will tell.

Once you'd been bathed, it was time to get dressed to leave for your appointment. Poor little thing, you had to suffer through being "dressed up" for your trip to town. I loved it, but I rather doubt that you enjoyed it much. After an uneventful car ride we arrived at your Doctor's office. You enjoyed the ride, but you weren't terribly thrilled about the Doctor's exam. You fussed, cried and yes, went "pookie." The Doctor wasn't at all taken aback by the accident, he merely commented that everything about you appeared perfectly healthy.

At your exam, you weighed eleven pounds exactly. The nurse measured you at twenty-two and one-quarter inches in length. That wasn't the measurement I came up with at home this morning, but I'm sure her measuring expertise with wriggly little critters is far better than mine, so I went with her measurement.

Once your appointment was over, and we were in the car, you were happy again. You looked so adorable in your little clothes. That was the first time you had been to town since you were born. You just had to be dressed for the occasion, you looked like a living doll.

On the way home, Arlene took us to the uptown mall, so I could pick up a couple of things. I had brought the front-carrier, but I didn't really want you to be around so many people yet. People can't resist looking at and playing with babies, and I really didn't want you exposed to people and their germs, until you were four weeks old. Today you were only three weeks old. Arlene said she would stay in the car with you, with the air-conditioner on, while I went in to pick up my things. After our quick stop at the mall, we headed for home. You certainly loved riding in the car!

August 12

You are a joy to watch when you aren't screaming. It's very frustrating when you cry for no apparent reason. Your Daddy and I feel like there should be something we could do, but at times there just isn't. That is very hard to accept. We know it's the truth, but it's still hard to accept.

August 13

I noticed that over the past few days you've become more expressive. You react with coos, chortles, or facial expressions, head tilts, and other body posturing to the conversation that we direct to you. It's really quite impressive.

August 14

A big day. A long day. First we went to see Dr. Smith; I was finally cleared to do light exercises. Yeah! Then we went to pick up a "drive-thru" lunch. Daddy drove us to the park by the lake where we picnicked under some trees.

It was your first picnic, and our first family outing. It was molded around two appointments, but it was a nice day. After our picnic, we made a couple of stops before going to see Dr. Jeffreys to have your angel tag removed. You had been a little doll all morning, but just before you were called in to see Dr. Jeffreys, you started to fuss. It was about time to eat again as we had already waited in his office quite a while.

Being a very modest and private person, I wondered how I would handle the first time I needed to breast-feed you in public, when I wouldn't be able to steal away to a secluded area to feed you. The situation presented itself today as we waited for your appointment. We had been waiting forty-five minutes. We were the next ones to see the Doctor. You were **definitely** hungry.

There were eight people of assorted age and sex in the waiting room. If we went out to the car for your feeding, we would miss your appointment. If I didn't feed and hence calm you, you would be all worked up and upset by the time of your mini-surgery. I was wearing one of the breast-feeding ("nursing tops") I made. I draped a receiving blanket across my shoulder and your head to maintain my privacy. Discreetly, and nervously, I opened the feeding access panel and connected you to your lunch.

I had wondered how I would handle it? I did just that—I handled it. My baby was hungry and I fed her. That's all there was to it. I felt uncomfortable and embarrassed, but once I was involved with the feeding, that feeling faded. The next time should prove to be a lot less anxiety-producing.

You braved your mini-surgery beautifully. It took all of three minutes, start to finish.

You were a sweetie when we took you up to the coronary care unit to show you off after your appointment. I remember that Diane was particularly amazed at how pretty you were. "My word, Vivianne, when you order up a babe; you sure make it a beauty."

You were so good and it was such a long day. Since you had been good all day, I thought you might prove to be a holy terror tonight. Wasn't that a terrible thing to think? Terrible, but possibly true.We made one last stop, at the grocery store, before we headed home.

Dad is fixing dinner for us tonight, as he has been doing occasionally since we came back from the hospital, and guess who's screaming! We knew that you were just fussy after a long day. You've eaten and your diaper is fresh. You were just plain upset and releasing the tensions of the day.

I put you into your crib hammock. Daddy served dinner and we ate while we let you cry yourself to sleep. That was the first time we'd done that—let you just cry, without any consolation, for a long period of time (ten to twelve minutes.) Let me tell you, it wasn't the "easy-way-out," there was nothing easy about listening to you cry. It was very hard on my heart. I know that there are times that we are going to have to do that. But let me tell you, for your own future reference, it was distressingly painful.

August 15

Today marked your first fashion show. We took some pictures of you in the outfit you wore to town today. We also took about fifty other pictures of you wearing different outfits. You're growing so quickly. If we don't at least do a fashion show once in a while to see how you look in the clothes you have, we may never get to see you in them before you've outgrown them.

I must tell you that you ate more today than I can recall.

I wonder if it's in response to healing, from your mini-surgery yesterday?

9:30 pm: With you in his arms, Daddy walked into the master bedroom to ask an exhausted Mom when your next feeding was due. You weren't due for another feeding for a while, but Daddy felt that you were hungry. Daddy had been holding you for me, so I could get some rest. My back had been spasming and was particularly painful today. I laid you down beside me to see if you were hungry. You went after your "food source" with true purpose, but 'ole "dinner buckets" (Grandma Ani-Poo's nickname for her breast-feeding daughter) wasn't only tired, she was literally tapped out.

I had been pumping my breasts for the last five days so there would be enough breast milk for Daddy to start feeding you once you became four weeks old. There was supposed to be less of a potential for nipple confusion if we waited until you were between four weeks and six weeks old before introducing a different nipple; and I wanted to avoid nipple confusion a second time. Today there was only enough expressed breast milk for three feedings. Daddy decided to open one of the cans of formula we had received as a shower gift and made a bottle for you. He fed you at 10:00 pm and said that you took only two and one-half ounces—not much of a feeding.

2:00 am: I pulled myself out of bed and shuffled my way to the kitchen to produce another installment of "relief Mother's milk" to add to our collection, before I went in to feed you. I thought that I would have to wake you up, but just as I finished pumping you had awakened and were asking for something to eat.

August 16

You, Mildieu and I are in the family room this morning.
Mildieu is on the couch next to me, supervising my writing, as
I record yesterday's events into your journal. You are full of
the "cutes," gurgling, talking, exploring and concentrating on
the things around you. As we each went about our separate,
yet related activities, Daddy came into the family room to ask
me which formula Dr. Kelley feels is best. He thinks we should
get some. My response is pretty flat.

It was nice to get some rest last night when I was so-o-o-o
uncomfortable; but I really don't feel good about using formula.
Dr. Kelley has said that using formula as a relief on occasion
doesn't usually cause any problems, and that there shouldn't
be any problem of your becoming dissatisfied with breast milk
after having the heavier formula. It doesn't happen very often.
But if it did happen with you, I'm afraid I would be devastated.

Daddy is trying to understand why using formula is such
a problem for me. But he doesn't understand and he's become
frustrated with my resistance to use the formula. Just another
day or two and I'll have pumped enough breast milk for Daddy
to feed you. I know he is eager to; it's something he's missed
being able to do with you.

If we hadn't needed to give in to so many things around
your delivery, I might not feel so negative about a silly little
bit of formula. I've just become a bit paranoiac about giving
up breast-feeding you, because so far it's the only thing we
haven't had to give up.

August 18

Your Daddy and I have been able to see quite a bit of
improvement in our parenting and infant care skills over this
last month. Things like having your diapers fastened comfortably
most of the time instead of by accident or when you cry we are

able to figure out what you need or want sooner are just some of the improvements. And no doubt you feel more secure when we hold you, because we feel more secure in how we hold you. I'm sure you've noticed it too.

Tonight will be Daddy's first night "on duty" as "Daddy buckets." He'll feed you during the night with breast milk that I expressed and saved over the last week.

August 19

Your weight today is 11 pounds 2 ounces.

This morning Daddy said he was tired from his Daddy buckets shift last night. He said he had to wake you up both times; that you fell asleep before even finishing your feeding, both times, and reawoke about an hour later, crying, because you were hungry. So he had to get up four times during the night to feed you instead of the two times he had counted on. For Daddy the "romance" of the night-time feeding duty was quickly erased with last night's difficulties. Daddy declined taking a night shift duty again next week.

August 20

Happy one month birthday, Tiffany! You're exactly four weeks old today. You've been through quite a bit in your short life. You were born, had to put up with an IV, a cardiac monitor, temperature sensor, a nursery full of screaming "roomies," then home to your own quiet room with loving, but very inexperienced and clumsy parents. Happily, none of this has taken any toll on your spirit. You continue to face life head on and love your work discovering everything you can of the world around you.

Speaking of enjoying oneself, your Daddy and I love watching you smile. We also love to try to get you to smile. You are making a lot more gurgles and coos than you used to do. You used to do more when you first woke up in the morning. You would have the most delightful and musical conversation with yourself as you greeted the new day. Now you gurgle and coo to yourself, Daddy, the puppies, Mildieu, or myself periodically throughout the day. You are smiling much more frequently and for longer periods of time.

I wish I could keep track of all the facial expressions you make, but there are just too many. I begin to wonder if your tongue will be your strongest muscle; you put it through such frequent workouts!

Your Great-Aunt Lucy came to visit you today, the first out-of-town relative you have seen. She thought you were beautiful and sat and gazed at you for the longest time. You gurgled, cooed, and smiled while she, Grandma Ani-Poo and Popie were there. You all enjoyed the visit.

August 22

You and I went into town again today. Grandma Ani-Poo and Grand-Aunt Lucy went with us. They were on "stand-by," just in case I needed help. I wanted a practice solo run of going into town with you; handling, managing, and maneuvering you, your stroller and all of your baby paraphernalia without help. I'm still not as coordinated with everything as I would like to be.

August 23

Today was our first trip to town all by ourselves with no one to help or on stand by. We went to the bank first to open your first savings account with the money your Great-Aunt

Nellie sent to you. Then we went to the card shop to buy some greeting cards. Then we went on our first "house call" to visit Brittany and John, neighbors who live a few miles out of town. You were ready to eat shortly after we arrived. Brittany, having had three children herself, understood that.

You gurgled and cooed while we were there, more than you had ever done before. You smiled when I talked to you, and didn't smile when I talked to Brittany. We both knew that you could tell when I was talking to you and when I wasn't. When I talked to you, you smiled and talked back! It was wonderful to listen to you talk. Your little voice is captivating and sweet. Your beautiful smiles are so completely disarming. My happiest times are listening to you talk and watching you smile.

Before we left, we all went to visit Brittany's animals. Her family has a pair of Alaskan Timber Wolves that are housed in an enormous enclosure, approximately six thousand square feet, the size of two large houses. Timber and Tundra, came out of the wooded area of their enclosure to greet us. They are large, beautiful and healthy animals with lush white fur. When their winter coat comes in, they will be even more beautiful.

That was your first encounter, up close or otherwise, with a wolf or any non-domestic animal for that matter. I imagine they just looked like extra-large dogs to you; or just extra-large white things, if you don't yet have an understanding of a "dog-creature."

We had a terrific time. As we left, I realized we had stayed for about three hours. You'd been a great little guest, right up to the last. Brittany complimented you on your gracious manner and your participation in our conversation.

August 24

You're continuing to smile and hold up your end of the "conversation" in response to being talked to. You are such a sweet, delightful creature.

You, Daddy and I went to Grandma Ani-Poo's tonight for your first dinner party. Great-Aunt Sherry and Great-Uncle Jack were there. You were a delightful little guest all evening; but I have to admit that I wondered how long that would last. After all, babies aren't designed to just sit there and enjoy parties, yet you remained the perfect guest. Your Great-Uncle Jack exclaimed, 'What a beautiful child!" and "How well behaved." You didn't know it, but your Great-Uncle Jack is not easily impressed, so I know he meant what he said.

Grandma Ani-Poo's friends, Josh and Connie, came to see you before we left. They had been dying to see you, so Grandma Ani-Poo had called them after dinner. Connie said they were getting ready for bed and that they would have to make it another time. Not ten minutes later, the doorbell rang. Connie had changed her mind and said she really couldn't wait to see you. Connie loves babies.

August 26

Tiffany statistics: 11 pounds 10 ounces.

Something new—you smacked your lips today. Your fist wasn't near your mouth, you just smacked your lips. You were so impressed with yourself once you realized that you had caused the sound, that you went through all sorts of facial contortions until you did it again. When you finally managed to smack your lips again, you made a huge smile and raised your right eyebrow as you looked at me. You're such a little cutie. Something else that's new; you're better now at finding your fist to suck on when you need it. Good 'ole fist. As you're getting better at finding it, you're having less and less interest in the pacifier. You never did really like it that much. I'm glad that you like it even less.

Tonight we'll have our first overnight guests since your birth. Mary, one of my girlfriends from high school, and her family are moving back to Los Angeles, after living in Oregon for the last few years. They will be arriving late this afternoon, stay for dinner and the night, then leave for Los Angeles in the morning after breakfast. Mary and Bob's daughter, Jessica, is four years old, so they have already been through a baby-stage. They will understand if you have a fussy night.

Mary, Bob and Jessica arrived in time to visit a while before dinner The grown-ups were busy comparing baby pictures while you and Jessica got acquainted. Soon it was time to eat. Mary played with and talked to you as I set the table.

We all sat down to eat. You were in the rocker carrier on the floor close to the table, but safely out of the "fall zone." As we started to eat, guess who decided to be hungry almost two hours early? You have developed a great sense of timing—you get hungry right when it's time for everyone else to eat. Some of the literature I've read said you can smell the food. Bob mentioned that also, as we started to compare "meal-interrupt-stories." The "smell theory" might make sense, but how could you know exactly when I'm going to eat the food?

Once Bob had mentioned the smell theory, the four of us launched into a funny debate about why babies cry during the adult's feeding time—and why they only cry once Mom starts to eat. Is it smell? Is it manipulation? Etc.,etc.

Could there be another force at work here? Moms and their little ones are very strongly attached. I wonder if that has anything to do with the fact that you don't get fussy when you

smell the meal cooking, but wait until just after I sit down to
eat it.

August 27

You were a very good little hostess last night.You didn't
fuss at all and allowed our guests to sleep soundly. Your Daddy
and I appreciated that as we did stay up late visiting and
would have felt badly if our guests hadn't clocked in enough
sleep to be refreshed for the next part of their journey. Mary
and Bob both thanked you personally at breakfast, for allowing them a good night's sleep. Our guests left right after
breakfast to avoid the mid-morning traffic.

August 28

Right after breakfast you and I went to town to run some
errands and to visit Cheryl, one of Mommy's nurse friends
from work. You became too hot riding around in the summer
heat and the air conditioning at Cheryl's house wasn't working
well. You fussed all afternoon; I imagine because you were
uncomfortable. We didn't stay as long as Cheryl's as planned;
and I cut the errand load short so I could get you home.
You developed a prickly heat rash while we were out. Poor
little sweetheart. It broke my heart to see that rash on you and
see your continued discomfort. You didn't have a fever, but you
were definitely uncomfortable.

August 29

This afternoon you seemed to feel a great deal better. Your
heat rash has lost it's fury. I'm not going to take you out in this
heat again until I make a sheepskin liner for your carseat.

Well, it's time for bed, now. I have completed making the sheepskin liner for your carseat, a terrific custom-fitted, reversible to flannel, carseat liner with bound edges for the seatbelts to pass through. We're ready for the blistering open road again.

August 30

Grand-Aunt Lucy, one of Grandma Ani-Poo's three sisters, arrived at Grandma Ani-Poo's last night. She will only be staying for three days. Grandma Ani-Poo, Grand-Aunt Lucy, Popie and I wanted to spend some time together. It also seemed a great opportunity for you and Daddy to have some time together—just the two of you. So you spent the afternoon with Daddy while we went out. It was the longest time that you had spent with each other.

I've noticed that you respond differently to me when you and I are alone, than when we are with Daddy or someone else. I feel our alone-time is very important, and I believe that it is important for you and Daddy to have this kind of time also. So far, I haven't been able to convince him that it's necessary. Maybe today he'll discover it for himself.

When we all returned home, Daddy said that you had a nice time together. He was surprised that you didn't take a nap, but said he thought of enough things to keep you entertained during your time together.

August 31

Listening to you talk is so much fun. I can't get enough of it. I keep noticing how your vocabulary—your different gurgles and coos seems to increase notably every few days. You are so fascinating.

September

Tiffi Statistics: 11 pounds 14 ounces.

Today I had a lot of shopping to do in Redding. Grandma Ani-Poo and Grand-Aunt Lucy wanted to spend the day with you. It was Grand-Aunt Lucy's last day at Grandma Ani-Poo's. We compromised. I took you down to Grandma Ani-Poo's so you could visit while I went shopping alone. It marked the first day that you went to Grandma Ani-Poo and Popie's to spend the day, or most of the day, without me. That gave them free rein to spoil you miserably, every grandparent's given right, since I wouldn't be there to hinder their efforts at indulging your every whim. As it turned out, Grandma Ani-Poo and Grand-Aunt Lucy spent a lot of the morning cooking, so Popie really did most of the babysitting. He certainly loves his grand little girl.

When I returned from my shopping mid-afternoon, you, Popie and I went out to visit Basette, one of Mommy's animal friends; a six year old Siberian Tiger to be exact. Basette lives outside the city limits at the wrecking yard owned by her owner's parents— Jeff and Lonnie. Basette's owner, Frank, owns a tire store next door to the wrecking yard. Your Mommy used to help train wild and exotic (a wild animal not native to this country) animals for movies and television before moving to northern California three years ago.

Having the opportunity to get close to and have a friendly relationship with wild and exotic animals had been a passion of mine for a long time. A little over four years ago, I seized an opportunity to do just that as a second career, or more correctly, a hard-working hobby; there really isn't any financial appreciation in such an endeavor until one has been in the industry for many years, if ever.

Jeff and Lonnie (Basette's human grandparents) weren't there today, so we couldn't get in to see Basette. You did get to meet the guys next door at the tire store. "The guys," Jake and Ron, work for Frank. You also met Precious, the Japanese Macaque (a small ape similar to a chimpanzee); John, the baby Capuchin (species of small monkey that was commonly used by ("organ-grinders"); and Sonny, Mac, and Tosha the Macaws (colorful long-tailed parrots).

September 2

Every day you smile and talk more, it's delightful. I'm very sure that you recognize me now, and that is a fabulously warming feeling. You are also making a new sound, a happy, laughing scream. It is so cute, I can't wait for Daddy to hear it.

September 3

Today you went to your first pot-luck gathering at our neighbor Rhonda's house. Everyone had a marvelous time and ate too much. Funny how people are more apt to overeat at a pot-luck. As everyone had wound down their eating to an occasional nibble, we started to visit more. I took you out of the front-pack carrier. Dolores, another neighbor, asked if she could hold you, now that you were "unwrapped." She held you for about an hour. You fell asleep on her shoulder. Rhonda wanted to hold you, too, but didn't want to disturb you; she waited for you to wake up. As soon as you woke up, you were transferred to Rhonda's shoulder. You seemed to enjoy the attention, and were a model guest.

September 4

This morning you and I went down to Grandma Ani-Poo's house. You, Popie and I went to the wrecking yard again to see if you could meet Basette. The wrecking yard was open. We visited with Jeff and Lonnie for a while before I took you outside to meet Basette. She was very well-behaved. She didn't even "fix" on you or charge toward you. (This is something "big cats" do with babies and young children almost one hundred percent of the time. They look at children as "hors d'oeuvres." A "fix" is an unbroken focus on a prey animal that the predictor has chosen to be his victim. It is almost unheard of for a big-cat not to fix on an unfamiliar child. Basette did "know you" in utero, or know of your presence. Basette and I have been friends for two years. Animals' senses being as highly developed as they are, I have always contended that she knew I was pregnant, and probably before I knew I was. She did start behaving differently around me—giving me more allowances, being protective—before I knew I was pregnant. I would like to think that her response toward you was due to our friend-relationship.

I slowly knelt down just outside her cage with you on one thigh and resting against my torso. I held you with one hand, and extended the other hand, placing my palm flat against the fencing of Basette's cage—a request for a kiss. I asked her to come over to the fencing. After a minute she did; she licked my hand through the fencing on her cage and chuffed at us. Chuffing is happy tiger talk; cheeks full of air softly pushed through the teeth in rhythmic bursts. You weren't really paying much attention to what happened, but Basette was being very nice to you. That very special encounter is something I will always remember and cherish.

September 5

You are such a joy! You become more generous with your smiles and your talkies with each passing day. You are putting more body movement into your efforts to talk. Sometimes you work so hard at trying to express yourself that you look like you're going to burst. If you can't get the "words" out, you cry out of sheer frustration. You seem to want so much for your feelings to be known. You try so hard.

September 6

Two of Grandma Ani-Poo's friends, Greta and her daughter Jeanie, came to see you today. They were both wearing red. They said they each had done so to capture your attention. Babies respond more to bright colors and stark contrasts. You talked and smiled at Greta for the longest time, and she loved it. You were quite a hostess.

September 7

Again I've noticed more animation in your talking. Your little voice is so beautiful, so delightful. I am in constant amazement at how rapidly you grow and develop. Over the last week or so you have been eating virtually all of the time. You aren't visibly growing—yet. I'd ask where you're putting it all, but I know where it goes. It's being converted to baby pudge! According to our baby books, that is a pre-growth spurt. In the next few days, you will begin a noticeable growth change, translating into outgrowing some of your clothes.

September 8

Today your feet discovered each other. You didn't seem to realize that they were there, or what they were up to. They, however, played "footsie" with each other. It was really cute. I wondered when you'd discover just who made it happen.

September 9

Today's statistics: 12 pounds 11 ounces.

Daddy called your Grandma Ruth (Daddy's mother) today. He is going to go down to Los Angeles to pick up some furniture and bring Grandma Ruth up to the ranch for a visit.

Tonight your Daddy and I went out on our first date since your birth. We went out for dinner and a movie. After dinner, and before we left for the movie, I called Grandma Ani-Poo to see how you were doing. Popie told me that my friend Doug had just called. He said that he, his sister Susie and his father Stan were in town. They had stopped on their way back to Los Angeles from vacationing along the California and Oregon coast. They wanted to see us before they left for home. We called them at their hotel room and arranged to get together at the ranch the next morning.

When we arrived back at Grandma Ani-Poo and Popie's house, they told us they had enjoyed you, that you had been a great little guest.

September 10

You were asleep when Doug, Susie and Stan arrived, so they were able to see you sleeping in your little crib hammock. When you awoke you were very well mannered, considering you have not had the chance to develop any manners yet. They all thought you were very pretty.

While the guys were out looking at our neighbor's new dam, you and I visited with Susie. You smiled and talked a great deal. Susie was really smitten by you. She couldn't stop saying how sweet you were.

"Your" guests stayed for about an hour. You were a great assistant hostess. It was nice we were able to get together while they were here. It will, no doubt, be quite a while before we get down to Los Angeles.

September 11

Today I started a difficult task, I started interviewing people to take care of you when I go back to work. You will be with them from about 2:00 pm until your Dad is done with his work between 5:00–6:00 pm. This is very hard to do. I have to feel very good about the person who cares for you while I'm at work. It's so difficult to entrust you, even to thing of entrusting you, to someone I don't really know while I'm at work. To further complicate my anxiety, there has been such a surge in child abuse in daycare centers. I should say there has been a surge in reported child abuse. I'm nervous and anxious about the whole thing. We have to be very thorough and very careful.

I located a couple of resources with checklists of what to look for and look out for in choosing child care. Armed with that information, I made up my own checklist and plan, to rule out potential problems at each care-giver situation.

September 13

Today I took Vicky (a nurse friend from work) out for a salad lunch that I have owed to her for almost a year! I forgot why I owed Vicky lunch, but I knew I did, and it felt good to have finally made good on our deal. We had a great time. We were at the restaurant almost two hours "nursing" our salads, as we hardly stopped talking long enough to eat anything.

After lunch I went shopping for a few small things. While I was in one of the children's stores, I ended up buying a jacket and three pieces of clothing for you; at least they were all on sale. Then I went to the discount department store for some vinyl hangers. I also succumbed to two toys for you. I couldn't help myself! Besides, it was fun. You needed a grab-it type toy, one of the items I had succumbed to. You also needed something to look at besides your teddy bear, while you're in your swinging basket. Your teddy isn't very colorful. How's that for rationalized justification!?! After I had finished my shopping, both planned and unplanned, I picked you up at Grandma Ani-Poo's where you had spent the day, and took you home.

September 14

This morning you tried to roll yourself over while I was changing your diaper; you rocked your knees back and forth to the right. You didn't make it over onto your tummy, but you tried a couple of times. Later in the day, while you were on your quilt on the floor, you rolled yourself on and off of your right side. It won't be long before you roll onto your stomach.

This evening you and I went out to an early barbecue rib dinner with Grandma Ani-Poo and Popie. It was your second restaurant outing, but your first dinner outing. On your first restaurant outing you were perfectly content until the food was served, then you were upset and started to cry. We took turns eating our meal and pacifying you. Sound familiar?

This time, you did a little better. You had eaten just before we left, but once I started eating the barbecued ribs you decided you were hungry. Why should you be left out when everyone else was eating? Right!?! Oh well, this time we only had to take turns feeding you at the table, not walking you in and out of the restaurant.

When we arrived home from dinner, we found that Daddy was back from his trip. With him were Uncle Greg, Aunt Margie, and a "new to us" truck. But Grandma Ruth wasn't with them. Daddy said she decided to fly up at the end of the month.

September 15

Uncle Greg and Aunt Margie spent a good deal of the day with you, taking turns holding you, talking to you and amusing you. During your visit you rolled onto and off of your right side a number of times; sometimes staying on your side for a while, other times just going back and forth. You didn't try rolling over via your left side at all, only your right side.

September 16

Today's Tiffi statistics: 12 pounds 15 ounces; 24 1/4 inches long.

We had the greatest conversation today. You made little gurgles, coos and chortles in response to the different things I said to you. After the conversation, you continued to talk, adding little happy screams. You weren't talking to me anymore. You were just listening to yourself talk. You made a lot of happy little screams and squeaks. You seemed to enjoy your own voice tremendously. It was delightful to watch you enjoy yourself so much.

September 17

Today I had three appointments in Redding; one with Dr. Smith at 10:00 am; an annual employee physical; and one with my Dentist at 2:00 pm. I wondered how you would fare being out for so long and having to sit in your little rocker-carrier during the Doctor's appointments.

You did beautifully. You were self-entertaining while we were at Dr. Smith's office. We then went up to Hilltop Hospital for my annual physical and lab work. From there it was off to Nancy's house, one of my nurse friends from work. You fussed off and on a bit while we were there, but nothing major.

When we left Nancy's we drove to the miniature golf course and parked under the shade of a large tree to eat lunch. First Mom, then Tiffany. After our lunch break we went to the dentist, forty minutes early. I had hoped to get home as soon as possible, so you could meet, your cousin Tess and her new hubby when they stopped by the ranch on their way to Iowa. Once at the Dentist's office we found that his lunch hour was from 1:00- 2:00 pm instead of 12:00- 1:00 pm, so we weren't able to get in early. There was a large, well-shaded lawn nearby. We sat on the lawn and played with leaves. After a short time I was able to rock you to sleep.

When we did get in to see the dentist, you slept through my appointment until the timer buzzed to signal that the x-rays were done. When you woke up, you looked around a bit, sucked on your thumb, then continued to look around quietly until I was done. I was very pleased.

We arrived at home just before 3:30 pm. Tess and Bryan were still there, so you did get to meet each other. You smiled, squeaked, and looked around a bit while they were there, but you didn't really talk. At 4:30 pm Tess and Bryan left. You didn't get to visit long, but you were at least able to meet each other.

Shortly after Tess and Bryan left, the tensions of the day caught up with you. You fussed and cried yourself to sleep after an hour or so of "shoulder time." Ten minutes after you fell asleep, you woke up hungry. You've taken to doing the sweetest thing during your feedings. Twice now, at about mid-meal, you'd stop nursing, look up at me and smile and smile and smile. It was wonderful. I couldn't see your smile directly, because your arm was out-stretched across your face, with your hand either placed on my breast or holding my blouse. But I could tell that you were smiling, even when you are attached to a breast, because your eyes drew up at the side. It was so sweet to look at your bright laughing eyes behind that tiny, plump, out-stretched arm. You are so captivating; I think that you have begun to realize that, too. After a full meal, you went right back to sleep.

September 19

You were certainly quiet today. You took three short naps, and only fussed a few times for short periods. It was unusual for you to take a nap during the day.

September 20

This morning I was surprised at how well and how long you slept last night. You were so quiet and restful yesterday that I thought you wouldn't be able to sleep much during the night, not having spent much energy. I wonder if that was because you were maturing into a more secure baby?

Today you had an early morning appointment with Dr. Kelley for your first immunization. You did very well. You didn't scream until you felt the needle of the immunization, and you didn't pookie on the Doctor this time. Dr. Kelley said that we could let you sleep through the night for up to ten hours without waking you! At last! I usually had to wake you up during the night to feed you.

After your appointment we went to Grandma Ani-Poo and Popie's to visit. It was your last chance to spend time with them for quite a while. They're leaving for a ten-week trip to the east coast tomorrow.

Popie decided to take us all out to lunch. You were very serene until lunch was served. We then had to take turns holding you for "shoulder time" and doing "laps" in the restaurant's foyer. Popie held you the most.

After lunch, we went back to Grandma Ani-Poo's, where Grandma held you most of the time. They wanted to get plenty of huggies in before they had to leave. It would be a long time before they could hold you again.

At 1:30 pm your left leg (immunization site) started to bother you. I gave you some acetaminophen (non-aspirin compound). At 3:30 pm we left for home. I wanted to get you settled in and comfortable at home before your leg started to bother you again.

At 5:30 pm, just before dinner, I gave you another dose of acetaminophen. You ate a full dinner and drifted off to sleep. You woke up at 10:00 pm to eat again.

10:30 pm: You fell asleep just as you finished eating. Your left leg didn't feel hot anymore, so I didn't give you any more acetaminophen. You seemed quite comfortable in your sleep. I couldn't help but wonder how you would sleep at night, not having to be awakened for feedings. You might wake up on your own with discomfort from your immunization, though you were much more comfortable this afternoon than I thought you'd be. I thought your injection would bother you for twenty-four hours.

September 21

You slept from 10:45 pm until I woke you at 8:45 am. That's ten hours straight! I always wondered how long you would sleep if we didn't wake you up all of the time. When you woke up you were happy, rested and hungry. You sucked down your breakfast quickly, then started to talk and sing.

It is 5:00 pm, and I haven't needed to give you any medicine today. Your leg is just slightly warm, and there is no sign of general swelling. Some babies have a lot of trouble with their injections. I'm glad that you aren't having any of those problems. Keep up the good work.

September 22

Today we went to a pot-luck picnic at our neighbors, the Randalls. The Randall's live in a one-hundred year old farm house on the other side of Cottonwood Creek. It isn't far from our ranch "as the crow flies," but the old bridge that used to be out here was never replaced after it collapsed many years ago. In the summer and early fall we can drive over the dry Cottonwood Creek bed. If it were winter or spring and the creek was full, we would have to drive the seven-plus miles into Cottonwood and catch another road going the seven-plus miles back out of town on the other side of the creek.

Peggy and Martha, two of the tellers from our bank were there. In a community this small almost everyone is your neighbor, very different than a metropolitan suburb. Your father and I were both raised in the suburbs of Los Angeles, California. This is very different for us. For you, however, this would be the usual, the way things should be. I hope that when you grow up, if you decide to live in the city, that you don't have any difficulty adjusting to the different way of life.

You really enjoyed yourself. Early in the afternoon you fell asleep. The Randalls rigged their bed with pillows under the edges of the mattress to create a place for you to sleep where you wouldn't be in danger of falling off. I was really touched by their efforts to make you comfortable and safe. They even dug out a crib blanket that belonged to their first son, now twenty years old, to cover you with. We didn't leave the party until early evening when it was too cool for the clothes you were wearing. I didn't know we would be able to stay that long. It depended on how you fared. You did just fine.

September 25

This morning you and I were in the family room; I was watching you play. You discovered your feet—a first. You wiggled your toes, moved your foot by bending and stretching your leg, and rotated your foot to the left and right while watching it intently. You were completely fascinated. After you finished marveling at your feet, you held your head up off of the floor perched on your elbows, while lying on your stomach. It was only for a few seconds, but it was a start.

Another first! We were still in the family room where you were lying on your tummy, and twisting your hips around. While you were quiet, I thought I'd wash the dishes. A couple of minutes later I looked over the counter to see how you were. You were on your back! Congratulations, you made it all the way over. I was so excited for you! Naturally, I wanted to watch you accomplish this great feat. After a lot of kisses and hugs, I put you down on your tummy and waited to see if you would turn over again. In less than a minute, you had turned your shoulders, the hardest part. Then something caught your eye. You studied it for a couple of minutes before finishing your turn, by throwing your hips over. So this turn-over was a "two-parter," as I guess the first one may have been, too. Your basic, installment turn. How about that? Two firsts in one day! That was a first in itself.

September 26

After lunch I put you down on your playquilt and jingled your play keys in front of your eyes and around your hand.

You watched this for a few minutes. I stopped jingling them and just dragged them over your hand every once and a while.

After a few minutes of this, you would hit them yourself by accident. You watched them move and listened to them jingle. You worked up to hitting them on purpose, occasionally smiling when they made noise. You knew that you were making that noise and movement happen! You kept this up for about five minutes. We both enjoyed it.

I took you to your room for a diaper change, then back to your playquilt. I put you on your back and started to play "keys" with you again, to see if you would remember the game. You were more interested in smiling and talking.

After dinner we had a fabulous conversation at the changing table. You used the greatest number of different sounds, that I had ever heard you use in a single conversation, or even in a single day! It was wonderful. You were so expressive, so animated! You are growing so fast! You definitely have developed your own, growing personality.

Back to the family room again, and you were ready for another discussion. During that conversation you were particularly active. After a couple of minutes I turned you onto your tummy to see if you would practice lifting your head up. You did exactly that. You held your head and chest up off of the floor on extended arms and looked around. You were up there for almost a full minute before taking a break. Another milestone! When you're hot, you're hot! The next time you held your head up, I managed to get a couple of pictures.

I wish that I didn't have to go back to work for a few more weeks. You've done so much just these last two days. I'm afraid that you'll do something new, and I'll miss it. Or that you would do something if I were there to cheer you on. This is going to be hard. At least Daddy will be there to cheer you on most of the time. You won't be spending that much time at the babysitter's. You just turned yourself over from your tummy to your back again.

September 28

For almost a week now, you've been taking naps during the day! Many times two naps, lasting up to two hours each. This gives me a chance to start your winter wardrobe.

You continue to fine-tune your efforts at playing with your keys and with gripping objects. No further progress in turning over yet. You are gaining more control over your head and increasing your time spent talking and smiling. You speak louder now, and, at times, longer too.

September 30

Today's stats: 12 pounds 15 ounces.

Daddy went to the airport to pick up Grandma Ruth tonight. You were already asleep when they came home. She was only able to look at you. The hugs and kisses would have to wait until tomorrow.

October

October 1

You are your usual sunshine self this morning. You just love greeting a brand new day. Grandma Ruth crawled out of bed and came into your nursery when she heard you wake up for your morning feeding. She caught her first Tiffi smiles, and you'd captured another heart. She was very touched by your sweet smiles and gentle voice. The two of you got along famously.

October 2

In two more days, I have to go back to work. I'm getting nervous about my nursing skills, after having been away from work for three months—chronologically; another lifetime emotionally. I'm even more nervous about leaving you while I'm gone.

I'm glad that your Grandma Ruth is here. It will be a lot easier leaving you in the care of a family member, instead of that of a care-giver virtually unknown to both of us. Even though I feel very good about the caregiver I chose, it will be nice to leave you with your Grandma for my first days back to work. To not have to deal with leaving you to go to work and a new caregiver both, on my first days back, is a blessing.

Beth, your soon-to-be-care-giver (babysitter), is a wonderful lady. I am happy to have found her. I interviewed and checked out fifteen different people. Many of them were wonderful ladies, but each time there was "something"—feeling, a negative feeling; about the lady herself, or more often, a negative feeling about the house—the feel of the house, or the feeling of the relationships between the family members, the area where you would spend most of your time, or the area where you would take your nap. Sometimes it was the outcome of the unannounced drop-by check I made, or the result of checking out the feel of the neighborhood. I would sit in my car in the neighborhood during business hours, evening weekday hours and during weekend days. With Beth I felt good about everything, no negative feelings.

October 3

Your enjoyment of looking at things while you hold your head up off the floor is really delightful. It must feel as though you have command of a whole new perspective of your world. You still marvel at your hands and feet every once in a while. At certain times they just catch your eye. You move them about slowly, as you study them intently. This afternoon while you played with your keys, you grasped one of them and tried to put it in your mouth. You're working your way toward a new skill.

October 4

I didn't sleep very well last night—I had an awful nightmare. This morning I'm nervous and hyperactive. This afternoon will be my first time back at work since you were born. I work the 3:00-11:00 pm shift in the coronary care unit at Hilltop Hospital, the hospital where you were born. Intellectually, I know that everything should go alright while I'm at work, but I'm still extremely anxious. I'm going to leave for work an hour early so that I can run a couple of errands, and walk around a little to try to calm down before I actually have to begin working.

It's midnight, and I'm home from my first day at work. Everyone is asleep except Grandma Ruth. she waited up for me. She told me every little thing that went on while I was gone, then went to bed. I really appreciated that. I had called Daddy and Grandma Ruth three times during work to see how things were going; when you'd eaten, when your diapers were changed, what you were doing. Everything sounded fine, but I was still nervous. I was away from you longer today than ever before. If I don't hold you and feed you now, by the time you wake up it will have been sixteen hours! I can't wait that long. I wouldn't be able to sleep. I've changed my clothes and showered off any hospital-acquired germs. When I finish writing it will be time for some hugs and your midnight meal. It'll be nice to spend some time together.

October 5

I heard you talking in your room this morning, so did Daddy. He got out of bed and went into your room to get you. I thought he just wanted to visit with you. Twenty minutes later I got up, as I thought your socializing mood would be over soon, and you would be ready for breakfast. I looked into your room, but you weren't there. I went into the family room and found Daddy feeding you. That was very thoughtful of him, to feed you so I might be able to sleep longer. I tried to go back to sleep, but it didn't work. I was able to just lie there for a while and rest.

As I rested, I thought about the night before. Overall, I did much better at work than I thought I would. I think it had to do with the fact that you were with Daddy and Grandma Ruth. We will see what happens when I take you to the babysitter for the first time. I'm not looking forward to it.

Grandma Ruth fixed breakfast for us. As we ate, we discussed your activities of yesterday. Grandma Ruth said you picked up your soft, musical rocking-horse block two or three times with both your feet, after it had fallen off of your tummy, and put it between your legs. She wasn't sure if it was accidental or intentional, but she was amazed that it looked so purposeful. Daddy said you laughed last night as he played with you and that for a few seconds your laugh sounded like a regular grown person. I'm sorry that I missed that.

October 6

You were full of smiles and talkies this morning. Daddy gave you your morning feeding so that I could pump my breasts for another meal for you while I was gone. It had only been six hours since I last pumped my breasts. Apparently it was not enough time between expressions, since I was not able to pump a full feeding. It is harder to express it manually than it is for the milk to flow if you were feeding.

I didn't have to work today, so Grandma Ruth and I took you to the mall for your first stroller ride away from the house. Overall, you were not terribly impressed. After about ten minutes of cruising, you were upset. Maybe your diaper needed changing!?! We went to the Women's lounge in one of the department stores where I started to change your diaper. Another woman with a baby came in shortly after we did. She brought her baby boy over to the changing table. You were perfectly happy until the moment this woman put her baby on the large changing counter next to you. You started to cry. It was as if you were crushed that we would do such a personal thing as change your diaper in the presence of so many people.

I felt badly for you. You looked truly hurt when you started to cry. A couple of minutes later you stopped.

The bathroom we were in caused all sounds to echo. That seemed to scare you, and you started to cry again. Each time you started to cry, the little boy next to you started to cry, too. I was sorry you felt so terrible. You settled down after having some hugs. We tried going around the mall some more, but you fussed every few minutes. Grandma Ruth and I grabbed a hot dog while you were calm. By the time we were finished, you were upset again. You just weren't impressed with this outing at all. Even hugs didn't make you happy, so we left. As soon as we were outside, you stopped crying and started looking around. Shortly after we "hit the road," you were fast asleep. Next time, we'll try going to the mall with the front pack carrier.

October 7

Today's statistics are 13 pounds; 25 3/4 inches.

This morning I heard your laugh, that real-grown person laugh that Daddy told me about the other day. You started to laugh when I laughed, as I tickled your nose with my hair. It was so disarming to hear such a deep-pitched sound from such a small creature.

I pump my breasts twice each night while at work. Even with that, I only get enough for one feeding. Possibly, once I have been doing it there routinely, I'll be able to express more during the short thirty minutes I have to eat and pump. Then you won't have to get so much formula while I'm at work. I'd like for you to get at least one feeding of Mommy milk each day that I work.

You had been particularly fussy for the last three days—since I started back to work. I'm sure this change in routine has confused and upset you.

October 8

For a long time now, I've been resisting taking a "nudie" picture of you—the typical unclad cherub-on-the-bearskin rug variety. I remember feeling so embarrassed when my Mom talked about showing a nudie picture of me to someone, anyone. Coupled with the embarrassment numerous other people have relayed about their similar experiences with this tongue-in-cheek blackmail, I decided that I would be different and spare you that future embarrassment.

Well, now I know why those pictures are taken. They're really for Moms only. Once their babies are grown, they can see and remember how soft, sweet and smooth that wee little body was. I tried, Tiffany. I really did, but I'm giving in too. I want a picture of your wee, soft, sweet little self "au naturelle." Then I, too, can see and remember the happy, laughing times we had while you were on the changing table, when you played with my elbow or with your own fabulous little feet as I changed your diaper, or the times you wriggled around as you protested or enjoyed your early-life baths. You are so precious.

October 9

The exploring you do with your hands now is becoming more discreet, more finite. You have even begun to use finer movements with your fingers. As you lay on the changing table you like to explore my elbow or the sleeve of whatever blouse I am wearing.

Watching you do this over the past few weeks, I noticed how your movements have become more and more sophisticated. You're growing so fast. I'm enjoying all of your new activities, and I realized that this growing wasn't going to slow down for about another twenty years. I'm already missing what you used to do, or used to not do, as you grow into your new activities.

October 10

Tonight will be your first night sleeping in your crib without your little crib hammock. You are physically just too big for it now. I wanted to wait until I have three days off in a row before I stopped using it, in case you have any difficulty adjusting. We just aren't going to be able to wait that long.

October 11

Timeline: today the first American woman walked in space!

Tiffi-timeline: you rolled over onto your back for the first time in two weeks. Too bad Grandma Ruth missed it.

October 13

Boy, did you have a little "fit" today. A true high-pitched screaming, "hot dog mad" fuss-fit! When you cried, Grandma Ruth came over to see what you needed, and you stopped crying. When she didn't pick you up, but instead, walked away, you started screaming! You'd done similar things in the last two or three weeks, but on a more subtle scale. There was no room for doubt this time. You were mad and you wanted everyone to know it! Quite a display for such a wee thing.

Aside from your mad-time today, you were full of talkies.

You become more and more conversant as time passes. Your "vocabulary" seems to take a jump once or twice a week.

Grandma Ruth is leaving tonight. We'll be taking her to the airport in about an hour. She said she'd really miss your precious, happy, little personality. I'm sure you're going to miss her, too. It was great that she came when she did.

October 14

Tiffi statistics: 13 pounds; 24 3/4 inches.

I've noticed over the past week, that you have gradually refined your sucking needs from your whole fist to just one or two fingers, or a thumb. A few times it was the last two fingers, then the first two, the first and third fingers, the middle two, then just the thumb, and, finally, just the first finger. It was as though you have been experimenting for size, flavor, comfort, accessibility, etc. The thumb seemed to be your favorite. You would still, occasionally, put your whole fist in your mouth.

I've just realized that for the last few days you were chewing on your thumb instead of sucking on it. Your drooling hasn't taken any hiatus either. I wonder if you are starting to teeth already.

October 15

Today was your three month Doctor's appointment and it looks like we've been doing a pretty good job of measuring you at home. Dr. Kelley's nurse came up with the same numbers we did this morning—13 pounds; 24 3/4 inches long. Dr. Kelley said that you were tall for your age and in the ninety-fifth percentile for weight. Sight and hearing were in proper order. You were very content during the entire visit. Dr. Kelley said there wasn't a thing wrong with you, that you were very healthy and had exceptional neck strength.

After your appointment, you and I went to check on Grandma Ani-Poo and Popie's house as they were away on their east-coast trip. We then went to see Basette and John (the baby monkey.) Basette didn't feel very sociable, but you and little John had a fabulous discussion as usual. We were surprised to find that the West African Brazzas female had given birth. The Brazzas is a small monkey with a blue-grey coat, distinctive white markings on their flanks and a small white "goatee" beard; their underlying skin color is a bright blue. They are very striking animals. No one realized the female Brazzas was pregnant! The Saint Bernard dogs, Bernia and Bernard, had recently parented two puppies. I guess watching two pregnant humans, Fred's daughter Sandy and myself for so long, started a baby boom in "Tiger Town" Tiger town is my nick-name for the place where Basette and the other animals live.

After returning from Tiger Town, I took you into your room to change your diaper. On the changing table, you put your feet up in the air and looked at them. You looked at your right foot then grabbed your toes with your right hand. A first!

As I sit here tonight, my mind is heavy with thoughts of tomorrow, the first day that I take you to Beth's, your babysitter. I'm not looking forward to it. I'm sure it's going to be a "toughy." I'm sure that you will be just fine, it's Mom that's going to be a mess. I want your first day at the babysitter behind me. It's raining now. If it rains tomorrow, Daddy won't be able to work, and could watch you while I'm at work. But I just can't stand another delay of your first day at the babysitter. Another time to have to try to suppress my anxieties; prepare myself mentally and emotionally, for a very stressful event. I want it behind me. I don't want to go through this painful crescendo of anticipation again. I'm going to take you to Beth's tomorrow, come rain or come shine. I told Daddy about my feelings and my decision; if it rains tomorrow, Daddy will have the whole day to himself to do whatever he wants.

October 16

It did rain, Daddy has the day off and I took you to Beth's for the first time. When I arrived at Beth's, half an hour early, I was fine. It was time for you to eat, so I fed you while Beth and I talked. Her fourteen month old son, Bryan, was taking a nap. I needed to leave at 2:00 pm to allow enough time to get to work in the rain. You finished eating at 1:45 pm. Two o'clock came and went.

Every time I thought of leaving I felt like I was going to cry, so I kept putting it off. Beth showed me where you would take your nap and where your diaper would be changed. I just couldn't make myself leave. At 2:30 pm, I finally left, with just enough time to grab a drive-thru burger, and get to work five minutes late. In the midst of my anxiety today, I forgot to eat lunch.

As I left, I could barely hold back the tears. I just had to give you one last kiss before I left. That did it, I was crying. Beth's eyes welled up with tears, too. She knew exactly how I felt.

It was still raining. I cried all the way to work. It felt to me as though the whole world was crying with me. I wasn't sure why I was still crying. I had fears of neglect and child abuse, which is why I checked out so many people before selecting just the right person to care for you while I was at work. I felt very good about Beth. She was pleasant, caring, honest, and genuinely liked you. You responded so positively to her. I knew she would be gentle and attentive. So why was I so upset?

I suppose it was the thought of having you in the care of

someone besides myself, your Daddy, or your grandparents who I knew loved you; it frightened me.

When I called Beth from work to see how you were doing, she was very understanding. She told me about everything the two of you had done: talking, playing, laughing; when you ate and how much, and when you went down for a nap. She knew all of the things I wanted to be told without even being asked.

Later that evening, when you were home with Daddy, I called him to see how you were. You had just finished eating and were about to play. He said you were just fine. I couldn't wait to get home to see you. I'd been so frazzled at work. The fact that there was a dear little one-month old baby girl there in our intensive care unit, who had been the victim of child abuse, compounded my anxiety.

I was asked to take care of her. I couldn't possibly under these conditions, today of all days, when I have a two-month old baby girl myself! I had to refuse. I couldn't stand to be in that dear, wee child's room for more than ten minutes. Poor, sweet baby. I couldn't wait to get home to hold you, hug you, protect you. The presence of that baby made the need more intense.

When I finally arrived home, you were sound asleep. I stroked your face and held your tiny hand. You stirred a bit. I wanted so much to pick you up, to hold you. You didn't seem to be sleeping very soundly though. I didn't have the heart to mess up your evening too—in case you would have trouble getting back to sleep. After all, you were fine; I'm the one that was a mess. You'd better be ready for some real "bear-hugs" in the morning though! I'll have to go take my anxiety out on your Daddy for now. You'll get tonight's hugs via second intention.

October 17

I was mentally exhausted last night when I finally went to sleep. I had numerous dreams and even more numerous bad images of losing you—child abuse, drunk driving, drowning, you name it! I sure felt a lot better once I was able to hold you this morning. Hugging you was so nice. It felt particularly nice to stay home with you today after yesterday's trauma.

October 19

You are eligible, by age, to progress to the next group of baby exercises. You have actually outgrown the first group by almost a month. You had already achieved their purpose, but I didn't want to move you into the three-to six-month old group of exercises before your time and risk harming you in any way. Shortly after your exercises, you ate and "went down" for a nap in your crib without being totally asleep, and with only five seconds of fuss.

Late this afternoon I had you in your rocker-carrier and you started to fuss. I tried to distract you with your cloth play-flower; jingling and squeaking it in front of you. After a few minutes, I put it face up in your lap, making it hard for you to see it. After another minute, you picked up both legs, to get a better look at it. A couple of tries later, you picked up only your left leg, the only leg the flower was sitting on. You did this a number of times—a fast learner.

We discovered a new game, and did you catch on fast! While on your back on your play-quilt, I pushed on your feet, bending your knees into your chest. You pushed straight at me with both legs and moved yourself away. I repeated my part and you repeated your part until we ran out of quilt. I picked you up off of the quilt and pulled you toward me again. You thought that was wonderful. We did the whole routine eight or nine times. You really seemed to enjoy it, you laughed quite a bit! Not long afterward, you rolled over onto your back twice.

October 20

This morning we worked on your new group of exercises. It was hard for me to lean over you on the floor. My cold had caused my head to be terribly congested and my nose to be just the opposite. I couldn't wait to get over this cold I picked up a couple of days ago. I haven't been able to kiss you, and I sure miss that. Once my cold is gone, we can really work on your new group of exercises. After our attempt at your exercises, you rolled yourself onto your back.

You've started to hold your nose with your fingers when you suck on your thumb. You've pretty much decided that your thumb is your favorite digit to suck on. I bet you thought you'd catch me calling your thumb a finger! Ha, fooled you.

Timeline: Today marks the first day of the Missing Children's Hot Line. Let's hope that it makes a difference in recovering lost and missing children.

October 21

Today you weighed in at 13 pounds; 24 3/4 inches.

Today, as you explored my elbow during a diaper change, you used both hands, a very sophisticated maneuver. You have done this during two of your diaper changes. Watching you grow certainly makes time fly.

October 22

Your first feeding of the day is so much fun now. For the first ten weeks, you would barely wake up for these feedings, then you would fall asleep again by the time you were burped. Now you wake up at the end of the feeding. You look about, lazily at first, then very brightly, but yawning the whole time. Those little-person yawns are so precious that I just want to hug and kiss you to pieces. I can't wait for this cold to be over so I can kiss you again.

October 23

I had to work today. It was your second day with your babysitter, Beth. We arrived at Beth's early enough for me to feed you before I left for work. I handed you to Beth so I could get your "gear" out of the car. You started to cry. I thought it was just an after meal fuss. When I came back with your gear, you were crying a little harder. Beth said, "You'd better hold her, Mommy." As soon as I took you from her, you stopped crying and snuggled against me. I held you for awhile.

After I fed you, I had to leave. When I handed you back to Beth, you looked at me. A frown started to grow across your face and you cried again. You recognized me now as Mom, and weren't about to settle for a non-Mom person. Poor Tiffany, I felt very bad leaving you. I'm sure glad that you weren't at this point the first time I took you to Beth's. I would have been absolutely devastated.

When I called from work to see how you were doing, Beth said that you had stopped crying after ten minutes. She had put you in her automatic infant swing and you loved it . She said you had no difficulty holding your head up as the swing went back and forth. I was glad you were having a good time.

I will try to change your automatic swinging basket over to the swinging chair again tomorrow. I have worked on it a couple of times and haven't been able to master hooking it up yet. It's a toughy. We'll get it put together in the next day or so.

October 25

It was such a pretty fall day that we just had to take advantage of the park. There aren't many pretty and dry days at this time of year. We went to pick up my friend, Cheryl, and her children, Randy (age 3) and April (five months). As we all headed for the park, we stopped by the hospital to pick up our respective paychecks. We spread out a blanket to sit on. You talked to April and to the tree while Randy played on the swings. You seemed to enjoy yourself.

October 27

This morning when I went into your room to feed you, you were about to roll over. You looked up at me when I called your name then finished rolling over. It was harder for you to roll over in the crib because it had more "give."

After breakfast, I struggled with your automatic swing trying to attach the swing attachment where the basket hanger had been before. I finally got your swing put together. The first time I put you in it, you weren't very happy with it. I think it was too soon after a meal.

We tried the swing again this afternoon, well after your last feeding. You loved it! You babbled and gurgled; you looked at everything you could possibly see; and smiled almost constantly. I'm so happy that you enjoyed your swing.

At 11:00 pm. you started to fuss, after you'd been asleep for a few hours. I waited three or four minutes to see if you would settle back down. When you didn't, I went in and found that you had turned yourself onto your back again. I picked you up for some hugs, gave you another feeding, and put you back to bed—on your tummy. You went right to sleep.

October 28

Today's Tiffi statistics: 13 pounds; 24 3/4 inches.

It's Sunday. I weighed and measured you this morning. You had grown one-quarter inch during the last five weeks, but you still weighed 13 pounds. You haven't gained any weight for five full weeks now. I'm working today and Monday and might not be able to get a call returned from Dr. Kelley; so I'll wait until Tuesday to call and talk to him about this. I don't want to wait the two weeks for your next well-baby appointment. You don't show a single sign of any other problems, but this lack of weight gain worries me.

October 29

It's Monday. It's a good thing I didn't call your Doctor today, I would never have been able to take his return call. The hospital floated me out to the telemetry unit to "special" a patient in "protective isolation." "Specialing" means a nurse takes care of only one patient. "Protective isolation" involves extra precautions taken to protect someone from environmental organisms and those of the caregiver. It's used for people with little ability to fight infection.

October 30

I talked to Dr. Kelley this morning about your lack of weight gain. He said he felt that you just needed more calories. He had originally suggested we wait until you were four months old before we introduced solids, to reduce the potential for allergies. Since you are demonstrating a need for more calories, he said we could start now. Some babies are ready sooner than others. I told Dr. Kelley that during the last week, I thought you had looked rather "longingly" at me as I ate some yogurt, and a couple of times when I ate graham crackers. I thought it was just my imagination, but Dr. Kelley said babies do show an interest in Mom and Dad's eating at a certain point and do long to share in that.

Dr. Kelley asked us to give you rice cereal only until your four month visit—two tablespoons of cereal in the morning and in the afternoon. He also told us that at this point in life babies gain about one-half ounce per day, and that you should gain one-half pound by your next visit. We will get started on your introduction to solid foods at your next feeding.

It was afternoon before we were back from the store and ready to start your first encounter with food. I tried to give you rice cereal before the breast-feeding, as the Doctor and all of the books I had read suggested. Based on the belief that since swallowing was hard , being a foreign skill at this point, you were more likely to engage in it if you were really hungry. Well, you didn't engage. I'd put a bit of cereal into your mouth with the "padded" (vinyl coated) baby spoon and you'd push it right back out at me. I put it in, you pushed it out. In-out, in-out.

You cried and cried. I hadn't wanted this to be so traumatic for you or you wouldn't want to do it. I've heard numerous "horror" stories of mothers' frustrated and maddening attempts at their babies' first feeding of solids. Now, I know why. I stopped trying and left the warming dish plugged in. I thought I'd try again after you finished the first breast. After the first breast, you were really fussy, so I decided to see how you would do after a full fourteen minute feeding. After a complete breast-feeding, you were much more relaxed.

We moved back over to the breakfast counter. I put you back into your infant seat and again tried to feed you cereal. I let you suck on my finger to help get the cereal down, you even got a bit of it down by swallowing. All in all you actually ate one teaspoon. I thought that was great for a first try! You had cereal all over your mouth and hands. You had a grand time squishing it in your hands and between your fingers. It was adorable! I asked Daddy to take pictures. You even enjoyed that!

October 31

Happy first Halloween! I've been making a leopard costume, actually a baby leopard costume for your first Halloween. I'll finish off the ears and tail of your costume this afternoon.

This morning, I again tried the solids before your breast-feeding—no success. Half-way through—still no success. I tried something a little different on the second breast. I disconnected you from it every so often and gave you a spoonful of cereal and let you suck it down at the breast. That really doesn't educate you to swallowing, but my first concern was that you gain weight. We could worry about how you'd do with pure swallowing once we got past your weight problem.

After the breast-feeding, I put you into your infant seat to finish your solid food, and you took a whole tablespoon. That's much better than last night!

The majority of the time that I put the spoon to your mouth you opened your mouth to accept it. Thank you! We had this down to a science. I'd put a little on top of the spoon and put it inside your upper lip and you sucked it down with your finger or thumb some of the time, and swallowed it on your own some of the time. I was so impressed with how well you did!

It was almost dusk when you finished your evening cereal feeding. I had finished your costume and it was time to put it on and go trick-or-treating.

You should have seen how adorable you were in your leopard costume. We took pictures before we left to go out trick-or-treating for UNICEF (United Nations International Children's Education Fund.) I thought it would be nice to start a tradition of going out for UNICEF right from the beginning. You were a real "hit" in the neighborhood. Many of our neighbors wanted a picture of you in your costume. You were very quiet the entire time we were out, you just leaned against me and didn't say a thing. You didn't seem unhappy, just quiet.

Once we were back home, and I had you all warm in your little snug sack, it was time to eat. That time, I completed your breast-feeding before trying the cereal. I put you into your rocker-carrier for your solids. You took one whole tablespoon again. That seemed to be the winning combination for us, breast-feed then cereal. You can't argue with success.

November

November 1

Shortly after your 5:00 am feeding, I heard you cry and thought that you might have turned yourself over onto your back. Daddy went in to check on you. I was right, you had turned yourself over. It was great to turn onto your back, but you rarely wanted to stay there, and you weren't yet able to undo the action. With your morning cereal feeding you showed improvement with swallowing and you took two whole tablespoons!

This afternoon I made the consistency of your cereal less watery, and you still did beautifully. You took the whole two tablespoons again You seemed to enjoy eating your cereal.

November 2

After we finished your morning feeding, the power went out. It had been raining most of the night and the winds were very strong. You were due for a bath, so I started it after the power had been off for ten minutes. The power doesn't usually stay off for very long, but just in case this turned out to be an exception, I wanted to do your bath while there was still some

95

water pressure and hot water. Remember, out here in the country, we have to pump the water up out of the well into a pressure tank. The house was still warm. You really enjoyed your bath. You almost played in it; that is you kicked at the water once.

The power had been off for an hour. I woke Daddy up so he could keep the wood stove going. We can't let the house get too cold for you. Besides, I needed to boil some nipples and prepare some sterile water for your formula feedings for when I went to work today. Wood stoves are very handy during power outages when all of your appliances are electric!

After your third morning feeding, I gave you your cereal. Your swallowing efforts were improving. At one point, you seemed stressed by it all and pushed your left hand, which was covered with cereal, up across your eye and onto your forehead, as if to say, "Whew! Won't this ever end?"

November 3

This morning, after you'd had your cereal, you were busy creeping across your quilt on the floor and working on rolling over. I sat down on the couch and ate some raisins. You were profoundly interested in my eating, I'm sure of it. You watched me for a couple of minutes, then you started making chewing motions while you watched me chew! You were imitating motion! You continued doing this off and on until I finished the raisins. It was really interesting!

Cheryl babysat with you this afternoon while I went to work and until Daddy was through with his work in town. I had left for Cheryl's early enough so I could spend some time with you there before I left for the hospital.

When we arrived at Cheryl's she said that she had worn

her red gingham blouse and red sweater especially for you. I thought that was very sweet. After the first few minutes there, you were unhappy. I think you knew that "something was up"; that it wasn't purely a social call. When you started to cry I took you over to watch April in her wind-up infant swing. The two of you watched each other. You stopped crying. April kept smiling at you. You weren't smiling back, but you were definitely studying her.

Once I put your blanket down on the floor, Cheryl took April out of her swing and put her down on the floor a few feet away from you. April immediately started to crawl toward you, smiling between each move. You looked a bit uncertain at first, but you weren't frightened. When April was within arm's reach, Cheryl pulled her back away from you, then April started all over again. At that point you thought it was great fun. You tried to creep toward April, but she was much faster than you were. April is one week shy of being six months old, almost twice your age. You still cried when I left, but I was sure that you would be playing with April in a few minutes.

Work was terrible. I "inherited" an extremely unstable gentleman as my patient and wasn't able to get away for two minutes to call and see how you were doing.

At 4:50 pm I was able to get someone to watch him briefly so that I could check on you. I had to call to see if our Tiffi-care connections had been made. Daddy was supposed to pick you up by 5:15 pm at the latest. Cheryl had to leave home at 5:30 pm. When I called, Cheryl told me that your Daddy's class had been let out two hours early and that he was there to pick you up twenty minutes after I left. She also said that she felt cheated, since she didn't get to play with you much. I felt much better knowing that transfer of care connections had been made and that Cheryl wasn't made late for her appointment.

I had to get back to my patient, so I wasn't able to call

Daddy to see how you'd eaten. I planned to call Daddy later if things ever settled down.

When I was finally able to call, Daddy said that you had done well with your cereal; you had taken about three-quarters of your serving. You're getting very good at this solid food business.

When I looked in on you after work, you were in the middle of your crib. When I went back a couple of hours later to feed you, you were right up against the crib bumper at the end of the crib. You were definitely more successful at creeping in your crib. I felt it was due to a fair amount of your creeping energy being absorbed in moving the quilt around when you practiced your creeping on the floor. I'll ask Dr. Kelley what he thanks about letting you be on the floor without a quilt, bedspread or other launderable covering on the carpet or linoleum.

November 4

Today's statistics: 13 pounds 2 ounces; 25 inches long.

You've gained two full ounces in six days. Great work, Sweetie.

After your second feeding this morning, Daddy put you down on your playquilt in the family room. You rolled yourself onto your back from your stomach, via your right side, and you did it three times in less than five minutes! You had just finished your feat as I came out to the kitchen. Right after Daddy told me about your accomplishment, he went to check the wood-stove. While Daddy was gone, you rolled over again twice within five minutes.

November 5

Today you rolled onto your back at will. You do it so regularly now that you consider it old news. In other words, you no longer herald the activity with an entire chorus of happy noises. You are also putting everything that finds it's way into your hand into your mouth—very normal, but at times unnerving. Everything within your reach must be "choke-proof," not small enough to become lodged in your airway.

November 6

Presidential Election Day

It's amazing watching you perform certain fragments of a task at one time or another; and then one day as we're watching you, we suddenly realize that you've integrated a number of those fragments into a complete task. Watching you grow is such a pleasure. You've been reaching for objects that were beyond your reach. You creep toward them or scoot yourself sideways in order to turn over to get yourself closer to the object.

Believe it or not, you watched your first Presidential Election tonight. An historical one at that. Ronald Reagan, ex-Governor of California, was reelected to a second term by the "largest landslide in American history."

November 8

Today, when I took you to Beth's before work, you cried; both when I went back to the car for your things and when I left for work. However, when I called to see if you had taken your bottle for Beth, she said, "Yes," and that you had a great time playing together. Beth said, "It was your best day together yet."

November 9

When I took you to Beth's today, you didn't cry when I went to the car for your things. You made very unhappy faces, and then started to cry after I came back into the house with your bag, and walked by you to put your things in your nap room. I held you for a while and hugged you. Beth and I worked at getting you to smile and forget your troubles. It worked. I was actually treated to a few smiles before I left.

When I called from work, Beth said you had taken three and one-half ounces of the breast milk. You played for awhile, then fussed, so she put you down for a nap. You are beginning to enjoy your visits at Beth's. I am so pleased, she is a wonderful lady with a wonderful family.

November 11

Statistics: 13 pounds 8 ounces; 25 inches.

You have gained eight ounces in the last thirteen days. Fantastic! The cereal really did get the job done.

You've come to spend a great deal of time with your index finger in the corner of your mouth. Seeing you in that position brought images of the sculpture "The Thinker" to my mind. That would make you—"The Young Thinker."

November 12

This morning you turned onto your back via your left side

for the first time. Later in the morning you did it three more times. When you're hot, you're hot! You almost turned onto your stomach. The only thing that stopped you was getting stuck on the arm that was under you. Same hitch as before when you were learning to turn onto your back. I was sure that you would overcome it in no time. Won't it be great when you can turn onto your stomach at will? That way, if you turn yourself onto your back and don't want to stay there, you could fix the problem yourself.

November 13

This afternoon you reached out for your rattle, grabbed it, held onto it and shook it. You're so amazing; changing, learning all the time.

You had your four month check-up today. Dr. Kelley asked questions to evaluate your development. He asked if you were turning onto your back yet. When I reminded him that you had started that at two and one-half months, he remarked, "That was amazing."

I asked him about the lighter-colored patch of skin on your left calf. He said it was called a hypopigmented macule. He didn't know if it would be permanent. If so, it would act as an identifying mark.

After your Doctor's appointment we went to Cheryl's house to visit. You were very quiet, like you were after your last immunization. You are such a good sport.

November 14

This morning I put you on the floor on your "choo-choo" quilt, the quilt with a train picture printed on it. You tried to grab at the printed apples in the trees every once and a while.

While you played on the quilt, you reached for your rattle with your right hand, then with your left hand, then with both.

This afternoon, when you were on your quilt, you were particularly animated. Talking, laughing, playing and turning over more than ever. You really enjoyed playing with the pictures on the quilt as you had done this morning. During your play, you almost turned onto your stomach. I gave you a very slight assist by turning you onto your side via your hip. You made it onto your stomach twice with that little boost.

November 15

This morning, you played with your ball. You were fascinated by it; touching it and rolling it to one side then the other.

After you played for a while, I readied you for a bath. During your bath, you held your legs straight up. You've come to the point where you enjoy just holding your legs straight up in the air and watching them. I pushed them closer to your face, and your eyes lit up. You reached out and grabbed your feet, one in each hand and pulled them a little closer. Then you started to push your fingers through your toes and laugh. You studied your feet intently, then laughed again. I could have watched you all day, but the house wasn't warm enough to stay in the tub too long.

November 16

This afternoon you rolled your little ball with both hands, from side to side, on the tray connected to your automatic swing chair. You stopped playing with the ball and started to explore your hands. All this happened as you were swinging in your swing. You were so intrigued with what you were doing. It was truly exciting to watch.

November 17

I forgot to tell you about something that happened yesterday during your morning cereal. You were helping it down with your thumb as usual. After switching thumbs a few times, you put your hands together, interlaced your fingers and put both of your thumbs in your mouth at the same time. Was that supposed to be twice as comforting?

November 18

You weighed in at 13 pounds 10 ounces, 25 3/8 inches.

Today, Daddy said that you had been holding your bottle when he fed you. He had told me that about a week ago; I thought he meant that you were just stabilizing it as you had been doing. When we talked about it today he indicated that he meant you had been holding it. So, when I put your "holds own bottle" sticker on your First Year Calendar, I will put it on one week prior to this date.

You can roll over onto either side now whenever you want. Often when I try to roll you back onto your stomach if you get fussy, you push against me at the half-way point. The times that I do get you all the way over, you push your bottom up into the air and flip yourself over to whichever side offers the least resistance.

November 19

For the last ten days, you stopped sleeping through the night. I work the 3:00 pm-11:30 pm shift, and I've had a hard time getting any sleep with your new schedule, even with Daddy doing a morning feeding. With all of the disruption, you're still the sweetest little one when I feed you during the night; so cute, so cuddly. I love my little snuggle-bug.

Your eyes haven't changed color for over a month now. During your second month of life your eye color seemed to vacillate between blue-grey, brown, and dark grey. It looks as though you're going to have very dark eyes, however, sometimes it's hard to tell if they're dark brown or dark grey.

Your eye-hand coordination has become so discreet. You find your "mark" almost all of the time by the first or second attempt. Now, when you put your hand on my face you don't just hit at it, you really explore it. You move your hand across my cheek to my nose grabbing it and pulling on it, then you move your hand down to my mouth and explore my lips, teeth, and tongue. You are absolutely fascinated with this moving, smiling toy, and it's fascinated with you!

November 21

You've developed quite a bit of mastery at playing with your ball; using both hands now on a regular basis. You're using both hands for most of your other toys, too. You are such a delight.

November 22

Thanksgiving Day

I had to work today, but Daddy brought you up to the hospital for turkey dinner so we could be together. He did a very nice job of dressing you for your trip. It was a cold night and I had set out your "Love" sweatsuit and hat to wear.

I certainly enjoyed showing you off to everybody. Believe it or not, there were some people there that hadn't seen you, in person, since you were born. Heaven knows they'd seen at least a hundred pictures. We took you up to the Nursery after dinner to see your nurse friends. You were very friendly and smiling to everyone we met.

November 23

Can you believe it? Santa Claus is already in town? It's only one day after Thanksgiving and there's an ad in the newspaper about having pictures taken with Santa. What the heck, I don't have to work today—let's take advantage of it. We might decide to use it as our Christmas card picture.

It was a little after 11:00 am before I finished dressing you in your pink flowered pinafore dress and white tights. You looked like a little confection. Enough writing, let's go see Santa!

When we arrived at the mall, Santa was out "feeding his reindeer," so we waited for him. While we waited, a boy about four or five years old came to stand behind us, he was with his grandma. He was a very nice and gentle boy. He talked to you expecting you to smile at him. You watched him talk, but you didn't smile.

When his grandma talked to you, you smiled and reached

out your hand toward her. She offered you her hand. You grasped her finger and held on. The boy offered his small hand. You grasped his thumb in your fingers. He looked at you, holding his hand and smiled a huge smile. You smiled at his big smile, and he laughed. You then gave him an even bigger smile. The two of you went through this exchange three times. You had made a friend. That reminds me, I didn't tell you about the boy you met at the hospital last night.

When we were walking back to the coronary care unit after our Thanksgiving dinner, there was a Dad with his young son in the visitor's lounge outside of the unit. The boy was about six years old When the boy saw you, he said,

"A baby. Can I touch your baby?"

I told him that he could come and say "Hi."

The boy's Dad told us that he had a seven-month old brother at home and knew how to be nice to babies.

The boy then said, "She's pretty." He came over and stroked your foot.

You looked down at your foot, then you looked at the boy; you didn't smile; you just studied him.

As we started to leave his father reminded him to say 'Thank you."

The boy said, "Thank you.".

We've run into some very nice young boys in our small travels. I don't remember many small boys being that nice when I was little.

This morning, as I dressed you, I turned you onto your tummy to button the back of your dress. You reached out with your right hand and touched the changing pad with your flat hand. Then you curled up your fingers in unison, making a scratching noise. You did this in two sets of two. It was very purposeful and very distinct. You did the same thing a couple of times on my face this evening. A new and complex movement to add to your repertoire.

November 24

You have a new habit of knocking the diaper-wipe container over at every diaper change, making it hard for me to do my one-handed diaper-wipe grab. So far, the diaper wipes we had bought came in tall cylindrical containers. Yesterday when I went shopping, I bought a different kind of diaper wipe. The container was larger and heavier. You still swung at it trying to move it around on the changing table. It did move; and you almost pushed it off of the table three times. But it didn't fall over; I could still retrieve the diaper wipe with one hand. You really work at finding things to amuse yourself—all part of growing up.

November 25

Today's Tiffi statistics are 13 pounds 14 ounces; 26 inches.

Your Aunt Lori called tonight to say that she was in Oroville visiting her sister-in-law Becky. Oroville is a two hour drive from our ranch. Lori, like so many of our friends, lives in Los Angeles. She and I have been friends for fourteen years, since we were sophomores in high school. She's been like a sister to me, so she's like an aunt to you. Aunt Lori, and her sister-in-law Becky will be coming up to the ranch tomorrow morning to see you.

November 26

Your Aunt Lori was so happy to see you. She said, "You are so very pretty."

She was right, of course. Are you beginning to believe that you are a truly beautiful baby!?!

I showed your Aunt Lori a game you and I play where I set you on both of my knees and raise and lower them alternately while saying "Boom-chiga-boom-chiga boom-boom-boom; boom-chiga-chiga-chiga; chiga-boom-chiga boom chiga-chiga-chiga boom-chiga-chiga-chiga boom-chiga-boom chiga-boom-boomboom" (right knee up on "boom," left knee up on "chiga" or vice-versa). You loved it, especially when I switched knees by putting two "booms" or two "chigas" together. You smiled, laughed, gurgled and babbled.

Your Aunt Lori played the "Boom-chiga" game with you. When she bounced you on her knees, she forgot the words, but you loved it anyway. Aunt Lori thought you laughed because you have a ticklish bottom. I think you laugh because you just like the ride. You and Aunt Lori had a nice visit together. While she was here, she gave you one of your feedings; you both enjoyed that tremendously.

November 27

This morning at 4:30 am, Daddy gave you your middle-of-the-night feeding. The next time you woke up it was 7:30, my turn to feed you. You were your usual sunny little self.

After we finished with your feeding you looked around the room. I started singing "Boom-Chiga-Boom"—your jingle to jiggle by, but without bouncing you. I held you up near my face. You smiled and babbled. You looked around; then looked at me again. I smiled. You smiled, laughed, and reached out to touch my mouth. You are so sweet, so exciting. I love you!

November 28

You have expanded your "in unison finger-curling" to experimenting on all kinds of surfaces now. Each surface gives you a different sound. You curl your fingers on one surface, then study your hand or tilt your head as you contemplate the sound and register it into your bio-computer, then you hunt for another surface, a new sound. I wonder if you'd truly notice it if you came upon a repeat sound? It's so cute to watch you formulate small tasks.

Today I went to get my hair trimmed for our first family picture. You came into town with me, but stayed at Cheryl's house while I was at the hairdresser. While I was in town, I went to Sears. They had mailed a gift coupon to us for a free Winnie the Pooh stuffed toy, to celebrate the birth of our new baby—YOU! The little pooh-bear was a cutie. You enjoyed playing with it once I introduced you to him. I think you liked his nose best.

All participating picture subjects have had a haircut now except you; you didn't need one. Tomorrow we will have our first family picture.

November 29

Picture day!

You did beautifully at the portrait studio. There was a line, naturally. There hadn't been a line all week but today—well, that's the way it goes sometimes. The photographer's assistant said the wait would be an hour or longer.

Poor Tiffany—poor Mommy. Up to this point everything had gone nicely. You were comfortable and happy. We wanted you to be refreshed, so we didn't interfere with the nap you took this morning, and actually ended up leaving a bit later than planned. I had dressed you last, just in case you spit-up before we left. I also put a bib on, to protect your dress until your picture was taken. I had geared this experience for success; to be an enjoyable experience for everyone. So much for the best laid plans.

One hour and twenty minutes later, you were getting fussy—completely understandable. I had prepared a bottle, just in case, so I wouldn't have to breast-feed you just before the picture was taken. Wouldn't you know, of all times to have a memory "brown out"—I had left the bottle at home. The nearest available place to feed you "ala breast" was, where else, the bathroom. This was, by the way, the first and hopefully only time you would have to eat in a bathroom.

What an experience. I was wearing one of the nursing tops I had made. A nursing top is a blouse designed with openings in a nipple-line seam or gathers; to allow for discreet breast-feeding in public. I had stitched the blouse's accesses closed, so that the blouse would be sure to drape properly for the picture. So I had to take my blouse completely off to feed you so I wouldn't get it wet for our photo. Wouldn't that have been the ultimate in "tacky?"

There we were perched in a bathroom stall. Me with my previously perfectly-pressed blouse off and gently draped over my purse, which was hanging from the top of the bathroom stall door. Naturally, there wasn't a hook in this, the only empty stall at the time. You were totally unaware of the spur of the moment redesigning of the situation that was necessary to accommodate you being hungry at this time.

As I said, you were hungry. You started to eat right away—until someone flushed a toilet. You looked around quickly, totally surprised, and somewhat traumatically disconnected from my breast in the process. I was still delivering milk, automatically, to the bathroom stall door two feet away.

We started again. You looked around and disconnected every time someone flushed a toilet, opened a door, turned on a water faucet, or flicked the trash can lid. The bathroom was busy, and with all of the interruptions we didn't have time for our usual full feeding of fourteen to sixteen minutes. We had just time to get enough milk in to you to "top off your tank," until we had our picture taken.

You were so frequently distracted that I doubt your sucking was very efficient. However, your tanks were sufficiently topped off; you were happy again. My skirt had milk on it now, but it wouldn't show in the picture. It was a good thing I had taken my blouse off, or it would have been wet, too.

Our turn with the photographer finally came. You were a little less than happy. By the time we had made some pose choices and were set up with the backdrop, you were tired but very cooperative. We were very proud of you, behaving so nicely despite the delay, and bizarre feeding. You could be such a dear when things were less than smooth, You are really quite remarkable for such a little one.

Surprise! Tonight you had your first feeding of vegetables in your "whole life." It was yellow squash. You looked so cute with squash all over your face that I asked Daddy to take a picture. Just after Daddy took your picture, the phone rang— once. That's Grandma Ani-Poo's signal. They must be back from their trip. I'll call them back after you're through eating. Grandma Ani-Poo doesn't want me to have to try to get to the phone if I'm busy, so she signals by ringing once and hanging up, to let me know she'd like to talk. I then call back when I'm finished doing whatever it was she might have caught me doing.

We'll go down to Grandma Ani-Poo's tomorrow afternoon so they can see your sweet little self, how you've grown, and all of the new things you've learned to do since they left ten weeks ago. We won't go until afternoon so they can have a chance to sleep in.

December

Daddy gave you your morning feeding. At your next feeding with me, you fussed and fussed on the first breast, as you've been doing the last few days, but settled down a bit at the second breast. I'm not exactly sure what all this is about. Over the last two weeks, you have become very fussy during your feedings. It wasn't very pronounced at first, but it has steadily increased.

Over this last week, I thought I'd pinned it down to the afternoon feedings. The last day or two have shown that it wasn't the feeding time itself; it's any time other than during the night, or your first morning meal! At today's, as with all of your "wee hours" meals, you nursed happily.

Grandma Ani-Poo and Popie were sure thrilled to see you. Grandma had tears in her eyes when she opened the front door and saw you. She grabbed you up into her arms before we could get through the door.

You were passed back and forth, you were hugged, cuddled, and nearly snuggled to death. You loved it! I was surprised at how quiet you were. You didn't fuss, but you didn't smile either; maybe you didn't remember them. You started to smile a lot, after you relaxed from all of the excitement, but you hardly said a word or should I say a "gurgle." After a couple of hours you started to laugh and did a bit of quiet talking.

Grandma and Popie had bought an adorable jogging suit for you. It was grey with pink cuffs and pink ruffled caps on the sleeves. They also bought a pink t-shirt for you that says "If you think I'm cute, you should see my Mommy." That should go nicely with your pink gym shorts, my "Lilliputian" fashion plate. (Lilliputians are a race of tiny people in the children's story *Gulliver's Travels*.)

You should have seen the family heirloom chairs that my cousin-in-law, Dot Winters, sent to you by way of Grandma Ani-Poo and Popie. They're wonderful. One was a rocking chair with a tooled leather seat. It belonged to my cousin Allen (Doc) Winters. He had it when he was a young boy. It's a child's chair, and is seventy-five years old.

The other chair is the most precious little chair I have ever seen. It is an armless bentwood chair. It's tiny and one hundred twelve years old. It belonged to my paternal great grandmother, Hettie Winters. The front portion of both front chair legs is worn off at an angle at the bottom, a condition created by little Hettie dragging the chair by the top of the chair-back. She took it everywhere she went. Isn't that precious! As an adult, Hettie Winters became the first Dean of Women at Stetson University in Deland, Florida.

December 2

Today's statistics are 14 pounds 1 ounce; 26 inches.

You took your night feeding very happily as usual, but you wouldn't nurse more than one minute at any other time today. I don't know what's wrong. Possibly I don't have enough milk anymore. Work has been so hectic lately that I can't pump and eat in thirty minutes. I don't get any milk out. I have to wait until I get off work to pump, and I haven't been getting off until after midnight. That translates into eleven to fourteen hours between milk expressions, depending on the progression of your feedings that morning.

I'm afraid I'm losing my milk production, that you haven't been getting much of anything when you suckle, and that is why you've been so fussy at your feedings. That upsets me. I want you to get the benefit of the antibodies and the lesser sodium present in my milk as opposed to formula. Not to mention the fact that I just enjoy nursing you. You enjoyed it, too; at least, you used to. I'm so disappointed at the thought of losing the ability to give you my milk this soon in your life.

I asked Daddy to warm the expressed breast-milk from the last night that I worked. You took it eagerly from the bottle, reaching for the bottle as you saw it coming. Few things have hurt me as deeply as that did. It did, however, tell me that it wasn't a problem with the milk itself, just the method of delivery, or should I say lack of delivery. Somehow, that didn't make me feel much better.

You didn't really nurse at all today. Each time I tried, you fussed and cried almost continually. I got all tense and teary. I couldn't bear to see you so unsatisfied with your feeding, especially when I thought you were unhappy with breast-feeding or that it might be because I was losing my milk. I don't want to lose the ability to breast-feed you until you are ready to be weaned to a cup. But the extra couple of months wouldn't be worth putting you through unnecessary anguish.

You have been taking the bottle so happily these days. If it isn't because of decreased milk production, I don't know what's wrong. I can't see anything that I'm doing differently from what I've been doing all along.

After the first two failed nursing attempts today, I gave up trying. I was so hurt that I couldn't even try again out of fear of your certain rejection. I'm a bit confused as to why I viewed that as rejection; it had been an emotionally painful day.

I went to bed earlier today to try to escape, then got up after you and Daddy went to bed, so I could spend some time alone.

December 3

Your night feeding went happily. I love those feedings most of all. You're so especially sweet and snugly at those times. If you won't take my breast at any time other than at night feedings, maybe it would work for me to pump my breasts during the day—at least that way you would get some of the benefits of the breastmilk and we can just nurse at night. I'll try again tomorrow!

Today's breast-feeding plan was to try different positions. I tried our usual cradling position this morning. The outcome was the same as yesterday—rejection. I tried laying you by my side on a pillow and supporting your head with my hand. You took my breast and started to settle down. You nursed for five minutes on the right breast, and then became slightly restless. I burped you and changed sides. You settled down quickly and nursed, holding my breast with your small soft hands. You became very relaxed and drowsy. After seven minutes, you fell asleep. Could it be that all you wanted was a change of position? How relieved you must have felt. Mom finally hit on the right way to satisfy your need. That's the first time that you've fallen asleep nursing in a long time. I was elated that the feeding went so well.

I put you down for a nap after a lot of gentle snuggling. I

was happy. I do so want to breast-feed you until you are ready to drink from a cup. I feel that it will reduce any problems of bottle-fixation, so to speak—instead of weaning you from breast to one hundred percent bottle, then weaning you from bottle to cup. Of course since you have been taking feedings from a bottle, approximately twenty-five percent of the time now, it wouldn't be as much of an issue for you. We would just increase the percentage of bottle feedings gradually. Well just take it one day at a time.

I was very relaxed at the next feeding and was sure you would be comfortable, too. Unfortunately, you weren't. We used the "side-lying" position that worked so well last time. No luck this time. We left the family room and I tried to nurse you while lying down. That didn't work either. I asked Daddy to fix a bottle for us. Maybe alternating bottle and breast-feedings is in order for a few days, to reduce the mutual frustration, until we find the winning combination(s).

December 4

You spent the majority of the morning smacking your tongue on the roof of your mouth. You were really going at it. Smack, smack, smack. Talk, talk, talk, smack. You were also getting different sounds by smacking your tongue in different places. It was so cute to watch you navigate your little tongue around, checking for your favorite sounds and experimenting with other sounds. Your favorite smack was with the pointed tip of your tongue on your upper lip, just to the left, on the outside. You made such a sweet little noise doing this. I could have watched you all day, too bad I had to work today.

We did very well breast-feeding today—thank goodness. There is still some dissatisfaction on your part. I'm no longer certain that it was all a matter of positioning. It could have something to do with supply. Even when you're happy with the position, you frequently become fussy after three to four minutes.

You could be getting what you need sooner and not wanting to suckle just for the heck of it as you used to. Last night and today when you fussed after three to four minutes, you'd start right in again if I changed breasts.

At your last feeding tonight, 9:30 pm, you suckled for a total of six to seven minutes, three minutes on each side. After seven minutes, you fussed and fussed, and wouldn't take a breast anymore. So, I asked Daddy to fix a three-ounce bottle, just to be sure that you were getting enough food. You took all of it. another piece of evidence that points to "lack of supply." At least, I felt better than I did two days ago when you resisted all breast encounters, except those when you were practically asleep.

December 6

Today we're going to the downtown mall to have our picture taken for this year's Christmas card, in a beautiful red sleigh. We're going early to avoid a long wait and messing up your day like we did last week. We should be gone and back home in time for your nap—should be. Anybody care to make a small wager on that?

We were home in time for your nap, and you did beautifully, as usual, during the picture taking. Sweet dreams, sweet Tiffany. I can't wait to see how the pictures come out; you were talking when the picture was taken.

Tomorrow we're going to Chico to see your Great-Grandpa Wayne and your Great-Grandpa Phil. Chico is a one and one-half hour drive from the ranch; it will make a nice "day trip."

December 9

Today you weighed in at 14 pounds 6 ounces; 26 1/8 inches.

You cried most of the way to Chico. We finally figured out what the problem was. We had to face your carseat forward due to the unusual angle of the back seat in Grandma Ani-Poo's car. Once we stopped and turned the seat around, you were quiet and happy, and soon fell asleep as you usually do during a drive.

We went to Grandma Ani-Poo's favorite restaurant in Chico. You were quiet and inquiring, until my meal was served, then you began to fuss. It had only been an hour since you'd eaten. I had breast-fed you in the backseat of the car when we stopped to turn your carseat around and soothe your frazzled nerves.

When we finished eating, Grandma Ani-Poo held you. Our waitress asked if she could hold you. So many people ask about you when we're out. How old are you? What is your name? Can they hold you? They tell us how pretty you are. In general, people seem fascinated with babies. Grandma Ani-Poo proudly presented you to the waitress. She bounced you in her arms gently for a minute or two.

This was fine with me—until she left the table. She walked away, to behind-the-counter area, which was half-way across the restaurant, while still holding you! Then she proceeded to take you into the kitchen to show you to the cook. I wanted to jump up and scream, "Where are you going with my baby?" I fought the urge, knowing I was overreacting. If she hadn't held the kitchen door open with her foot, enabling me to see you, I probably would have jumped up and screamed at her. The thought of her carrying you away from me was frightening.

She didn't even ask if she could take you "on tour"; she just walked off with you.

She probably only had you for a couple of minutes, but it seemed forever. I couldn't relax. I couldn't take my eyes off her. I would never let anyone walk away from me with you again, unless I knew and trusted them. I can't describe how frightening that feeling was. Never again.

After we left the restaurant we went to see Great-Grandpa Phil. Phil was my late maternal grandmother's steady boyfriend. They met sometime after my Grandmother divorced Wayne (Great-Grandpa Wayne.) Phil and my Grandma Minnie had been "sweeties" for over ten years, before she died. He loved my grandmother very much. I ended up adopting him as my second Grandpa. Great-Grandpa Phil lives in a very small house that is filled to the rim with his personal treasures. You can barely walk through it. He gave us each an ornament for the Christmas tree, a walnut shell painted silver or gold with a red ribbon hanger and a quarter inside. He had made them himself. Great-Grandpa Phil had given me one of these about eighteen years ago; I still have it. He also gave us four colorful butterflies, on suction cups, to put on the window. You were fascinated with their colors.

Great-Grandpa Phil really enjoyed listening to you talk. Whenever you said something, he would stop talking and look at you and smile. Then he would look to us and say, "Aw, would you listen to that." He certainly was happy to see you. We took a picture of all of us together.

After leaving Great-Grandpa Phil's we went to Great-Grandpa Wayne's. Wayne was my grandmother's second husband and the only grandfather I knew when I was growing up. He's in his early eighties. My Grandma's first husband, my Mom's father, died when my Mom was sixteen. Great-Grandpa Wayne was supposed to be a tough mountainman. He is, in reality, a very kind and caring man.

You were past due for a nap when we arrived at Great-Grandpa Wayne's. We couldn't raise anyone at his house; but just as we were pulling away Popie noticed someone that looked like Great-Grandpa Wayne coming out of a house down the street. It was him!

Since you were overdue for your nap we didn't take you out of the car. We didn't want your encounter with Great-Grandpa Wayne to be a negative experience (more out of concern for him than for you). You would get over it, he might not. Wayne came into the car to see you. You brought a huge gentle smile to his face. As we visited, you faded off to sleep. Grandma Ani-Poo stayed in the car with you while Popie and I went into the house to visit with Great-Grandpa Wayne for a few minutes.

Great-Grandpa Wayne said, "How 'bout that little one, isn't she something!?!" with a big soft smile and a twinkle in his eye. We didn't stay long, as you had had a very long day. And your Great-Grandpas appreciate short visits more than they do long ones. Great-Grandpa Wayne came out to the car with us to get another look at you and we were off. We forgot to take a picture of him—darn! We gave each Great-Grandpa a picture of you.

When we arrived home, I thought you would want to go right to sleep after such a long day. You didn't. I changed your diaper and you were ready to play; twenty minutes later you were ready to eat. You fell asleep right after you finished eating. Good night, sweet dear. You've had two very long days now. Tomorrow we'll stay home. We'll sleep when you like and play when you like. You need a day of just being at home enjoying life.

December 10

Today, you greeted me with smiles, laughs and "ih's" (a new word). While on the changing table, you started to play with your feet once they were out of your sleeper. When I finished changing your diaper, I just watched you play with your feet for awhile.

You managed to get your right big toe into your mouth for the first time by yourself. It was so cute. I had been looking forward to the time when you would put a foot into your mouth; I always thought that was such a sweet baby activity.

When we were playing on your quilt, I decided to let you play with the little training cup that came with your food warming dish. I had been thinking about this for a few days, wondering if it was too soon to try you with a cup. I thought I'd just give it to you to play with and knock around. My hope was that after a few weeks of trial and error you'd get good at holding it, which would make your bottle-to-cup transition easier.

Since you had just rolled yourself onto your back and were looking right at me, I handed you the cup. You grabbed it and put in right into your mouth. Right-side up and top-side in! Amazing!

After a minute, you dropped it. I gave it to you four times. Three of those four times, you put it in your mouth—right on target. The other time, you went through the right motion, but missed your mouth with the tip. I was really impressed! I had no idea that you would pick up on that so quickly. I suppose you looked at the cup as if it were your bottle, and you knew what to do with that. Now I'm not sure what to do. If I let you keep playing with an empty cup, you may give up working with it. Should I just not give it to you anymore. Or should I put a little formula in it? The milk comes out of a training cup faster than it comes out of a nipple.

As you played, I called Dr. Kelley's office to ask his nurse for advice about the training cup. I also asked her about increasing your time between daytime feedings to three hours. She said every three to four hours is fine. She also said to begin mixing cereals, vegetables and fruits for a more balanced meal.

She said that it was fine to give you some formula in a cup, but you should have something to eat first so that you wouldn't gulp your formula too fast. She said that once you've eaten something to then let you take some formula from a cup, then the rest from a bottle, since the cup wouldn't satisfy the sucking needs you still had at this point in your life.

December 11

This morning your Grandma Ani-Poo and Popie spent some time with you while I went to Redding to do some shopping. They really enjoyed their time with you. It was the first time they were able to spend some relaxed time with you alone. You laughed, played, and talked. They were thrilled. You were very quiet the last time they visited with you.

This afternoon as you played on one of your quilts, you reached for your ball. You gathered it into your right arm and drew it in close to you. You also rolled onto your side a few times and made it all the way to your stomach twice!

December 12

When I called Beth from work today, to see how you were doing, she told me that you were having a terrific time playing together. You were pulling on your feet and playing with them. Beth is such a wonderful lady and really enjoys you.

December 13

You took an ounce of formula from your little cup this morning, holding it firmly. You did very well. All I did was hold my finger over the air intake hole to keep the milk from flowing too freely.

After a successful session of cup-drinking practice, you were ready to play. For a change of pace we moved your playquilt into the sunken living room, which is bordered on two sides by two carpeted stairs. It was sort of like a giant playpen. We do have to be careful in there, as one of our two wood-burning stoves is there. You played with your cloth flower—the one with a different texture—and a different surprise nose in each petal. You held it in one hand, by one of its large petals, lifted it well off of the floor, and moved it through the air. Such strength.

You worked on creeping while we were in the living room. Over the last couple of weeks you seemed to be "testing the waters" as far as creeping goes. You made efforts toward it on occasion, then took an extended hiatus before attempting it again. You'll try it again, when you're ready.

While we were playing on the bedspread on the living room floor, Grandma Ani-Poo and Popie dropped by. You romped all over the bedspread. You pushed yourself backwards while raised up on your straightened arms until you ran out of bedspread. Then you rolled over and grabbed a foot in each hand. Your legs were split apart with your knees to your chest. It was so cute.

You were so fussy tonight. It was bedtime and you were tired, but fought sleep. You became overtired, fussy and crabby. Poor little Tiffi, you just didn't want to end the day. I tried another half-feeding, even though it had only been ninety minutes since your last one. It didn't help. Walking up and down our sixty-foot hallway with you over my shoulder didn't work either. That long hallway is usually great for walking you to sleep. I gave you the last bit of the half-feeding as I rocked you and sang to you in your room. You watched me constantly, eventually you just stared through me and lost focus. Your head became heavier. As more time passed, your eyelids became heavy, heavier, heavier, and finally closed. It was so precious watching you finally give in to sleep. I love you, Tiffany.

December 15

This morning, while we were on your playquilt, you picked up your cloth flower by one petal and swung it about in the air. It reminded me of a bronco buster with his free hand waving in the air. Once you tired of waving your flower, you discovered your orange squeaky bear toy. That squeaky toy had been one of your favorites since "day one." It's about the size of a small adult fist; it was an ornament on one of your new-baby gifts. You fell in love with it at first sight, probably because of it's almost neon red-orange color. You were holding your squeaky bear by the head with one or **both** hands for long periods of time!

You seem to have developed an activity trademark lately; you bend, kick, bend, and kick your left leg. You just pump away, during feeding, changing, whatever. I'm not sure why you do it. You must be aware of what you're doing.I guess you enjoy it.

Here we were at five months and not yet able to stretch out your feedings. You still eat every two hours; sometimes every ninety minutes, except when you're sleeping at night. You're still getting four ounces at each feeding. You eat the full four ounces most of the time; you don't ask for more, except on isolated occasions, then we give you more. In the morning, I'll call Dr. Kelley's nurse to see if we should increase your amount per feeding.

December 17

Today's statistics: 14 pounds 14 ounces; 26 3/8 inches.

This morning, after getting up, you played for quite a while on your side. You didn't manage to turn over onto your stomach, but you weren't really trying to either.

While you were playing, I called Dr. Kelley's nurse to ask about increasing your amount per feeding. She said to increase you to six ounces of formula at feedings. In other words, I should offer you a full bottle after breast-feeding.

I am concerned that my milk production is down. The last week and a half of work has been so hectic that I haven't been able to get away for a break to pump my breasts. I have been going up to the third floor nursery area to pump my breasts before I go home. Combine that with not getting off work until just after midnight. It added up to too many hours between expressions, a definite precursor to decreased milk production. With you not waking up until five to seven hours after I pump before leaving work, it just hasn't been adequate stimulation to produce enough milk. I feed you every two hours on the days I'm home. Apparently, that periodic increased stimulation hasn't been enough to carry us over on the three days per week that I work.

It wouldn't be fair or practical to be so obsessive about the breast-feeding, waking you up at night to increase your feedings and hence my breast stimulation to increase milk supply. Neither one of us would get any sleep, making us both edgy and irritable. It's much more important that we enjoy these fast moving early months of life than to waste them spending too much of our energies to recapture breast-feeding.

You'll be taking your formula from a cup in another six

weeks or so. I'll just keep breast-feeding you first, when I'm home, and supplementing it with formula afterwards. If that doesn't work with you, I'll just breast-feed you once a day, during our favorite time—your "wee hours" feeding. We can continue that for as long as I can produce enough milk.

I'll miss breast-feeding you. I was never sure exactly when to start weaning you. I had decided on somewhere between eight and twelve months, whenever you were working well with a cup. It now looks as though my work schedule and your subsequent decreased interest have decided the time for me.

When I put you down for a nap today, you were very quiet. I thought you were going to go right to sleep. About five minutes later I heard a strange sound coming from your room. I went to see what it was. You had a hold of your plastic ring of flowers and were banging it on your mattress, and, I mean, you were really **banging** it, with a good deal of energy.

December 18

This morning, Daddy gave you your bottle. Midway through the feeding, you took your bottle out of your mouth with both hands, turned it sideways somewhat and then put it back in your mouth; you're so talented.

After breakfast, as we were sitting on the couch, I sat you up in my lap. You have gained more control of your upper torso. You sat up rather nicely in my lap. How exciting! I wondered when your little internal clock would start saying, "It's time to sit up."

You leaned forward to play with your feet, knees and my leg. I don't know if it's because you aren't yet able to hold your whole torso up, or if you lean over that much just because it's what you want to do; I think it's the latter.

At the next feeding, you fed at the breast for a number of minutes and then I offered you a bottle. While you ate, you became intrigued with your right foot. You started playing with it and pulling at it with your right hand. You were having a difficult time doing both that and eating as you strained to watch what you were doing. But you just couldn't give up on your activity. It took quite a while to finish that bottle, but you were sure cute to watch!

After your feeding I sat down on the floor with you. You did very well sitting up with a stand-by "training hold." I wasn't really touching you at all times, just guarding you from falling "training wheel style." This time you held your little self up rather straight. That was fun! I'm really going to enjoy the different things we can do together once you can sit up. I'll be able to play with you more. For example, I'll be able to get a foot or so away from you and play with you, with both hands, instead of holding you with one and playing with the other.

I'm really going to miss you tonight. I'm working a double shift, sixteen hours. I'll only see you for a short time tomorrow before Daddy takes you to Beth's for the day so that I will be able to sleep. Our Christmas guests will be coming the following day and I haven't been able to finish cleaning the house. After I sleep in, I'll buzz through the house to clean it up and reduce that "overly lived-in look" before I pick you up at Beth's.

9:30 pm: I went to the nursery to pump my breasts. I was only able to get two and one-half ounces. That was after ten hours of not pumping. I'm losing my milk faster than I thought I would. We will still continue our wee-hours feedings as long as possible.

December 19

Well, I'm managing to stay awake. I wasn't able to pump my breasts at all the second shift, but it didn't feel like there was anything to pump.

As I drove home, at 8:00 am this morning, the grass and the ground looked particularly pretty, like wet diamonds. I thought it might have snowed during the wee hours, but it was just an unusual frost. Your first snow hasn't happened yet, but I wouldn't be at all surprised if it did snow this winter.

When I walked into the house, you were awake and in the family room. Daddy was just preparing a bottle for you so I was in time to give you a breast feeding. You were so happy to see me and I was very happy to see you after so long. You nursed for about eight minutes. Then I gave you the bottle that Daddy had fixed. I gave Daddy the breast milk that I had expressed last night and asked him to please mix your solids with it, since it wasn't enough for a full feeding.

You took five ounces of the bottle, then I sat you up on my lap. You had very good full-torso control. You're getting close! We played for awhile as Daddy packed your bag for Beth's. You gave me some great huggies before Daddy took you off to Beth's, then I went to bed. I slept rather well, considering it was during the day. I have never been able to sleep very well during the day.

At 4:30 pm, I left for Beth's to pick you up. I was so happy to see you. You were getting rather tired and spacey. You had that pre-sleepy look. We visited with Beth a bit before leaving.

December 20

Your Grand-Aunt Betse was here tonight. She came up from San Diego, California to meet you. When she arrived, you had a mouthful as well as a faceful of dinner! She thought you looked sweet. Once I had washed your face, she thought you were pretty. I guess only Mommy and Daddy think that a face full of food is cute.

December 21

It was 3:30 am and I was awake. It had been eight hours since your last formula feeding. You were still asleep, but my breasts were full and very tender. It's been about twenty hours since our last breast-feeding.

I awakened you for a breast-feeding. This might be the last one, so I wanted to savor it. You were your usual sweet "wee-hours" self. It was a little hard for you to nurse at first because I was so full and tight, but you settled in shortly for a nice feed. You were very relaxed and dozed off a time or two briefly. I offered you a bottle afterwards. You took three ounces of it before you drifted off to sleep. When you were through I didn't move for a while. I just watched you sleep.

I held you up to burp you. You were limp and cuddly. You were so cuddly and sweet that I had a hard time bringing myself to put you down; after all, this may have been our last breast-feeding. After about fifteen minutes, I finally put you down. I have felt very good about the extra benefits you've received from my milk. I'll miss breast-feeding you, but it's all part of your growing up. It just came sooner than I wanted.

December 22

This morning while you were playing on your quilt on the floor, Daddy went over beside you and sat down on his knees. He sat you up between his leg. You held your little torso up beautifully. You leaned forward to reach your musical cube and your little orange, squeaky bear. You looked so "mature" sitting up and exploring your universe. I wished we had a roll of film. I would have loved to have taken a picture of you and Daddy then.

Grand-Aunt Betse came up from Grandma Ani-Poo's to see you before I went to work this afternoon. She, Grandma Ani-Poo and Popie took you to Grandma's for the day; and they were very excited about it. They're taking your swing, stroller, and your infant seat. They intended to show you off to the neighborhood. Your Grand-Aunt Betse kept exclaiming at the fact that you held your head up three inches from her arms as she cradled you. She was definitely impressed with your young abilities.

December 23

Tiffi statistics: 15 pounds 12 ounces; 26 3/8 inches.

We picked up our Christmas tree. We also reserved the last video camera in town for use with the VCR we had reserved for Christmas Day. Your Grand-Aunt Betse, Grandma Ani-Poo and Popie will be here Christmas Day. I wanted to have your first Christmas on film. We don't have a VCR, but we will someday.

This evening, we took you down to Grandma Ani-Poo's while Daddy and I went to your Grand-Uncle Jack's Christmas party. We took turns being with you and spending time at the party. It worked out beautifully. A number of people asked about you. Roy, your second cousin Janice's husband, was there. He hadn't seen you before, so he left the party to go meet you.

It was late when we left Grandma Ani-Poo's after the party. You'd had a lot of excitement during the night, with people leaving the party next door to visit with and entertain you. You really fought going to sleep. It was 11:00 pm before you finally gave in to sleep.

December 24

Today your first Christmas Eve. You were full of energy and really kept me busy. Daddy went to pick up the VCR and video camera, but a certain adaptor cable hadn't been returned yet.

When Daddy returned, I went back to the guest room to finish putting together our first family photo album.

Daddy didn't know what I was up to, so I wrapped it up as a Christmas present to all of us. Daddy had to leave again in an hour or so to pick up the missing VCR cable. He was going to stay in town until the cable was brought in. We were worried it might not come in time, and we wouldn't be able to film your first Christmas. Some day we will buy a VCR to use for home movies. Until then we will rent the equipment to film special occasions.

The video equipment came in about fifteen minutes before the store closed. Once Daddy returned home, it took a long time to get the whole thing working (not having dealt with the stuff before).

We haven't decorated the Christmas tree yet; we need to do that before we can take time to do any filming. We usually bought our Christmas tree and set it up a week or so before Christmas, but this year money was tight. We juggled bills to rent the video equipment and would have done some more juggling, if necessary, to insure that you had a tree for your first Christmas. This year we were lucky enough to get a free Christmas tree. It was one that the school children had used for the classroom. When school was out of session, the trees were put out for disposal. The school janitor rescued them and offered them to whoever could use them.

I finally finished the housecleaning for Christmas Day. Daddy watched you while I decorated the tree. You enjoyed watching me put the ornaments on the tree.

December 25

Tiffany's First Christmas!

By 8:00 am, I finished making a batch of shortbread and the puffed cranberries for dinner tonight, and doing two "batches" of laundry. I thought you were still asleep, but when I went into your room, I found you lying on your side watching your mobile. You broke into a full-body smile when you saw me. Merry Christmas, Tiffany! It was time to get you ready for your first Christmas happening. Grandma Ani-Poo, Popie and Grand-Aunt Betse would be arriving at 9:00 am.

Daddy came into your room while we were having some nice huggies. He gave you your morning Tiffi-feed, while I dressed. The family arrived mid-feed. Grandma Ani-Poo finished feeding you while Popie brought in the presents. Daddy set up the video-camera. He wanted to film the first time you saw the Christmas tree.

You and I made our grand entrance. You were far more interested in the big dark thing (camera) "on" Daddy's face, than you were in the Christmas tree.

You were so cute in your little red Christmas romper. You seemed to still be sleepy. After a bit, we were sure of it. You were very unimpressed with the package opening and associated goings-on. All you wanted were huggies, and there were plenty of "takers."

Funny thing, there were more presents for you than for anyone else! You should start a fan club. Popie played Santa Claus, and distributed the presents while Daddy and I took turns at camera duty and helping you open your presents. We

showed you each present. You liked the stuffed animals best, the musical toys second. You reached out to hold the stuffed bunny that Janice and Roy gave you. You were so excited with that bunny that you started to drool. Another gift was a stuffed Koala from Vicky. You were particularly fascinated with his fluffy, long, white-haired ears.

Two and a half hours after your last feeding, you became fussy and very tired. Grandma Ani-Poo fed you while Grand-Aunt Betse and Popie walked up the hill, to the east side of the ranch, to see the new lake our neighbor had developed. After your feeding, you were ready for a nap.

Sleep well, sweet Tiffany. All of the glitter and pretties will still be there when you wake up. We ate breakfast while you napped. Actually, it was more of a brunch. We wouldn't do any more filming until our "star" had rested.

After everyone left, I straightened up the package-opening aftermath and started packing your things for Grandma Ani-Poo's Christmas dinner.

As I cleaned up, Daddy started filming again. We really wanted to capture some of your smiling and, particularly, your charming deep laugh on video tape. We especially wanted a permanent record of your deep baby laugh.

You must have felt that we were terribly silly. A constant barrage of tactics to get you to laugh, so we could catch it on tape. Just watching us should have been good for a laugh.

We filmed getting you ready for the picture with your Christmas bear that Grandma Ani-Poo and Popie had given you, a beautiful bear that played different Christmas caroles when you touched one of his hands or feet. The bear was just as big as you were. I decided to take your picture next to it every year at Christmas so we could see how much you have grown each year. There will come a day when you will never believe that you were the same size as that bear. We even captured some footage of you sitting up alone. It was only for a second. But you were sitting alone. We will always enjoy this film.

When we arrived at Grandma Ani-Poo's house, it was time for you to eat. You took the bottle out of your mouth and moved it around as I balanced it. Grand-Aunt Betse was fascinated. After dinner, we all went over to Uncle Jack's to watch the Christmas video we made earlier. Everyone enjoyed it.

When you watch the video tape of your first Christmas, I want you to know that this was something of an "off day" for you. Although you look to be an adorable baby, doing the usual baby things, sometimes happy, sometimes fussy, you are, in reality, an extraordinary baby. You usually fuss less and are more outgoing than you will see on this video. All babies need to fuss at things occasionally. It's part of growing and living.

You've been very interested in your surroundings from your first week of life. You are very happy and enjoyable. You laugh at us and with us. Most of the time you smile, laugh, explore, and study the world. You are rarely fussy with it.

Permanent recordings of events, being the only visual record of life at home, have a tendency to become regarded as the "norm." This is not always accurate. In this case, it is not the norm. Just know that, though this will look like a normal day, it was an unusual day for you.

December 26

Merry day after Christmas. You were so cute this morning, all rested and happy. You were much more interested in visiting with me this morning than you were in eating. You pushed the bottle out of your mouth—talked, smiled or both, then pushed it back into your mouth. I merely balanced the bottle for you. You did all of the navigating.

I set you up in your automatic swing in the family room. You started waving your arms with glee. I hung the little battery-operated monkey that Grandma Ani-Poo and Popie gave you on a perch. I hung it where you could see it while in your swing. When you saw it, you stopped waving your arms and started talking to the monkey and squeaking at him. I hadn't even turned him on yet!

December 28

Just since Christmas, I've noticed that you appear to look at people and things with more intellect; there's more understanding behind your gaze. More than existed just two days ago!

You sat up between my knees today, but you really didn't need the support, at least not at first. You held your body erect, looked around and played with things on the quilt. You also lifted things from off of the quilt and waved them around in the air! All while sitting up. After a couple of minutes, you were leaning forward and did need the support. You leaned farther and farther forward over the next couple of minutes. You then put your arms in front of you, laid down sideways and turned over onto your tummy! Impressive move. Once on your tummy, you made some new faces. You looked particularly mature making those faces. I couldn't say the same for myself if I tried to make those faces.

A week ago today, we experienced what I was afraid would be our last breast-feeding. It was. Seven days have passed and, although I have had tender spots in my breasts, there isn't much milk in there. You have accepted being a completely formula-fed baby most graciously.

Something else happened concurrently. You have been sleeping to your maximum number of hours between feedings during the night again. I don't know if it is all due to your switch to being fully formula fed. Some of it could be because you're growing up—couldn't it?

Since you gained fourteen ounces in one week and have had a few nights of sleeping eight to ten hours, I'll let you try to sleep twelve to thirteen hours to see how you do; you're old enough now.

December 29

Today you sat up for more than five seconds without any support. As the day progressed, you preferred sitting up to any other position. You held your head up straight, and leaned forward, with your nose only inches from the floor, then you raised your torso up again. Other times you would lean to the left, supporting yourself with your left hand, either on your knee or on the floor. By the time evening rolled around, you were sitting up for two to three minutes at a time without help! Isn't that exciting! I called Grandma Ani-Poo and Popie to let them know.

Before I went to bed, I dressed you in the purple pj's that your Uncle Greg and Aunt Margie gave you. The top fit perfectly—"but Sam, you made the pants too long." That will give you room to grow, but for now you looked as though your feet were crooked.

You resisted going to bed. My guess was that you were too excited from your new accomplishments. You chewed on the vinyl foot of your pink blanket sleeper that was next to you on the changing table. Then you put the cloth foot back into your mouth, bit down on it and pulled it out from between your gums—frustration. It was time for bed. You fussed feverishly for about ninety seconds. Then it was off to dreamland for my sweet, little, growing girl.

December 30

Year-end statistics: 16 pounds 1 ounce; 26 3/4 inches.

I watched you while you played on your quilt. You hugged your koala toy. It was so adorable, I wanted to get a picture of it. Once I had the camera, you weren't hugging it anymore. You were waving it and smiling at me, so I took a picture of that.

After a moment or two, you burped. Then, as any lady would, you covered your mouth with your hand. If you don't believe me, I caught a picture of that too! You then proceeded to suck on your thumb and your pinkie finger at the same time. Adorable!

A little later, I put you in your swing to take a picture for Uncle Greg in the "pj's" he gave you. You're becoming quite a photographer's model. You pause and look at the camera while it is in front of my face. You did the same thing on the quilt earlier and a couple of times yesterday. You're certainly a sharp little one.

When you were tired of the swing, I sat you up in your infant seat on the carpet. I sat in front of you recording in this journal the things you had done earlier in the day. Your little seat belt was on and you played with your cloth flower. You waved it around with one hand, dropped it on your legs, then kicked your legs in and out wildly. You laughed and squealed because you were causing the flower to move so much that all of it's little noise makers were sounding off. You were delighted!

Then you became interested in the carpet although it was very hard to reach it over the side of your seat. You stretched and stretched, grunted and strained to get your fingers to the carpet; such effort. I tried to get you interested in your teething necklace, but you were determined to touch that carpet. You finally made it. Once you were satisfied with carpet "feels," you started banging on your cloth flower with the teething necklace.

This went on for a few minutes. I had at least as much fun as you did just watching you. You're so delightful. I wish I could have gotten to Daddy's camera for some pictures. I had just finished the roll in my Instamatic while you were being adorable earlier today.

December 31

It's fashion show time again. We need to get pictures of you in your sweet clothes before you outgrow them. You were most accommodating. I put you on your little one hundred twelve year-old chair for the first time to take a picture. You were dressed in a jumper that Grandma Ani-Poo had given you and the Nike's (jogging shoes) that your Aunt Jill had given you.

It was a toss-up as to which was cuter, you sitting on the antique chair or the picture of you in the bathing suit that your Great-Godmother Evy sent to you. You can judge for yourself, Tiffany, now that you're old enough to read this.

At your next feeding, we were sitting on the couch in the family room. After you ate I sat you up on my lap for a burp. You became interested in the box of tissue. You reached down and picked up the tissue I had just wiped your face with. It was wet. I took it away when you started to put in your mouth.

You reached down and pulled out a fresh tissue—from the box! You looked at it from a couple of different angles, then moved it toward your mouth. I took it away. You reached for

another tissue! You pulled it out, laughed and smiled. I think
you liked the noise the tissue made as it came out of the box.
You were really intrigued by it. I wanted to get a picture, so I
tried putting you on the floor in front of the large study-pillow
with the box of tissue next to you. I hoped that you would still
play with it. You did. You pulled out tissue after tissue waving
them in the air, smiling, laughing and drooling. It was hilarious.

At work tonight I learned that there were five Moms in
labor in the hospital. That's a lot of New Year's Babies. Many
of the people at work were trying to out guess each other as to
which baby would be born closest to midnight.

January

January 1

Happy New Year Baby!

This morning after the Rose Parade, I took your picture in the "Baby" New Year outfit I made for you. While Daddy watched the Rose Bowl, I inflated the stacked balloon ring-walker that Grandma Ruth gave to you. You were too young to use it as a walker, but I thought you would enjoy the new perspective of your surroundings it would allow you. It would support you in an upright position; who cared if you couldn't actually "walk it" yet.

You loved it! You leaned one way then the other and then all the way back, looking behind yourself—upside down. You had the greatest time. You laughed and leaned, and the walker moved! Your eyes grew wide and you gave a huge smile! What a happy baby!

When I first put you in your walker we were on the vinyl flooring in the dining room hall. After a while, I moved you onto the carpet in the family room where it would be harder for you to move the walker. I didn't want to push you into walking. I just wanted you to enjoy yourself. On the carpet, you didn't try moving, just bouncing and playing and looking at everything in the room, from a whole new perspective. I handed different toys to you to play with. You'd hold them, then let them go and watch them fall. You also had great fun studying them as they fell.

I neglected to mention earlier that you have been sitting unsupported for long periods of time. Congratulations.

January 2

Today you're moving the walker a lot, and on the carpet, no less! You could move it in all directions. You bounced in it making the jingle balls in the top ring jingle. That warranted a Tiffi laugh. You even seemed to dance to a couple of songs on the radio while you bounced in your walker. What a fabulous toy. I especially love it because the inflatable rings are clear, so I can see all of your little movements.

Early in the afternoon you said a consonant! You definitely said ah-gah. I thought you said it the day before yesterday, but I wasn't sure. Today I'm sure. Congratulations! A first!

You're able to sit up for as long as you want and hold your torso more erect than before. You sit and sit and sit. I had to put you on your tummy once and a while as a rest break.

Later in the afternoon we were playing peek-a-boo. You and Daddy were peek-a-booing at me. You laughed and laughed, a new louder and heartier laugh. It's delightful!

January 3

Your Grandma Ani-Poo and I are going to take you to the mall today for a stroller ride. Wouldn't you know, I had planned for us to go after your morning nap, but you wouldn't take a nap! Shucks.

You will probably be fussy and unhappy with the outing like last time. I was so hoping you would enjoy going out to the mall for stroller rides. There are so many different things and people, especially kids, to look at.

I wanted to take you anyway to see what would happen. Grandma Ani-Poo tried to reassure me that you would nap for most of the stroller ride. Well, you didn't nap for one second. But, you enjoyed yourself tremendously! Whenever we came near a baby we would all say, "Hi."

We went to the deli for a soup and salad lunch. You, of course, wanted to eat, too. I gave you a bottle so that Grandma Ani-Poo and I could eat lunch at the same time, for a change. I put the back of your stroller down and rolled a small towel up and tucked it under your bottle as a prop. I tucked receiving blankets on either side of you, so that your bottle wouldn't fall to the side and out of the stroller. You took your bottle all by yourself. You're so talented. I was impressed.

That wasn't all. I thought you would make a grand mess. But, you made less of a mess than usual. We won't make bottle propping a habit, just an occasional time to smooth out a meal. I much prefer to hold you when you take your bottle. It's a lot nicer.

You looked so adorable in the denim jumper and white ruffled sweater that Grandma Ani-Poo gave you and in your little size two Nike's that you wore today. Grandma had a great time showing you off. Whenever we would go by someone who took an interest in you, Grandma Ani-Poo would say, "That lady over there wants to see Tiffany. Let's take Tiffi over to see her." I think she was looking at everyone to make sure that anyone who looked at you, however briefly, would get a chance to meet you.

We had a wonderful day. I would like to take you to the mall for a stroller ride, or for a ride in Grandma's neighborhood at least twice a week; we don't have any sidewalks or smooth surfaces in the area where we live. Mildieu kitty sat on my lap as she "helped" me write this.

January 4

Today you fell over while sitting up. It was a gentle and slow fall. It's the first time that I let you fall without me as a protective bumper. I'm glad that the first roll over was a soft one. It makes my allowing you some independent sitting time, a lot easier.

Me overprotective? No! I need some time, Tiffany. You're my first baby. I want to do everything right. I want you to be safe. I want you to be happy. I also want you to be independent, but I can't accomplish that until I'm a little more comfortable being a mother. I'll lighten up a bit with time, effort, and a little experience.

Today you are throwing things down while in your walker, not dropping but throwing. You'd throw a toy down and watch it hit the floor. A few minutes after you started throwing things, you would hold your hands out in the air. You would open, close, open, close your hands almost rhythmically as you held them out.

I wondered if you were aware of your actions. But as you went through the motions, you had a fixed gaze on an object, or just gazed all around, as if you weren't really conscious of your hands. Watching you open and close your hands was adorable. Would you like a pair of castanets?

January 5

It's Saturday morning—cartoon day. After eating, you sat up on your playquilt. You became tired after a long while of sitting. I started to put you on your tummy. As I put you down you had both legs folded under you, as in a crawl position. Your arms were on both sides along your face. You looked so cute. I can't imagine that you were comfortable with the position that you happened into, but it was adorable.

Later when you were sitting up again, I surrounded you with "ground bumpers" and went to the kitchen to fix my breakfast. You were doing just fine, until you realized that I wasn't there. You started crying. Not your usual, nobody's here cry, but a frightened cry. I guess you are afraid to be left alone while you're sitting up. You must need the security of knowing someone is close by when you're feeling vulnerable.

January 6

Today's statistics: 16 pounds 10 ounces; 27 1/4 inches.

I had you sitting on my lap on the couch in the family room for a burp, after your morning feeding. You were facing me. Mildieu kitty walked into the family room and caught your eye. Turning your head to the left, you watched her walk around to the front of the couch . When you couldn't turn your head to the left any more, you rotated your head fully to the right. Then you proceeded to follow her with your eyes as she walked along the front of the couch again. Mildieu finally jumped onto the couch, after she was satisfied that she had fascinated you. Your movements, in following her with your eyes, were very sophisticated.

We went to Grandma Ani-Poo's for dinner tonight. It was the first time Popie first time has seen you sit up alone. He was delighted. You were very gracious during most of dinner. You chewed on your little Nike's, that were near you on your quilt. I had taken them off, so I could put you on your tummy. You didn't fuss until you were hungry. Thank you, Tiffany.

January 7

This morning, I opened your rocking-stacker toy. I put it in front of you while you were sitting up. You reached for it and knocked it over right away. You then proceeded to take off the first two rings and play with them. After a couple of minutes, I took the other two rings off and moved the stacker so you wouldn't fall onto it and hurt yourself.

Amazingly enough, before I moved the stacker you had hit at it with one of the rings. You also hit a number of other things with the rings. You seemed to be listening to the different sounds you created by hitting the rings on different things.

You had a marvelous time playing with the colored rings; banging them and chewing on them; sometimes holding one in each hand. I should know by now not to be surprised when you do amazing things. What can I say? I can't help myself.

January 9

This morning, while you were in your walker, you moved yourself eighteen inches toward me to get the pretty receiving blanket I was holding. After playing tug-on-the-blanket with you, I went into the kitchen to fix my protein drink. I looked over the breakfast bar to check on you. You had propelled yourself two and a half feet to the coffee table in an effort to try to reach Daddy's watch!

I offered you a pretty pink toy, but you still reached for Daddy's watch. You pulled it onto the floor and strained to find it for almost a minute. Then you reached for the pink toy I had placed next to the watch. When you dropped that, you again strained to reach for it. You are a very clever little girl.

This afternoon I wanted to take you to have your picture taken, a double exposure pose. We'll go after you wake up from your morning nap so that you feel refreshed.

I'm not quite sure how, but you always seem to know when I have planned to do something, and have structured it around your nap. I think I'm being very organized. I have most everything set up the night before. Somehow you sense this and won't take your nap. It happened again, today.

I had wanted to get your picture taken. I was going to do it yesterday, but you had scratched your nose the night before. I thought we should give it an extra day to heal, as I prefer to have your picture taken free of "boo-boos."

It's raining today, but since it will be a number of days before I will be off for more than one day at a time, I decided we should go for it and dressed you for your pictures. I took a longer route, thinking that since you were due for a nap, you might sleep; longer drive—longer nap. Sure enough, you fell asleep.

I had tried to feed you before I dressed you, but you wanted no part of that. When we arrived at the mall, you wouldn't eat in the car. Obviously you weren't hungry yet.

We went into the studio. You were a wee bit tired, but sweet as usual. You did have a hard time sitting up straight for any length of time; you were too interested in your pretty shoes. It was the first time you had worn them except when you tried them on. You were also fascinated with your new socks. I'm sure your pictures will turn our very well. How could they not? As soon as we arrived home you were ready for a nap.

January 10

This morning, we met Grandma Ani-Poo and Popie in Cottonwood for a breakfast of tea and biscuits. You had eaten just before we left, and were very happy and fuss-free during our breakfast. You pulled your hat off during breakfast. A first!

You reached up with your left hand and pulled it right off over the front of your head. Speaking of your left hand, you seem to be showing a preference for it. It isn't a sure thing, but you seem to favor it a fair amount of the time, at least for now.

After breakfast, Grandma Ani-Poo wanted to go to the western shop next door and look for a turtleneck sweater. Once we were there, I noticed they had baby clothes. Naturally I went to look, so did Grandma Ani-Poo. She ended up buying a hooded top for you that said "Cowgirl." This was the first time you'd been present when clothes were bought for you. When we arrived home, I put your new top on. Grandma and Popie arrived soon thereafter. We were in separate cars.

Popie hadn't seen you use your walker yet, so I put you in it. You really went to town. You moved forward with both feet, bounced up and down two or three times, and pushed yourself forward with a smile on your face and arms outstretched! You moved around, much more than you did the day before. You have this walker business down to a science; a fun science.

January 11

Your hair has really been growing the last two weeks. Not just in length, but there are new hairs on your head. I also see a fine little peachfuzz starting to grow on your arms. Over the last few days, I've noticed a visible difference each day.

January 12

Your Uncle Greg and Aunt Margie are here from Los Angeles; and, unfortunately, I'm sick. I woke up with a terrible sore throat. Shoot! Now I can't get any huggies. I better get this throat cultured to be sure it isn't beta-Strep (a highly infectious organism). We can't risk you getting that. At least your Aunt Margie is here to take care of you, but I'm going to miss playing with you, Sweetie. I'll go to the emergency room before work and have it cultured, and I'll request to sit at the cardiac monitors today, so I don't expose any patients to me. I can't afford to stay home.

January 13

I felt terrible not being able to snuggle you. It's for your own protection, but it is very hard. When Daddy got you up this morning after your bottle, he put you into your walker. You were just full of talkies. I heard you say "Ahh wah (gurgle, bubble) wak nee!" Two new consonants.

I was in bed, just waking up, and feeling terrible when I heard your charming voice. It made me feel better. I was so delighted at your little song and new sounds. I wanted to run into the family room, scoop you up into my arms and say, "That's beautiful, Tiffany. How exciting it is to hear you make new sounds."

January 14

Daddy took care of you all day, again, today. Mommy's still sick. Tonight, you had a very hard time getting to sleep. Daddy put you down for sleep at 6:00 pm. You woke up just before 8:00 pm. Daddy fed you and you went back to sleep in about thirty minutes.

I called the hospital to check on my throat culture. It was negative for beta-strep. It seems I have one of the two new flu bugs that's circulating, and I don't want you to get that either.

You awoke again just before 11:00 pm. I put a pillowcase on as a mask and went in to get you. Your weekend had been so "different," with changes in your eating and sleeping patterns and no Mommy, I wondered if you were having "Mommy withdrawals."

I picked you up and got a great big cuddle. You knew my voice, but you didn't seem to know my face with the pillowcase over most of it.

You'd had a **pookie.** I'd cry, too, if I had a mess like that in my pants! I changed your diaper and fixed a bottle for you. You wolfed down the first half of it, then didn't want the rest. You fussed, cried, squirmed, and pushed the bottle out of your mouth with your tongue. You pushed it way out with your tongue. You tongue is becoming more versatile. Anyway you fussed and cried and fussed and cried. You weren't hungry and didn't want to eat anymore. So I held you on my shoulder and walked with you. I talked and hummed, as much as I could with a very painful throat. After about twenty or thirty minutes, you seemed more comfortable. You took a bit more milk. And after a few more minutes of walking and snuggling, you were ready to go to sleep. Poor Tiffi, such a tired little girl.

January 15

Finally, I get some hugs again. I went to give you your morning feeding when you woke up. I was afraid to kiss you on the mouth or face, yet. But, it was wonderful to get hugs again. How I've missed that.

Daddy was playing a new game with you today, "Huggie huggie, peek-a-boo." He snuggled you to his shoulder then held you out at arms length and said "Peek-a-boo." You loved it.

I went back to work today. When we arrived at Beth's, you played another game. I was holding you on my lap. You arched your back and stretched your head backwards, and looked at her upside down. Then you looked at her right-side up. Beth then turned her head upside down after you did it a second time. She then looked at you right-side up and you followed suit. This went on for a few minutes. Beth enjoyed it as much as you and I did.

January 17

Today, we went out to breakfast in Redding with Grandma Ani-Poo. We saw one of the nurses who took care of me when I was in labor and after you were born. She commented on how pretty and how well behaved you were. You smiled and talked to her a bit.

You enjoyed shopping today. You've become an excellent shopper. You were very interested in everything at the mall. While there, we took pictures of a lion-taming act to send to the Animal Protection Institute (API) in order to gather evidence against a man who severely neglects his animals. He was here last year, but I didn't know about it until after the show was gone. All I could do then was gather information, after the fact. Last year the API asked me if I had pictures; I didn't. This year I have pictures.

Unfortunately, they didn't have a show while we were there or at a time when we could come back. But, I did get pictures of the six lions, three adults and three cubs, who were spending too much time in a too small transport cage. We also took pictures of the transport vehicle, a single forty foot rig for all of the equipment, cages, and six lions. The vehicle had no climate control for the trailer and almost no ventilation. I'll call the API when we get home to tell them what's happening. I'll also call the mall manager to see if I can find out where the act is going next.

After we left the uptown mall, we headed over to the downtown mall. When we arrived, you were asleep. We put you into your stroller. Today would be the last time that you'll be able to wear your little Nikes. They are getting too small. Grandma Ani-Poo offered to buy you a new pair of jogging shoes. You slept through the entire fitting.

January 20

Today you ate your first meat. It was turkey. You must have liked it, you certainly ate enough of it. I didn't weigh you today, for your usual weekly weigh-in; tomorrow is your six month birthday. I'll weigh you then.

January 21

Tiffany's one-half year statistics: 17 1/2 pounds; 27 5/8 inches.

Happy one-half year birthday today, Tiffi! You've grown almost 3/4 of an inch over the last week. You made a new facial expression, today. You squinted your eyes, pursed your mouth tightly, and laughed a tight little laugh through your nose. It was so cute. I wish I had a picture of it.

January 22

You're "making" such darling little body language today—coyly tossing your head left and right with a smile. I took some pictures of you making your new little face; it's new since yesterday.

When I started pointing the camera towards you, to take pictures, you increased your talking and head tossing. I missed the shot of when you had your head tossed completely sideways. Darn, it was so sweet.

After our photo session, it was time for Mommy to do her exercises. As I did my exercises, I had you on a quilt on the living room floor. Mildieu came to visit with you. She sat on the edge of your quilt. You looked at her, and talked to her, coyly tossing your head as you spoke. You also reached toward her, while playing with one of your toys. It was very sweet.

When Mildieu left, you concentrated on me doing my exercises. When I leaned my head one way, you copied the motion. You smiled, when I counted out loud. That always gets a smile. You like listening to me count, when I do my exercises.

January 24

Today I had an all-day class for nursing continuing education. Grandma Ani-Poo and Popie came to the house to be with you. They were excited about taking you to the mall themselves. Popie had never seen you "cruise the mall" before.

You arrived home a few minutes before I did. Popie said you had a wonderful time and that some of the merchants remembered "that pretty little girl," from last week. Grandma Ani-Poo and Popie sure are proud of you.

Shortly after Grandma Ani-Poo and Popie left, I sat you in your swing with me on the floor next to you. We played peek-a-boo with a small blanket. One time, you pulled the blanket off of your face by yourself! Then, you played peek-a-boo by putting the blanket up with one arm and covering my face—by accident at first, I imagine. But I said, "Peek-a-boo" when you moved your arm down. A minute or so later you did it again. Then, again and again. What fun. What a bright little girl.

January 25

Today while you were playing on your quilt, you played with the empty margarine tub with the red pet food lid inside. You've always enjoyed playing with that, but today you did something very different. Instead of just shaking it and listening to it rattle, you picked it up, and turned it top-side down while you looked up into the inside with a lot of intellect in your gaze!

January 26

Today Jennifer, my friend, Donna's, daughter, came to be with you while I worked. Jennifer is a very special, compassionate young lady. She loves babies and knows how to take care of them.

One of the times I called to see how things were going, Jennifer told me you had crawled off of your quilt. Crawled! How exciting! I wish I could have been there. That was a definite milestone. Maybe you will do it again tomorrow. I can't wait to see you crawl. Jennifer said you had crawled about four feet when she was playing chase with you.

January 27

Today you were tired, and didn't feel like crawling about and pioneering. You went to sleep at 5:30 pm, and woke up at 10:00 pm hungry and uncomfortable. After a bottle and a lot of hugs, you fell asleep.

January 28

Today's statistics: 17 pounds 12 ounces; 26 1/2 inches.

You woke up at 3:30 am, ready to eat. You didn't get back to sleep for about an hour. At 8:00 am you were awake and ready to eat again. No self-entertaining time this morning, you just weren't comfortable. Daddy gave you your morning bottle. You took five ounces. You weren't yourself. You fussed the entire time. We weren't sure if you were just tired, or if you had a bottle that just didn't agree with you. Maybe you were sick.

At 10:00 am, I tried giving you a bottle to rule out hunger and then put you down for a nap. You only took one and a half ounces. You didn't go right to sleep. I thought I'd let you fuss a while in your crib and see if that would help. If you need a fuss-out we usually give you fifteen minutes.

After ten minutes of fussing, your cries sounded different. I went to pick you up. I checked your diaper and thought I'd better check your temperature. As I checked your temperature, you vomited. Poor Tiffany.

I hugged you with one arm wrapped around you and, my face next to yours as close as I could as, I took your temperature. When you vomited again, it made you even more uncomfortable. It hurt me to see you like this. You pushed your little head against my arm and looked at me. It was such a painful, pitiful, and tear-streaked face. It broke my heart.

Both emeses (vomitus) were very large, adding up to five or six ounces, probably both of your last two feedings. Your temperature was 101.2 degrees. Poor sweetheart, you've never been sick like this before.

Fortunately, your regular six-month appointment was today at 2:15 pm, so we knew you would see your Doctor today. I called Dr. Kelley's office to see how much acetaminophen I could give you for your fever.

You stopped crying just before I called the Doctor. You just melted against me when I picked you up from the table. I figured you needed a few more minutes of hugs before I tried giving you your medication. I medicated you about seven or eight minutes later.

At 1:00 pm, you took a whole bottle. I had been checking your diaper, but there was no stool and alarmingly little urine. Your body must have been using your fluid to regulate your temp; not to mention how much of it you had vomited.

The news media has called the flu that is going around at present, the worst in this nation's history. I sure hope that isn't what you have. I'm terrified of you getting the sore throat I had with my flu. It could be so dangerous for you to have that degree of throat swelling. You didn't catch the flu when I had it. I was very careful. But why are you sick now?

When I woke you from your nap, to leave for your Doctor's appointment, you didn't talk or smile. You lifted your head up heavily and gave me a sorrowful look. That was very unusual for you, sweetie.

Dr. Kelley said you have the tummy flu. He said to watch for higher fevers, and that this would probably last three to four days, including recuperation. I'm sorry that you're sick, sweetheart.

Aside from your flu, the Doctor felt that you were developing well—an otherwise very healthy baby. He mentioned that the Association of Pediatricians had determined that once babies have gone through their course of meats they can drink adult milk. You are also now eligible for any strained food. He also said to increase your solids to three meals per day, to let you eat as much as you want, until you start to play with your food, then to supplement you with a bottle. Your need for milk now is for the calcium.

Once we arrived home, it was time for Tiffi to relax. Time to rest and get rid of this nasty flu. Strength to you, sweet Tiffany. We'll get rid of this flu as quickly as possible.

January 29

You slept well last night. Nine hours. When you woke up today, you had a smile for me. No vomiting since yesterday morning. You weren't your usual bright self this morning; you were still sick, but I could tell that you felt better.

Grandma and Popie will be with you today while I am at work and until Daddy is done with his work. You were happy and smiling by noon, feeling much more like yourself. No fever or vomiting today!

When I called to see how you were, Daddy answered the phone. He was already done with his day's work and had let Grandma Ani-Poo and Popie go home. Daddy said you were doing well. I was so glad.

January 30

I wasn't worth much at work last night. I was preoccupied with how you were. I was delighted to see your happy and smiling face welcome me this morning. I'm sure you're over your illness, but I'm going to keep you inside today. Starting tomorrow, I will be off for five days. It will be a chance for us to spend a lot of time together. Our first large amount of time without me working since I was sick. It will be a real treat!

February

This morning Grandma Ani-Poo, Popie and I took you to the mall in Chico. While there, Popie wheeled you in front of a three-way mirror that was in a children's clothing store. He said you talked, tossed your head, waved your hands and then your feet. You had a marvelous time playing "Tiffany Says" in the mirror to "all of those" babies!

When we arrived at Grandma's house after our trip, there was a message from Daddy on their telephone answering machine. It said Daddy had gotten a job! We sure hope it lasts. The last few jobs only lasted about a month or so each. A steady job would give us a chance to pay off our bills and finish building the house! Daddy and I shared a bottle of champagne to celebrate the new job.

February 2

Timeline: Today **Tiffany** Chin won the Championship of Women's Figure Skating at the American Nationals Competition.

February 4

Statistics: 17 pounds 14 ounces; 26 1/2 inches (after eating).

This morning, we went to breakfast with Grandma Ani-Poo and Popie. You were wonderful, and charmed everyone. After breakfast, we went to Dr. Kelley's office for your six-month immunization. You did very well. We weren't able to immunize you at your last appointment, because you were sick.

After your Doctor's appointment, we checked the baby store to see if your playpen had come in. It had been backordered for about a month. I wanted you to have it before you needed it, or should I say before I needed it. That way you could have a chance to become acquainted with it, and enjoy it before you saw it as a restriction of your crawling activities. The playpen just arrived on the truck. What timing!

February 5

This morning, you watched me set up your playpen. I let you look at it and get accustomed to it being there. After your nap, we played a bit, then I put you into the playpen. I stayed with you so you wouldn't start to associate being put there with my leaving. You enjoyed it. The vinyl bottom let you move around on your tummy with less effort. You thought that was a good deal.

It was almost time for bed, and your continuing pleasant disposition showed me that you tolerated your immunizations very well again. This time it did seem to upset your stomach for a few hours. You spit up more than your usual little amounts for a couple of feedings. In all, you required three doses of acetaminophen for comfort. You had needed two doses with the last two rounds of immunizations. That is still very good. There was never more than a dime-sized raised, reddened area around the immunization site.

February 6

The raised red area of your injection is closer to being quarter-sized this morning, but it doesn't seem to bother you at all. After breakfast, while you were sitting on the floor, Mildieu walked into the family room and sat on the floor about three feet away from you. She looked at you, then jumped up onto the kitchen desk facing away from you. You were very intrigued with her. You looked and looked at her, and made little talking noises. When Mildieu didn't acknowledge your remarks, you sorted of grunted at her. You sounded like a car that was having a hard time kicking the engine over. After grunting at her a couple of times, Mildieu turned around and looked at you. As soon as she turned around, you started babbling sweetly to her, tossing your head from side to side. It was fabulous. I was so impressed. So was Mildieu. You worked to get her attention, and once you had it, you started talking to her.

February 7

You give hugs now; real "whole body" hugs! It's so sweet. You reach out with your hands, grab hold and pull yourself snugly against us. It melts my heart. It's so dear; so intentional. I love it!

February 9

Daddy had to work overtime today. Grandma Ani-Poo and Popie came to play with you before I had to leave for work. Later, they told me you really enjoyed playing in your playpen. I was glad to hear that.

February 11

Today's stats: 18 pounds 3 ounces.

This morning we went to Grandma Ani-Poo and Popie's. They visited with you while I went to see Basette. You should have seen Little John (the baby Capuchin monkey.) He has really grown. He's still very sociable and very gentle. His parents, however, have become quite rowdy. Poor dears, they had always been sweet and gentle. I'm afraid they've had too much of the wrong kind of attention and too little of the right kind. They really "raked" at my hand as I offered them some raisins. I gave them a stern talking to and they behaved better with the next offering.

Sonny, the Macaw, took his raisins with only a gentle token nip-of-the-thumb afterwards—typical Sonny. It's been three months since I last saw these animals. Some of them have changed, behaviorally. It's been too hard to get down here to see them once I went back to work, after your birth.

When I saw Basette, she was lying on her den-box, facing away from me. (A den-box is a small enclosure inside of a cage, providing privacy and protection from weather.) I went through the doorway to the animal compound, and stopped to call to her, to see what she would do.

She rolled over and looked at me, chuffing, then sat up "sphinx-style," still chuffing. I walked over to her, chuffed back at her, and told her how beautiful she was. I asked her if she would come down and say "Hi" to me. She jumped down off of the den-box and rubbed against the cage in front of me. There was a new layer of hardware cloth over the nine-gauge chain link fencing, so I couldn't get a kiss through the cage. (Hardware cloth is a large diameter wire woven into a cloth with one inch or two inch separations. It can be used as a fencing material.) Attached to Basette's permanent cage is a small transport cage which is unshaded. I've termed this unshaded area her "sundeck." After Basette rubbed against the cage in front of me she ran over to the "sundeck area" and plopped down into the "brush me" position. The separations between the bars of the sundeck cage were larger than other areas of her external cage; they were also vertical, allowing for better brushing access. She seemed upset with me when I didn't brush her. Actually, confused, would be a better description.

I was touched and delighted that she wanted to be brushed by me, after I hadn't come to see her for such a long time. Since it had been so long, though, I wasn't sure it would be a good idea. Basette changed position and moved closer to me. When I still didn't brush or pet her, she became upset, then overexcited. I felt badly about not obliging her offer. I wanted to, but I was afraid that she would become overstimulated since it had been a long time since our last contact. (Overstimulation leads to aggression in tigers.) It would be best to wait until our next visit and see what her mood was at that time.

After I went back to Grandma Ani-Poo's, we visited and played for a while. Grandma Ani-Poo suggested that we go out to lunch. I hadn't brought your yellow infant seat, which you usually sit in when we go out to eat.

Since you had just eaten, it seemed extremely unlikely that you would want to eat again while we did. Did I really say that? Famous last words. We decided to go out to lunch, and let you sit in a high-chair. A first, and you did beautifully! You were extremely well-behaved. You seemed to feel quite important sitting in a chair like everyone else. You were a perfect restaurant companion. Wait until we tell Daddy.

February 12

You have definite cuticles on your fingernail areas now. I hadn't noticed them before, but they are very prominent now.

February 13

Today, you burst forth with a bunch of consonants. It was so exciting, a literal explosion of new talkies. "Ah-gah, wah-nah, ah-hah-dah-nah-mah." It was delightful! We talked and talked and laughed. When you used those syllables, you involved your whole mouth, and to a great degree. Every muscle seemed to play a part in the forming of the syllables. This was as exciting as when you first started to babble. I don't want to miss a single minute of it.

On the way to Beth's today, you said, "Ah dah-dah nah." Are you trying to say "Dah-dah (Daddy)?" We'll have to keep track of that. I hoped you would say it again soon, when Daddy could hear it.

February 14

Happy First Valentine's Day, my little dear. You are my Valentine, and you are a sweetheart without a doubt. I Love You, and your Daddy Loves You.

You and I went to the mall this morning; you were dressed in your "Valentine-appropriate outfit" and sported your heart bib. You looked adorable. We looked at all of the pretty displays and shopped for a card and a gift for Daddy.

Many people stopped to talk to you; you smiled and talked back to them. So many people commented on how sweet, happy, and well behaved you were. We even saw Le Ann there, one of the nurses I work with. She said, "You were pretty and sweet. A real dolly."

When it was time to eat, we sat on one of the benches. With your heart bib on you served yourself, while reclining in your stroller. You're such a delight.

After we left the mall, we went to the hospital to pick up my paycheck before heading home. You were able to see some of your adult friends in the personnel office. You have developed quite a fan club.

February 15

Today, we went over to see our neighbor Halli. She even had a gift for you, one that she had meant to give you at Christmas. It was a beautiful pressed-glass child's dishware set, with impressed patterns of nursery rhyme illustrations. A very lovely gift. "Thank you, Halli."

February 16

You said you first word today "Dah-dah"! Daddy had taken over your morning feeding and let me lie down for a while. After you finished eating and had been playing on the floor, you started talking. I could hear you from the bedroom. During your talkies, you came out with a clear and definite "dah-dah"! Daddy was, of course, thrilled! In response to his reaction, you said it a few more times. He then came to tell me about it. He didn't realize I had heard the whole thing. Happy first word, Tiffany!!!

This being Saturday, it's cartoon time. It's also time for your first meal in your own high-chair. You really enjoyed it. You were fascinated with the large tray in front of you. At one point, you were so full of exuberance you screamed "Ih"; rocked back and forth against the cushion and the tray, grinning and talking. You ate all of your breakfast and hardly noticed that the cartoons were on. You were too busy discovering your high-chair.

After your nap we went to the downtown mall to buy another half dozen large velcro-closure cloth diapers. On our way there, we were having a wonderful person-like conversation. You said,

"Ah-gah."

I replied with the same thing. I repeated whatever you said and included, "Dah-dah." When you paused for a longer period, than just an end of statement pause, I would say, "Dah-dah."

You answered with, "Dah-dah," more than sixty percent of the time!!

Then I said, "Bah-bah."

You said, "Ah-bah."

Then I tried, "Mah-mah," while we were waiting at a stop light, I looked at you and made definite movements with my mouth.

You watched me intently and said, "Mah-gah." Then while still watching me you closed your jaw and lips together as if you were trying to mimic my movements, at least, if not the sound.

You did this a few more times during the day. Smart baby!

While we were at the mall, the manager of the baby store there was taken with the fact that you were so happy and smiling. You smiled at her when she talked to you.

She asked if you were always that happy and pleasant. I said you were, most of the time.

She replied, that was remarkable. She turned to a customer

in the store and said, "Have you seen this darling baby? She's so happy."

The customer then called her daughters to come and see the smiling baby.

You loved the attention, and I was, of course, very proud.

February 17

Today, we watched some of the Daytona 500 stock-car race during breakfast. You enjoyed your high-chair so much, that after breakfast, I set your high-chair by the couch next to me. I put some things on the tray for you to play with. You were fully involved for about ten minutes, as I watched a bit more of the race.

February 18

Tiffi statistics: 18 1/2 pounds; 27 1/4 inches.

This afternoon at Grandma Ani-Poo's, you were so cute. You were playing with your Snoopy teething ring, trying to tear it apart as you do facial tissues; but it wasn't that easy! You tried a couple of times. Then you tried again, scrunching your shoulders up against your head, pursing your face into a tight knot and letting out a terrific grunt as you forced your arms apart with a jolt. All of that, only to find that the darn teether was still intact. The thing just refused to be torn, but you kept on trying. Such perseverance!

"Dah-dah" is well established into your vocabulary now. You say "Dah-dah" and "Dah-dah-ah-wah-nah" many times a day, to a tune of your own composition. It's delightful.

February 21

Happy seven month birthday, Tiffany. Today, we went to Chico to shop at the mall there, "a la stroller." We went to the children's store that has the "small gauge" three-way mirror; the one you enjoyed so much the last time. You had a great time there. You reached out to touch the baby in front of you and ended up touching all of the babies all around you! It was a lot of fun watching you.

We stopped at a hot dog shop for a soda. You had a "bott-bott" (bottle). A young lady working there heated it for you. She asked how old you were and your name. We were all surprised to learn that she had a six and a half month old baby girl also named Tiffany!

Once you had finished your bottle you were full of talkies. You reached toward me from your stroller, touched my thigh, and rubbed your hand back and forth across it. As I reached to touch your hand, you took hold of my finger and moved it closer to you. Then with both hands, you latched onto my forearm and pulled it closer to you. You looked up at me, let go of my forearm with one hand, and stretched that hand toward me, leaning forward. You wanted to be close. You wanted a hug. Your small movements were so touching, so intentional.

You were really a model companion. Since we had left when it was time for your nap and you had just eaten, I felt sure you would sleep during the drive. As it turned out, you only slept for the last fifteen or twenty minutes of the trip. You never did fall asleep later during your stroller ride.

When we arrived at Grandma Ani-Poo's house, I changed you into a sleeper. I gave you a bottle, before we left for home. About half way home, you fell asleep. I am sure you'll sleep long and hard tonight, sweet Tiffany.

February 22

Today, we went to Redding. Some of the pictures we had taken in for developing were ready.

On the way to town, you were talking almost constantly, saying, "Dah-dah "and "dah-dah-ah-gah-wah-nah."

I said, "Dah-dah."

You said, "Dah-dah or dah-dah-dah," or "Ah-dah." More than half of the time you responded with, "Dah-dah."

When you paused for a bit I said, "Mah-mah," turning my head only slightly toward you, so that I could still see the road—I was driving, remember.

You responded to "Mah-mah "with a huge smile and "Gah-gah "or "Dah-dah." After a couple of times, you watched me as I formed my sounds, very purposefully, while looking at you. (We were at a red light.) You quietly moved your lips as though you were trying to form the sound. It was exciting and delightful to watch you study my mouth as you tried forming the sounds.

Later we did our little conversation again, and it was a conversation. You would say something, then I would say something. You didn't talk while I was talking. That's a fully bonified conversation in my book. It was wonderful. We conversed again, over a bottle, while at the mall, again on the way home, and at home before bed when Dah-dah could join in. It was terrific.

February 23

This morning, you had your first attempt at your orange training cup—a big cup with handles and a screw-on lid. You tried it, or rather you tried at it. You plugged it in appropriately and poured it in, down and around your mouth. You even managed to drink some of it.

It was such a pretty orange color that you had to play with

it, turning it over and over, spilling most of it on your high-
chair tray. That's ok. That's what it's there for—fallout.

Yesterday, when we were at the mall, I bought two soft
vinyl books for you. After breakfast, we sat down on your
playquilt and read them together; then you played with them.
It was so cute. While on your playquilt, you spent a lot of time
leaning over to one side or the other. You turned yourself
almost on your tummy as you reached for something, then
pushed yourself back up. You did this again and again.

Occasionally, you actually did end up on your tummy. Then
you twisted one way going after something else, and on and
on. You never really crept anywhere but you were very busy
twisting and reaching. You were good at pulling what you
needed toward you, via gathering your playquilt in toward
yourself.

February 24

I get so much enjoyment out of watching you play in your
crib just after you've awakened. I watch you from behind your
bedroom door so you don't know I'm there. I love seeing how
you play, when you're alone, uninfluenced by anyone. It isn't
really any different. At least I can't see any difference, but I
believe it's important for you to have some time to yourself. I
think a different type of learning takes place when you are
alone. Not lonely, just alone; there is a big difference between
the two.

February 25

Today, while we were reading one of your vinyl books, you

put your hand on the picture of the kitty and said, "Kuh!" A new word!

Tiffany Stats: 19 pounds; can't find the tape measure today.

You weren't your usual sunny self today. You slept well last night. You did play patta-cake with your hands all by yourself on the changing table this morning, undirected. You still smiled and laughed, yet at the same time, you were fussy and cranky all day. It's as though you weren't sure if you were happy or unhappy. You didn't have a fever.

In the morning, you took a thirty-five minute nap. In the afternoon, you took a one hour nap. During the day, you had three stools, two regular and one loose and squirty. I've checked your temperature twice today—normal. If you were chewing more than usual, it wasn't a lot; so much for teething. I'm sorry you're not feeling up to snuff today. All I could do was give you more hugs and love.

February 27

Yesterday, I wondered; today, I really wondered if you were teething. You had two stools before your nap this morning!

After your first bottle this morning, you held your hands together, behind your head, sometimes straight over your head, like a victorious boxer. All of this seemed to impress you.

You play patta-cake a lot more now. Sometimes, in response to Daddy or me starting the game, you'll play a few rounds. Then you'll grab your hands together, interlock your fingers and laugh and squeal with delight at your accomplishment. It's hard to tell which of us enjoys the game more.

This afternoon, there is going to be a pot luck in the coronary care unit, to celebrate the birthdays of two of the nurses. I don't have what I am assigned to take, so we'll have to go to the market. You loved the market. I put you into the shopping cart, nervous about your safety, as usual. I only had to get two items so I shouldn't have worried. I always had one hand right next to you. There are a number of things that I can't help but worry about. Your continued safety is one of them.

Your head was constantly turning, watching the people and especially the endless ocean of colorful things on the shelves. How exciting, all of those colorful cans and packages were to look at. It would have taken forever to see all of them.

When I took you to Beth's before work, I told her of your activities over the last two days. She agreed you were probably teething. I called Beth from work, as usual, and she reported feeling a lump in the area of your lower central incisors. Wow! Your first tooth erupting!

February 28

You wanted no part of me feeling your gums for your erupting tooth, this morning. I couldn't really feel anything discernible on your gums. Darn. I guess it just wasn't big enough for a novice to detect. Maybe I'll be able to find it tomorrow. As I took you from your changing table out to the family room, I asked you if you were ready for your "bott-bott" (bottle). You tried so hard to form your mouth for the sound "bott-bott." It was touching watching all of that effort from such a wee creature.

March

March 3

You really are a little trooper. You are teething, and thus, fussier and crankier than usual. But you're such a delightful baby ninety-nine percent of the time. Many babies are cranky and constantly crying during teething. Who could blame them? I'm certain it's no picnic. With all of the discomfort that must accompany teething, I feel that you are handling it quite graciously.

Patta-cake is a regular part of every day now. You patta-cake in any number of positions, even when lying on your side. You patta-cake toys together. You patta-cake one hand against your vinyl book. You thoroughly enjoy yourself.

This morning you even played patta-foot! You had a hold of each foot with your hands and patted them together while I changed your diaper. You are a true joy to watch and to be around.

March 5

Did you have intentions of skipping crawling and going straight into walking? You want to pull yourself up by almost everything you come across. Whenever I hold you standing near something, you grab for it and hold yourself upright next to it, smiling your biggest smile.

March 6

Today, you explored your inflatable walker from the carpet level. You became intrigued with the swivel coaster wheels. You would push it away by the bottom ring while lying on your stomach. Then you grabbed the bottom ring between your fingers and thumb and pulled it back toward you, watching how the wheels turned and rolled. Such intense study. You tried to pull yourself up on it, but it didn't cooperate. It just rolled away. You rolled that walker back and forth with your hand for more than five minutes.

You've begun to add different inflections to your voice when you talk. Your experiment started by saying a certain word, saying it hard, then soft, then quiet, and finally loud. You made one sound quality right after the other. You've also been experimenting with talking at different pitches. A rather high and delicate pitch, your regular pitch, and one a little lower than your usual pitch. It's lovely to listen to, and easy to see that you are impressed with your new ability.

March 7

You certainly have become an active eater lately. At some meals, you expend more energy than some people do in two days. It's a challenge trying to bottle-feed an almost constantly moving mass of muscle. Twist, turn, sit up, turn around, lean over, lie back, talk, kick, bend. Whew! You burn up a whole meal's worth of calories before you even get the contents of the bottle inside of you. Heaven forbid that you should miss something that might be happening, somewhere in the room, the house, or the world while you do something so mundane as eat. Life is so stimulating.

March 8

Statistics: 19 pounds 7 ounces; 28 1/2 inches (after eating).

You've become particularly active when you're turning over on the floor. You sit up, then roll to one side until you are on your stomach. From your stomach you can turn in all directions and reach for something, anything. Once you had one object, you twist off in another direction after something else, or just because you feel like it. If you aren't preparing yourself to crawl, you are certainly getting ready to do something.

You are the "growinest" little thing. Your hair continues to thicken; I trimmed it around your ears the other day. I don't believe I mentioned, your hairdo was less than fashionable. It was square at the edges and shorter over the ear toward the back of the head than at the front; it wasn't easy trimming a constantly moving target.

Fast growing also means fast fingernail growth and frequent trimming. Within the last month, you have taken a definite dislike to having your nails trimmed. It has become a real challenge. I'm often only lucky enough to get one shot at it. Needless to say, your nails are frequently in varying states of trim.

March 9

This was a special day, Tiffany! I stood you up in a corner of your playpen. You grabbed onto the rail, one hand on either side of the corner, and smiled a huge smile. You looked at me with sparkling eyes, then looked down at your feet and squealed with delight. You stood anchored at your hands and feet, with your bottom rotating about. You delighted in this new sensation—you were standing up all by yourself.

You did this twice more, with a little rest in between. Each time, you stood longer than the time before. Daddy saw you the third time, when you stood almost five minutes; laughing, grinning, looking at your fabulous feet, and making sure that everyone was watching your efforts.

March 10

Today involved more practice at standing up. We need to get rid of our sharp-edged coffee table. I don't want you to hurt yourself by falling on or across it. I'll see if I can find a round-edged table in the classified ads.

March 11

Now you're getting daring; standing up in your playpen with only one hand—"bronco style," while you frequently reposition the other hand. That leads to a few one-to-two second attempts at standing without any support, and without falling as you change the position of your supporting hand.

March 13

Today, I had an appointment to have our income taxes prepared and another appointment to take Libra to the Veterinarian. She appears to have injured her eye. You spent most of the day with Beth. I called Beth a couple of times during the day to see how you were doing. The second time I called, Beth said you had something to show me when I came to get you.

When I arrived at Beth's you were finishing a nap. I came into the room where you were napping, Beth was with me. You woke up when you heard my voice. You were still sleepy, but greeted me with a big smile, making me feel warm all over.

Beth speaking for you said, "Mommy, I have a tooth!"

A new tooth!

I had a feeling that was what you wanted to show me. I felt your gums. Sure enough, there was a tiny sharp peak in your lower gum, just left of the center. A hard, sharp peak. It felt very much like a piece of glass.

Beth said she had wondered if that was why you slept so much that day. But unlike most babies' teething behavior, you ate very well, solids and bottle. Beth had nothing but compliments for your gracious behavior during a difficult time.

Bless your sweet little heart. Punching that first tooth is supposed to be very hard; but "punching teeth" didn't seem to bother you much. God bless Tiffany and her new little tooth.

What's that, Tiffany? You say you want steak and eggs for breakfast!?!

Well, maybe next year.

March 15

We went to the mall today dressed in your new pink sunsuit and "Thumbelina" hat. You were adorable. Lots of people stopped to talk to you, and there were lots of children "strolling" around for you to visit with. I bought a set of bunny ears at one of the stores for you to wear on your first Easter.

March 16

Tiffi statistics: 19 pounds 5 ounces.

You said, "M-m-m-m" a couple of times early this morning. You said it with your lips tightly closed.

Today, we're going to your first baby shower. It's for Mary, one of the nurses from work. Mary and I started working at Hilltop Hospital at the same time. The shower will be held at Alice's house. Alice is one of the nurses that took care of you when you were in the intensive care nursery.

As I got dressed, you sat on the floor in the bedroom. You did your usual stretch-onto-your-tummy and twist-to-reach-something moves. Your cloth flower toy was out of your reach. You stretched your arms out for it, but still couldn't quite reach it. You grabbed two little handfuls of carpet and pulled your whole self along on your tummy, then started to fuss. You hadn't yet realized that you had pulled yourself close enough to the flower to reach it. Then you put your hand out toward it, touched it, and grabbed it. You laughed and squealed with delight.

I fought the urge to immediately scoop you up to hug and congratulate you. Instead, I complimented, congratulated, and clapped for you; letting you savor your accomplishment for a bit, without touching you. You stopped what you had been doing and clapped your hands, too. Then I scooped you up and gave you some big "bear-hugs."

We had a marvelous time at the baby shower. There were a lot of girls from the hospital there. You charmed them all. Lisa, my favorite labor and delivery nurse, was there. She spent a lot of time holding and talking to you. There was another baby girl there. Her name was Kristen. She was born on July 23 at Hilltop Hospital, two days after you were born. The two of you had been roomies in the nursery. How about that?

March 17

Happy St. Patrick's Day!

You spent St. Patty's Day with Grandma Ani-Poo and Popie. I tried to catch up on reading my parenting books and magazines and work on our photo album.

Grandma Ani-Poo said you went for a long stroller ride through the neighborhood and through the large walnut orchard at the end of their street. You saw a bunch of people during your travels. I had forgotten to put your shamrock on! I think the people would have pinched and squeezed you even if I had remembered to dress you in green. Babies rarely escape pinching and squeezing.

When you came home from your time with Grandma Ani-Poo and Popie, you were tired and your gums seemed to bother you. I put some numbing ointment on your gums, and to my great surprise, there was another tooth—your lower right incisor! And your upper right incisor area is lumpy! Boy, when you start teething, you don't mess around. I can now see the whole top border of your left lower incisor and just the tip of your right lower incisor.

March 18

It was such a beautiful day that Mommy got brave and took you for a walk down our dusty country road. We are minus two of the neighborhood dogs that used to confront Teaki and Libra whenever we tried to go for a walk before. There are very few fences here in the country, consequently the animals go wherever they've a mind to. Teaki and Libra always accompanied anyone who went out for a walk.

After our walk, I decided to try putting you down on a quilt, on a sparsely grassed area of lumpy ground, that will someday be your backyard. I knew you would enjoy being outside tremendously. I hadn't done this before because the puppies didn't have a fenced area where they could be when we needed to do something outside—"dog-free." I hadn't been up to fielding the anticipated, repeated overtures and investigations from them before, or them possibly being too playful in their activities around you.

I sat right next to you on the quilt. Fortunately, Teaki was the only one there for the first ten minutes or so. Libra was visiting with someone else. Keeping track of one dog at a time made it much easier. I knew Teaki had no intention of hurting or scaring you, but she is very big and playful. So I had to be careful. She brought a stick to you as a "present." Teaki always takes a present to whomever she to visits.

Teaki was interested in you and you were very interested in Teaki. She followed my commands and behaved very well. A couple of times, she came too close. The first time, it scared you; the second time, you were just uncertain.

After about ten minutes, Libra came home from her travels. Libra's movements were much more subdued. She wanted very much to get closer to both of us. Libra hurt her eye the other day. She had to have hot compresses on it, and medication put into her eye six times each day. This was a crummy situation for her. Hence, she is very hungry for some attention that doesn't have any medication associated with it. Libra, very gingerly, offered her paw to you. You reached out to touch it. It was very sweet.

Libra and Teaki stayed close for a while longer, then I asked them to leave. They went a few yards away and waited, returning a few minutes later. They soon developed a routine of visiting for a few minutes, going a few yards away for a few minutes, and so on. I didn't even have to ask them to leave after the second up-close visit. They developed their routine and stuck to it of their own accord. You thoroughly enjoyed watching their activities. We played that way for almost two hours.

Daddy went to Los Angeles the other day and won't be home for a few more days. You will be spending the evening with Cheryl, Randy and April until I get off work tonight. When we arrived at Cheryl's, you were ready for a nap. Cheryl set up a porta-crib for you in April's room. When I put you into the crib you let out a shrill painful wail. You couldn't relax. You kept looking around the strange room. I was right next to you, but you didn't stop your frightened cry until I picked you up.

I had arrived there forty-five minutes before I had to leave for work, so I could give you some buffer time if you needed it; it was a good thing I did. I tried putting you down again thirty minutes later, but you wanted no part of it. You reacted the same as before. Poor Tiffany. I felt terrible. I picked you up and cuddled you for a few minutes. Cheryl said she would stay with you. It was hard to leave.

I called Cheryl from work at 4:15 pm. You had just gotten up from a one hour nap; Cheryl said that you cried for about seven minutes after I left, then fell asleep. I called again at 9:00 pm. Cheryl said you had a wonderful time playing with April and Randy, had eaten a good dinner, and went to bed at 8:00 pm with very little trouble.

I left work, on time, at 11:15 pm and drove to Cheryl's house. I gently knocked on the door. And who, to my surprise, came to answer the door! It was my sweet Tiffany. I was amazed. Cheryl said you had woken up at 11:15 pm. Oddly enough, that was exactly the time I had left work.

We had a safe trip home. Grandma Ani-Poo and Popie were there to spend the night so that we wouldn't have to come home to an empty house. You went right to sleep. Good night little princess. I'll see you in the morning.

March 19

I have to tell you about your ability to wave "bye-bye"; actually waving "Hi" would be more accurate. The action involves your whole arm, which is slightly bent at the elbow, with extra wrist and finger action. It's absolutely precious. So many big steps for such a little girl.

For your lunch, I moved your high-chair onto the linoleum of the kitchen area and handed you your two-handled training cup. It didn't seem to be too hard for you to drink out of it as far as the flow of milk. But when you tried to "chew" on the spout, the milk ran out of the sides of your mouth. Half went to your stomach, half dribbled around your face, etc. It's all part of learning.

March 20

Today was the first day of spring. We went to the downtown mall this morning, with Cheryl, Randy, and April. We didn't last long at the mall, as Randy had too much pent-up energy, so we went to the park so he could run some of it off.

At the park Cheryl watched Randy and April play, and I fed you a bottle as we sat on the grass. When you smiled at me, I noticed your left upper incisor glistening. The area of your right upper incisor was feeling very pointy. Unbelievable—you've made another tooth already.

When we arrived back at Cheryl's house, it was 1:30 pm. You were quite overdue for a nap. You had only taken a fifteen minute nap at 8:00 this morning. Randy and April went down for a nap. You have been very reluctant lately to nap in unfamiliar places; I knew you wouldn't take a nap there, so I didn't even attempt putting you down. You fussed off and on while we ate lunch. I picked you up and set you in my lap, so you wouldn't wake the children.

I looked into your mouth to see your new tooth again and

saw yet another new tooth. Your right upper central incisor! Goodness sakes, sweetie. So little fuss considering how long you've been awake, not to mention the fact that you cut two new teeth today! You're quite a little lady.

March 21

You're eight months old today! 28 1/8 inches long.

I took Mildieu and Libra to the veterinarian, this morning. Libra needed her injured eye checked to see if the damage had healed, and Mildieu needed her first feline leukemia booster. (Leukemia is a fatal blood disease, a form of cancer, demonstrated by a pronounced increase in the number of leukocytes (white blood cells) in the blood. The (Felv) vaccination is the first anti-cancer preparation on the market for any species, and it's working! Definitely history in the making, and our Mildieu is one of the pioneering pussycats.)

Grandma and Popie stayed with you while we were at the veterinarian. Grandma said you pulled yourself up onto your walker, as she held it still. That was really something. For the past week you have been pulling yourself up to the couch and the coffee table from a sitting position on my thigh, when I was on the floor. But this was the first time you pulled yourself up from floor level. Look out world—Tiffany is on the move! When I returned home, you mustered the strength to do it again.

This afternoon, we went to your first wedding shower. It was for Stephanie, one of the nurses at work. Unfortunately, we didn't get to stay for all of the festivities. We had another commitment. You were also overdue for a nap, again. I didn't want you to two long days in a row without a nap. That just wouldn't be fair. We stayed at the party for an hour then left. Then it was off to home and nap-time for Tiffi.

March 22

This morning, when I went to get you, you were sitting up in your crib. That was the first time I knew of you getting to a sitting position without an assist. Later in the morning, as we played in the family room, I sat you on your knees to see what you might do. You leaned forward onto your hand and pushed up with your legs until they were straight! You were standing on "all fours." Another step towards crawling or walking! You weren't sure what to do next. A little later you crawled backwards a couple of feet! It was really something to watch.

March 23

When we arrived at Beth's today, we found that Jason was getting over a bad cold. I was unhappy that Beth didn't tell us ahead of time, so we could have made other arrangements. I didn't want you to catch a bad cold.

March 25

You definitely have a runny nose. It started last night. This morning it's really running strong. You were a bit of tired, but didn't seem to feel bad otherwise. I certainly hope it doesn't become anymore intense.

Your cold did intensify during the day. I called your Doctor to ask whether I should use a vaporizer or a humidifier. They said either would be effective, but a humidifier was safer. So far, I haven't needed to give you any medicine, just lots of hugs. That wasn't too hard.

March 26

The little peachfuzz hairs on your legs are really developing now. Not as much as they are on your arms, but they're getting there.

You had such a rough time this afternoon. You had thrown up almost half of each feeding since lunch. With your last bottle before bedtime, you cried before and after vomiting. I'm sorry that you felt so awful. Your temperature was 101.4 F.

Daddy threw out the bottles we had made up for tonight and tomorrow, and washed and boiled the nipples. We'll start from scratch in case your vomiting has anything to do with contamination of your bottles, or our preparation of the formula for those bottles.

It hurts me terribly to see you like this. I wish I could hurt for you. It must be frightening to feel so bad and not understand what's going on. I'm going to stay home from work tomorrow unless you feel a lot better in the morning. I called Dr. Kelley's office. They told me to watch for higher fever, and to be sure that you didn't throw up more than you took in. You obviously can't go to Beth's tomorrow.

You woke up a couple of times during the night. The first time was at 10:30 pm. You were crying; I gave you a bottle, assuring that you were hungry. The extra fluid would be good for you, too. Once I put you down to sleep, I made a little nest for myself on the floor next to your crib. I was afraid to leave you. If you vomited during the night, I might not be able to hear you from the master bedroom. If you didn't signal any discomfort, I would be afraid the emesis might get into your windpipe, if you fell back to sleep in it.

March 27

You seemed a little better this morning, but you were a long way from feeling good. I was surprised that you felt any better. You didn't get much sleep last night. You awoke frequently, rustled around, and complained some before getting back to sleep. Hence, I imagine the sleep that you did get wasn't very restful. I'll stay home from work today to be with you.

After throwing out the old bottles of formula prepared and the new group of bottles, we were just about out of formula. We only had enough for one and a half bottles. I just couldn't make myself take you out to the store in your condition.

If Grandma Ani-Poo isn't available to go shopping for us, I'll have to call around until I found someone who could. Grandma Ani-Poo and Popie said they would be happy to go shopping for us.

Grandma Ani-Poo and Popie arrived shortly after my call to them. We all sat in the family room. with you perched on Popie's lap. When you looked at me, you said, "**Mah-mah**"! You definitely said, "Mah-mah." You said it three times! I was so thrilled! It brought tears to my eyes. Grandma Ani-Poo and Popie were ecstatic. It was so wonderful to hear your sweet little voice say, "Mahmah!"

You woke up early this evening. I picked you up for some hugs. We played quietly, sitting in my "nest" by your crib. You imitated my motions. When I "patta-caked" you responded with some patta-cake. When I waved bye-bye, you waved bye-bye. This went on for a few minutes. It was very sweet and a lot of fun. I put you back in your crib after rocking and singing you to sleep.

You woke up a few times, during the night. One time, you were unable to get yourself back to sleep. I fixed a bottle for you and rocked you gently as you drank. You fell asleep, but woke up a couple of minutes later. You were very uncomfortable, and cried and moved as if you had a tummy ache. Soon after you woke up, you vomited. Poor Tiffany.

You didn't want to rest on my shoulder or cradle in my lap any longer. You wanted to sit up. You turned yourself sideways, perched on my right knee and faced my left side. You twisted your upper body toward me, leaned against me, wrapped your tiny arms around my waist and hugged me. You hugged and hugged and hugged. I was so touched. I enjoyed the feeling that you were happy to have me there for comfort. You looked up at me, with loving eyes, and whispered, "Dah-dah-dah-dah," as if to say, "I'm glad you're here." I was so moved, that I couldn't help but cry.

March 28

Sweet Tiffi had a rough day. You were tired and never really comfortable. You took three naps, all very short and restless. During one of your naps, I took some clean clothes into your room. Just putting the cloth diapers into your diaper stacker woke you up. Instead of your usual big smile that you usually greet me with, you wore a very tired and painfully bewildered expression. It broke my heart to see that expression, knowing that you must have felt terrible.

At around 9:00 pm during a bottle, and just before trying to go to bed again, you vomited about half of what you had just taken in. It was curdled. You had cried a very painful cry for a minute or two just before you vomited. You continued to cry afterward. It was a very painful wail. You kept on crying—you were still hurting.

I was afraid you might dry-heave, since you were still in great pain and discomfort. I called out to Daddy in the other room. When he came in, I asked him to bring us some wet paper towels and washcloths. He also fixed you a bottle of water. While he fixed your bottle, your wailing tone became a little softer. I wasn't sure if you were feeling a bit better, or were becoming exhausted. You looked up at me briefly and hugged me, your tiny arms wrapped around my chest. I squeezed you a little tighter and you looked back up at me as if to say, "I'm glad you're here with me." Dear little Tiffany, I Love you. I'm sorry you're hurting.

You seemed to feel better after having some water. But the improvement only lasted a minute before you were in pain again. Daddy felt your stomach, it was spasming. Your pain lasted almost twenty minutes. I called Dr. Kelley. His associate, Dr. Williams, was on-call. He said to give you one-half ounce of water every hour until your tummy settled down, and to then give you only water or clear juice until you could see Dr. Kelley the next morning.

Fortunately, in less than thirty minutes your tummy had settled down. You were still uncomfortable. Quite possibly you were more frightened or confused than anything else. What a terrible ordeal for such a wee creature. Anyone would have felt horrible experiencing what you did. To not be able to understand why it was happening, what it was, that it should stop soon, must have been terrifying.

About thirty minutes after your tummy settled down, I gave you another ounce of water. Thirty minutes after that, I gave you one ounce of apple juice, mixed with an ounce of water—to give you a few more calories. You must have needed them. You'd been burning your reserves for the last hour or two.

You don't usually like apple juice, even watered down, unless it is mixed with your cereal. But you vacuumed up the two ounce mixture and melted to sleep in my arms. I put you into your crib and curled up in my little nest on the floor.

You woke up three or four times during the night. Twice, you were able to get yourself back to sleep. The other times, you needed a hug and some cuddles. Each time, you melted off to sleep on my shoulder in less than two minutes.

March 29

You were feeling much better this morning. I was so relieved! You were tired and I knew that you didn't feel good, but you did feel much better. We made an appointment with Dr. Kelley for this morning. I haven't slept for more than two hours total for the last few nights. The two days before you were sick, I wasn't able to sleep. I wasn't sure why. At any rate, being that tired and fatigued it wouldn't be safe for me to drive. I wanted to avoid it if at all possible. I called Grandma Ani-Poo and Popie; they said they would gladly drive us into town.

Dr. Kelley found a **roaring** ear infection in your right ear and a significant infection in your left ear, too! A middle ear infection could cause nausea and vomiting. The rest of your exam proved to dismiss any stomach or intestinal involvement. The nausea and vomiting appeared to be from the ear infection. I was sorry that you had such a terrible infection and in both ears! Poor Tiffany.

Your Doctor and I were both glad that it was something common easy to take care of, and that didn't present any long-term or serious problems. Dr. Kelley prescribed an antibiotic for you to take for ten days. We were also to make an appointment for a check up in ten days. I felt much better once the Doctor had seen you and we knew what the problem was.

Dr. Kelley complimented you on how cooperative and pleasant you were during your exam, considering how uncomfortable you were. I told him that you were very pleasant natured and because you were amiable, it was necessary to be particularly alert for signs of illness. Even when you were tired and sick you would smile, laugh and be cooperative.

Once we returned home, Grandma Ani-Poo watched you while Popie drove me to the market to do the bi-weekly shopping; we were out of almost everything. I hadn't wanted to take you out when you were sick.

You awoke during the night hungry, so I gave you a bottle. Afterward, I put you in your crib and then settled into my little "nurses nest." A minute or two later, you pulled the crib bumper down wanting to look out. I heard you moving about and was watching you. When I realized you might see me, I started watching you through just a slit of my eyes. I knew that if we started overtly watching each other, you wouldn't be able to get back to sleep anytime soon. You smiled and tossed your head when you saw me there, saying, "Ah-dah-naa-naa" quietly. You were surprised to see me there. You hadn't realized I was there on the floor. After a few minutes of trying to get my attention, you lay back down.

A few minutes later, I heard you stir again. I peeked at your crib through a slit of my eye and watched you pull the bumper down. You looked around for me amongst my covers. Once you found my face, you smiled and started talking. After a minute, you lay down again. It was as though you were just checking to see if I was still there.

March 30

You slept a total of six and one-half hours last night. Quite an improvement over the night before. Three and one-half hours of that sleep was continuous! You didn't talk to yourself much when you woke up, but you did talk a little. I knew you were feeling a little better.

During our play in the late morning, you pulled yourself up to the couch from sitting on the floor—twice with no thigh boosts. You also pulled yourself along on your tummy, and with some attempts at crawling too! When you fell from your crawling or cruising efforts, you made things a lot less scary for Mommy by falling to a sitting position instead of falling flat on your back. You demonstrate such terrific balance while reaching and bending for a dropped toy or other item of interest, holding onto a piece of furniture or whatever as you stand. It's so much fun to watch you! You work so hard (grunt-grunt). You show such concentration with your raised or wrinkled eyebrows. You're such a delight. It was wonderful to see you feeling like your usual sunny self again.

April

April 1

You have progressed to the point of pulling yourself up to nearly everything you come in contact with. And that's no April fool!

April 2

You pulled yourself up to your walker this morning. You crept around at a regular rhythm, slow but steady. You crept over toward the kitchen floor. When you reached the vinyl flooring and heard your hand make a smacking sound as it hit the floor, you stopped. You smiled, then smacked the floor with your other hand. You gave a big squeal of delight. You proceeded to play patta-cake with the floor for a while. You then changed yourself to a sitting position and smacked away a little longer.

April 3

Now you cruise and creep over the entire house in your walker. You go all over the family room leaving zillions of little "walker tracks" in the carpet. You go into the kitchen and head straight for the laundry room (full of no-no's). It kept me busy making sure you couldn't get in there. I barricaded the laundry room doorway with a large couch cushion to prevent your entry. We haven't hung the door to the laundry room yet. I'll have to ask Daddy to hang that laundry room door soon.

April 5

Big News! You tried to stand up today in the middle of the floor! You backed up onto your straightened legs with your arms—an all fours position. I even caught a picture of your first attempt! You tried it three more times before I had to get ready for work.

April 6

When I went into the nursery to get you this morning, I found you sitting up in your crib smiling at me! If you're not careful, you're going to get good at that. It also meant you were feeling much better.

I've noticed over the last few days that you're becoming much more self-entertaining. You will sit and explore something for a while; creep over to something else, or just another area; and sit up and see what that area has to offer. Then you start all over again.

As Daddy and I were playing with you this afternoon, we hid his wrist watch under his hand, after you had become interested in it. You picked and pulled at his hand. When he let you open his hand, you grabbed the watch. You repeated the action three times. Another milestone accomplished— looking for hidden objects; though I don't think you're aware of that.

April 8

This morning when you finished your first bottle, you called for me to sit you up; I didn't respond. You called again; I still didn't come for you, but watched you from a position where you couldn't see me. After a couple of minutes you turned yourself over onto your tummy—something you rarely do. Maybe I could get that tactic to work again! Once on your stomach you started creeping, then crawled! Knee to knee to knee to knee for five feet! Seeing you crawl was great!

Well, it is time to start babysitter shopping again. Daddy hasn't been able to find anything other than short-term jobs in our area, so he's going to leave for Sacramento to look for work. He'll have to sleep in the camper there during the week and come home on the weekends. With him gone, I'll have to find someone that can be with you until I get off work on the weekends. Your Daddy had been watching you then.

I am not looking forward to shopping for a new sitter. It was so hard to find someone I felt good about the first time. Beth's wonderful, but she only works until 6:00 pm and she doesn't work weekends. My work hours are from 3:00 pm to 11:30 pm and I have to work every other weekend. I'm terribly concerned about finding a nice, loving person willing to work our hours.

I'll check with the new Child Care Referral Office, which recently opened in Redding, to find all of the licensed persons in our area. And I'll put "feelers" out again for sitters that people who I knew are using, and feel good about. Last time only one of my friends was able to recommend someone, and that person didn't have any openings. She did have a waiting list. We are still on that list.

When you awakened from your afternoon nap of one hour, I found you **standing** in your crib smiling at me and saying "hello" (a la Tiffi). I was so excited! I had been looking forward to the time I would find your sweet little face peering at me over the crib rail. It was so precious—just as I thought it would be. I called for Daddy to grab the camera and come see you. He arrived in time to get a picture. It was at this time, that Daddy told me he found you standing up in your crib a few days ago. He thought you had been doing it before, so he didn't say anything to me. He didn't realize he had witnessed a first.

April 9

This morning we were finally able to take our Easter pictures. I felt so bad and so tired Sunday from not sleeping for so many days, I just couldn't get myself going. I wanted your pictures to be taken when we were happy. I like our photo sessions to be fun for you, too.

I was happy to finally take pictures of you in your bunny suit. The focus may not have been perfect. Those ears didn't want to stay on long enough for me to focus, at least not without a little conscious effort on the part of the "wearer." The "wearer" was much more interested in her Easter basket to bother keeping tabs on what her ears were "up to" or "down to," as the case may have been.

We took some funny pictures too. I can't wait to see the picture of you in your first pair of boots; standing up, of course, with your hands holding onto a stool. You looked so funny— your minute little self in a pair of boots that went up beyond your knees. As usual, I can't wait to get the pictures developed.

We went to visit some of our neighbors, Jeanie and Ralph, this morning. Jeanie and Ralph live on the main road into

town. Little Cottonwood town, that is, not Redding. While there, you took six well-placed little steps as Ralph held your hands. When we left Jeanie and Ralph's, we went to the Child Care Referral Office to get started on screening a new sitter. Our next stop was Dr. Kelley's office for your follow-up appointment, because of your dual ear infection. You still had fluid in your right ear, but the infections were gone from both ears. The remaining fluid would reabsorb in time. I told the Doctor that you had started saying, "Mah-mah," but were now saying, "Nah-nah." He said that the fluid in your ear could be effecting how you heard some sounds.

Once home, I made some appointments for us this week to meet three ladies—prospective babysitters. I scheduled two appointments for tomorrow and one in a few days. Wish us luck.

April 10

You had your first teething biscuit today! Fortunately, I had put a bib on you and "parked" you in the middle of a quilt in the family room, just in case it was messy. It was a good thing. Those teething biscuits are a mushy mess. They turn into live foam when they come in contact with drool.

Babysitter screening update: We did meet three nice ladies. Kathleen, who was very nice, just couldn't make our hours work for her. She had a housekeeping job on certain mornings and couldn't get home until 3:00 pm, that's too late for us, since I have to be at work by 2:45 pm. She did refer us to another lady named Winnie, who was highly recommended by a friend of hers who had gone through three other caregivers in the last six months. We will definitely call her! Barbara, our second scheduled appointment, was also a super lady. I had good feelings about her, and our hours worked for her most of the time.

After leaving Barbara's, I stopped to call Winnie. She said we could come over. I had very positive feelings from our first encounter. Winnie seemed like a great choice. I still have to do my usual unannounced drop-ins and "staking out" of Barbara's and Winnie's neighborhood before I sign any child care contracts.

It was exciting to have more than one promising person, although choosing who was going to care for you wasn't really any less scary than it was the first time.

When the ladies we interviewed talked to you as I held you, you would look at them, usually smile, then become shy and turn your head partially away from them. Then you partially buried your face as you leaned into my chest. Then you looked at them again. It was so sweet.

You waved bye-bye at least once to everyone you met today. You're getting quite good at it. You waved bye-bye to me, too even though I wasn't leaving you. You waved also as you said, "Nah-nah."

I haven't told you how adorable you are when you say "nah-nah." You put such effort into it! You squint your eyes, wrinkle your nose, and move your mouth and jaw with such purpose. You stretch out the "n" sound, "Nnnnah". It's great!

April 11

I called Fran, our other child-care possibility, to get her address. I neglected to get her address when I talked to her before. It turned out that she lived over five miles out of town on a windy dirt road. I didn't like the idea of going that far out on that country road in the wee hours of the night with you in the car. After thinking about it, I called to explain our concern and cancelled our appointment. I felt I could afford to do so already having two such fine prospects to choose from.

Barbara and Winnie were both wonderful. After a lot of

"pro and coning," I decided on Winnie. If you stayed with Winnie, you wouldn't have to be on the highway in the car at night as much as if you stayed with Barbara. Winnie lived in Anderson, seventy percent of the distance home from work, while Barbara lived in South Redding, only twenty percent of the distance home from work. I didn't really like the idea of you being on the interstate highway at night all the way from South Redding three nights a week.

I would like you to be with Barbara occasionally, if she would allow us to do that. It would give you the chance to be acquainted with her before you become afraid of strangers. Just in case Winnie didn't work out, or for the times when her charges, or her own children were sick. If we start with Barbara now, hopefully you will become acquainted with she and Winnie before you reached the point where you are afraid of strangers. That point, in your life, will be coming soon.

Tomorrow we'll "drop-in" on Winnie, as a double-check, to make sure everything is ok. We'll drop-in on Barbara on one of my days off next week and talk with her again.

April 12

You are full of new vocalizations, and there is a new character to your "talking." The sounds are more complex. Even if they are some of your "old words," there is a new complexity in the way you say them. Your new vocals seem to be made up more of compound sounds than just simple sounds.

Now that you are over your ear infection, I've started switching you over to whole milk. I'm doing it gradually, in case there is a notable difference in taste that you might dislike. An added benefit is that any allergy you might demonstrate would be less intense. Today I gave you seventy-five percent formula with twenty-five percent milk. In four days, I'll change it to fifty-fifty. After another four days, I'll change it to twenty-five percent formula and seventy-five percent milk. Four days after that, it will be one hundred percent milk.

We dropped-in on Winnie today, and everything was appropriate. The next step was to "stake out" the neighborhood. We'll drop in again next week to give you a chance to become acquainted with Winnie, before spending a long time there without me.

Beth is on vacation in Hawaii all of this and next week. She doesn't know anything about Daddy having to look for work in Sacramento, or about our having to change sitters. I'll let you stay with her for a week once she returns. I can't just stop taking you to her before you have the opportunity to spend some time together to say goodbye. We'll also go for visits once and a while after you're with your new sitter. Beth's family has become like a part of our own. We won't be able to just stop seeing them.

April 14

Today, while standing up at your walker, you let go of it as Daddy balanced you at your hips. He let go of you without you really knowing it. He said you stood on your own for almost five seconds! Congratulations!

April 15

While standing at your walker this morning, you let go and stood on your own for three seconds, completely on your own. You did it three more times! Soon you'll be standing alone at will! It was exciting, yet, on the other hand, you're growing so fast—too fast.

While it was nice out, we went to town to shop for a toddler's walker for you. You needed something more "directable" than your walker; something slower, too.

April 16

I took some wonderful pictures of you playing with the Toddler "Model T" walker that we bought yesterday. Today, you enjoyed playing with the walker itself. Yesterday, you were far more interested in the box it came in.

April 17

You've had a runny nose for three days now and have thrown up three times in those three days. I made an appointment with Dr. Kelley to see if the fluid that had remained in your ear had become reinfected. He had an opening this afternoon.

At Dr. Kelley's this afternoon, he found another ear infection. The infection was in your right ear. At least it wasn't in both ears again. Poor sweetie, you're such a little trooper. I feared something was wrong when you didn't talk to yourself when you woke up this morning. The last two days, you started to cry for no apparent reason. It didn't last long; but it was so unlike you. The Doctor prescribed a different antibiotic this time. We'll go back for another check-up in ten days. We picked up your new prescription on the way home.

April 19

You woke up singing to yourself today. I can't tell you how happy that made me feel. You seemed to feel fine and happy yesterday, but you didn't talk to yourself when you woke up. Oddly enough that seems to be our best indicator of how you're feeling, since you are so incredibly good-natured. You woke up singing today, so I knew you felt wonderful, and after only two doses of your new antibiotic.

It's a beautiful day out and very warm. Let's go "malling"! You haven't been to the mall for awhile because of your previous ear infection, we must go out and enjoy this beautiful day.

We went to the mall in Chico. It was a great day for a drive. We stopped by Grandma Ani-Poo and Popie's house on the way, and they decided to join us.

While we were in Chico, we also went to see Great-Grandpa Phil. You talked to Phil and reached out to hold him, and just generally made a fuss over him. He was spellbound! You really made his day, if not his whole week!

April 20

You now crawl with great speed. You seem to be intent upon exploring the inner depths of my "mall-ing" bag, a large tote bag I use as a combination purse and diaper bag when we go malling. Seeing you crawling around with such progressive speed reminds me of a doll that was sold in the toy stores several years ago. I don't remember what she was called. She was battery operated and would crawl when you turned her on. Her arms were fixed and straight. Her legs were fixed and bent at right angles with the soles of her feet turned in at the toe. I remember thinking how cute she was, but I also remember thinking that she couldn't possibly look anything like a real baby crawling. Each little fixed leg would alternate at "stepping." It looked so unrealistic.

I was wrong. As I watch you clip along with your arms fixed, straight and determinedly placed, your legs bent at almost right angles and seemingly fixed; and the soles of your feet turned in at the toe, you move almost exactly as that little doll moved!

I am learning more from being with you everyday than I did from all of the books and tons of parent/child magazines I studied. I knew I couldn't learn how to be a mother form those things. Not knowing anything about babies, however, I couldn't help but learn a lot of things that would help.

You've taken to sometimes turning your tongue on it's side in your mouth. I think you do it because it feels different, or maybe it's just fun. You will occasionally stick your tongue out, while other times you have it at the corner of your mouth with a slight twist in it. This is fabulous. It gives you an appearance of intense concentration; I love it.

April 22

We went to visit Beth today; she's back from Hawaii. I told her our unhappy news of having to change babysitters. She understood, but was obviously upset. She's going to miss you; and we are both gong to miss her. She is a super lady. Beth bought a gift for you in Hawaii, a tank top shirt that says "Aloha" with a young boy and girl pictured on the front. That was very thoughtful of her.

April 23

Today was your next to last day to be with Beth. As we visited before I left for work, you crawled up the step from her "sunken" living room. It was your first attempt, and you made it easily.

Daddy said he could tell that Beth was upset when he picked you up that evening. We have made very special friends in Beth and her delightful family.

April 24

Today, I could tell you'd discovered that the other rooms in the house existed even if there isn't someone in them. In your walker, you propelled yourself into the kitchen and across to the laundry room. Oh-oh! Foiled again! The laundry door is in now! Too bad, Tiffi. The laundry room door is the kind that slides into the wall; a pocket door. If it isn't closed all the way you could open it. Once you discovered you couldn't penetrate the laundry room, you took a couple of laps around the kitchen island then headed into the dining room. Then it was down the hall and off to the master bedroom.

While I was getting ready for work, you were in your walker again. You rolled yourself over to the sliding glass door in the master bedroom. It was covered with a "drape." Actually, it was a bed-sheet. It would be awhile before we could concern ourselves with proper draperies for all of our thirty-two windows. You hit at the drape; you then lifted the drape up and—surprise—there was the outside! You looked out, then dropped the sheet. You picked it up again and rolled along the sliding door inside the sheet, and generally had a marvelous time.

Today was your last day with Beth. We arrived almost an hour early, so we could have plenty of time to visit. We were all a little tense and afraid to talk about it. We've become quite close and it was very hard to leave. Beth is a super lady and has been wonderful to you.

Beth and I hugged and cried when I left. I seem to recall doing the same thing the first day I left you there. We will stop by to visit Beth sometimes when we're coming back from Redding.

April 25

This morning, you were in your walker. I was about to get myself ready to take you to town for some professional pictures, but I had some laundry to put away first.

You were in the family room in your walker. I was going to take the laundry and set it on the living room brickwork behind the large woodstove. Then I would take you into the bedroom with me so I could put the laundry away and get dressed. But I didn't get a chance to get you; you followed me as soon as I left the kitchen. You had rolled your walker down the hall to the brickwork where I had put the laundry. I congratulated you on following me. Then I went to the bedroom doorway and asked you to "Come get me." You did! Hurray, Tiffany!

Once I was ready, it was time to get you ready. I called to you, "Come on, Tiffi, let's get you ready for your pictures." I walked to the guest room where your on-the-hanger clothes were. We haven't put the moulding or the closet rods in your closet yet, so we keep your hanging clothes in the guest room closet for now. You came right after me. This was really fun!

You were your usual sunny and cooperative self during the picture taking. So much for the horror stories we hear about taking childrens' pictures. At least, so far. This may change once you become afraid of strangers.

We had your picture taken at two studios. You wore the beautiful dress that Jan sent to you. They were both having a special. We took advantage of both so we'll have plenty of pictures for everyone who wants one.

The studios such cute little props for their pictures. I couldn't wait to see how they'll turn out. Both photographers asked me if I would trade you for free pictures—fat chance! They were just being complimentary.

April 26

Today, you stayed with Barbara. She agreed to be our back-up Tiffi-watcher, so I set this day up for you to start getting acquainted. There were four other children there. You were completely absorbed in watching them play. I stayed for about thirty minutes as buffer time. You weren't upset at all when I left. You were too busy entertaining yourself.

I shopped for a couple of things for you, then went home. I spent time doing the deep-down type of house cleaning that I seem to have a very hard time getting done anymore. You know, the "fun stuff"—cleaning all of the crevices throughout the house, slider door and window tracks, where the carpet meets the wall, and spaces where you find fuzzy crumbs, dead bugs, and other assorted icky things.

I also crawled around the entire house on all fours, looking for potential hazards that I might not catch looking from my usual perspective. I made a room-by-room list of things that had to be done, as soon as possible, to further child-proof the house.

I called Barbara at 12:30 pm to see how everything was going. She said you were a doll and were getting along beautifully. You had eaten your lunch in a high-chair on the back patio and watched the other children play. After lunch, Barbara put you in a playpen on the patio to protect you from any overactive play by the other children (ages four to five). What a wonderfully organized and considerate lady Barbara is.

At 6:00 pm I picked you up. You'd had a wonderful day. Barbara said you enjoyed crawling around or sitting in her lap to watch the other kids play most of the time.

April 27

Today's statistics: 20 pounds 2 ounces.

We went to the shopping center in Anderson where the Sheriff's Department was sponsoring a free identification card with photograph and fingerprints (footprints in your case), as a means of identification for when a child is missing. Three days ago, California became one of the first states to pass a law that all children must be fingerprinted before entering school. Many people felt that this was an infringement of a person's right to privacy. I feel it is extremely important to be able to identify a missing child.

However, I don't feel that fingerprinting is enough. There needs to be a standardized code of identification, one that can be fed into a nationwide computer network of authorities, and would result in a near instantaneous, nationwide description of a missing child, in addition to the fingerprints.

The Sheriffs said that your photo would be ready May 4th. After we pick it up we will put it in our safe-deposit box.

April 28

We all went to the uptown mall today, Daddy included, to look at the entries in a photography contest that were displayed in the mall. We also did some coupon shopping, and picked up an infant gum and toothcare set. Now that you have teeth cleaning your mouth with a damp cloth after eating wasn't enough anymore.

Back at the ranch—I wondered how you would accept the infant gum massager. It was designed for babies over seven months old, and had a handle large enough for you to hold. I handed it to you. You looked at it, put it in your mouth and chewed on it while rolling it around in your mouth. Did you like it!?! I guess so, I had a hard enough time trying to talk you out of it. Two points for little Tiffi "two-teeth" (two on top and two on the bottom).

April 29

This morning, after breakfast, you wanted to explore the whole house via crawling. I perched here and there to watch your activities. Then I started to play chase with you as you headed down the hall for the nursery. You giggled and squealed, crawling as fast as you could.

Once you reached the carpet in the bedroom, you started laughing. You laughed hard enough to short-circuit your high-speed crawl. You tried to roll to a sitting position, but your belly-laughing wouldn't permit it. You ended up rolling onto your back. I crawled over to you and gave you a big kiss and hug. You laughed and talked, then headed off again.

You really seemed to enjoy that little episode. I don't know which of us enjoyed it more! Such happy little laughs and big belly-laughs. I think you are a very happy baby.

Right after lunch, we went into town for your Doctor's appointment. Your follow-up exam for your double ear infection went beautifully! Both eardrums were perfectly clear; what a relief.

Later in the afternoon, we played in the family room. You demonstrated that you had mastered opening and closing the "trunk" of your toddler Model T walker. You lifted the trunk lid up to reach inside. As you let go of the lid to put your arm

in it, it closed to the level of your arm. You lifted the trunk lid
again, with your right arm, and took your left arm out. Then
you let go of the lid to reach in with your right arm. The same
thing happened; the lid closed onto your arm.
Now you tried lifting the lid and pushing it until it stayed
open by itself. It did have a "locking" position. Once you were
through taking everything out of the compartment, you pulled
the lid closed, at the cut away area in the center, so it didn't
hurt your fingers. You did this three or four more times.

At dinner, I had included cottage cheese in your menu.
Today made the second time I offered it to you this week. You
wouldn't take it either time. At this point in your life, you seem
to intensely dislike cottage cheese, or maybe you just don't like
bumpy foods.

April 30

I tried fixing you a scrambled egg for brunch. No luck. You
wouldn't take it by yourself, and when I tried feeding it to you,
you wrinkled up your face and pushed your tongue out. That
happened three times. Then you scrapped the egg off your
tongue. I'm not sure if it's the taste you dislike or the texture.
I bet it's the texture, it's lumpy. I have yet to find a lumpy or
bumpy food that you like.

Today will be your first day with Winnie. I'll pick you up
when I get off work tonight. I hope this new arrangement won't
be too difficult for you to adjust to. You've always been a very
sound little sleeper. I would hate to mess that up for you, and
for me.

The first time I called Winnie from work, to see how you were doing, it was only 4:30 pm. She said you were trying to take a nap. You were more than ready for one when you'd arrived there. But just like your first day at Barbara's, there was too much new stuff to look at and children to watch for you to want to take a nap.

Winnie also said that one of her "after school" boys came today wearing a hat shaped like a bug with long legs sticking out of it. He came up to you, made a scary noise and really scared you. Winnie said that it took a while to convince you that everything would be safe and alright again. Poor Tiffany.

I called again at 7:30 pm. You were still awake. You hadn't eaten any solids for Winnie; she tried three different times, but you only took your milk. Winnie said that except for the "bug-hat" incident you had a great time. You especially liked playing with her daughter, Stacey, crawling around and playing with the busy-box. She said you didn't cry after I left. Sounds like your first day was a big success.

I was so eager to see you when I left work. I was anxious about waking you and Winnie up, and how traveling around with you in the car, in the middle of the night, would affect you.

Winnie let me in. She picked you up from the playpen in the living room where you were sleeping, as I put your things in the car. You awoke with a smile. You were far from being completely awake, but you were still generous with your smiles.

You stayed awake all the way home, protesting occasionally. When we arrived home, I fixed a bottle for you. You took about half of it, then went to sleep with only a small amount of fuss. Twenty minutes later, you woke up unhappy.

I tried letting you fuss for a bit to see if you could get yourself back to sleep. You did try, but cried and fussed off and on for another twenty minutes. I went to your room to give you some hugs. You collapsed on my shoulder. But when I put you down ten minutes later, you cried and fussed again. I tried leaving the room for a while. I waited across the hallway in the guest room to see if you would settle yourself. You were just tired, bewildered and unable to get to sleep.

A few minutes later, I went back in, picked you up and snuggled you against my shoulder. You were happy and comfortable there. We rocked and swayed and listened to music boxes. At a little after 3:00 am I put you down. You fussed as I left the room, then cried. Three minutes later you were quiet and going to sleep.

You awoke again before 4:00 am. I fixed a bottle for you and we rocked while you drank. I hoped you wouldn't need two bottles during the night regularly because of this change in schedule. I could hardly deny you of it for now, but I need sleep, too. This new schedule is disruptive. I can certainly understand you needing extra comfort and support in the beginning. We'll see how the next week or so progresses before I worry about it.

May

May 1

When I woke up, it was 7:30 am. When I checked on you, you were sound asleep. I went back to bed until you woke up at 8:30. At least you were able to catch up on your night's sleep, so did I.

You had a nice morning. You have taken a definite fancy to playing in the pantry. I cleaned off the bottom shelf of any hazardous items, and stocked it with "pain-free" and safe "household toys." You played in there for thirty minutes after I redecorated. I thought you'd like it because it's a small area, two feet from shelf edge to shelf edge. The horse-shoe shaped shelves are easy for you to reach from one end to the other.

You took a regular-sized nap (two hours) this morning and a short one before we left for Winnie's house.

At Winnie's, I sat you on the floor and one of the two little girls that were there came over to play with you.

She asked if I had brought any toys for you to play with.

I told her I had, and handed a couple of them to her.

She then offered them to you. You were very happy talking and playing with the little girl, as Winnie and I watched.

I didn't stay very long. I thought I should kiss you goodbye and leave while you were enjoying yourself. It was hard to

212

leave so soon. (I usually stay twenty minutes with you at the sitter's before leaving for work.) I wondered if you cried when I left or after I left. You didn't cry when I left. Neither did I. I was sort of "choked up" like I was yesterday. I almost cried yesterday, but was able to stop it. Just like at Barbara's, I got out of the door, then the tears came. I can't help it; it's very hard for me to leave you the first few times with someone new.

I called at 7:30 pm and found that you hadn't cried after I left. I was both happy and sad. On the one hand, I wished that you'd miss me. On the other, I want you to be able to function and enjoy yourself when I'm not there. It's an emotional tug-of-war. If, and when, you have your own children, you will understand what I mean.

I was out of work on time tonight. When Winnie woke you up, you didn't fuss at all. She handed you to me and I was greeted with a very sweet and sleepy Tiffi smile.

You slept part of the way home, a very small part; but, overall, you were sleepier in the car tonight than you were last night. When we arrived home, I warmed a bottle for you. You took most of it. I stole some more hugs and squeezes then put you down in your crib. You delivered one small grumble, then fell asleep.

May 2

You slept very well last night, bless your heart. I will be very happy if we are able to have this new arrangement without messing up your sleep pattern or doing anything to lessen your sunny disposition.

You woke up at 3:30 am and weren't able to get yourself back to sleep. When just huggies didn't help you get back to sleep, I got up and fixed you a bottle. After your bottle you fell asleep. Tonight was definitely easier for you than last night.

May 3

We had some fun game time this morning. We played peek-a-boo through your bolster-shaped toy with the clear vinyl at both ends.

We also played with your shape-sorting ball, dumping out all of the shapes. You picked up a shape, then I put that shape in the appropriately shaped hole, with the hole facing you. You tried to put some in, too. You put two in by yourself and a couple of other times with help. The rest of the time, it was just hit and miss and enjoy the noise.

After your morning nap we went to visit Basette and the other animals. Little John (the baby monkey) was now as big as his parents. He is still sweet, and you still like talking with him. His mother is pregnant again (if I haven't already mentioned it.) After talking with Little John, we stopped by to see the baby Brazzas. The baby girl Brazzas monkey was still buff colored. She had yet to display the bright colors of an adult, but she had developed her little white "goatee." (A goatee is a small neat beard trimmed to a point.) She had begun to venture from the security of hanging onto her mother's body all of the time. She came over to visit while you and I talked to Lonnie. That little one was very friendly. Benson, the dominant male of the group, was actually being a friendly and tolerant father. He was usually an unsociable grouch.

Afterwards, we went to Grandma Ani-Poo's to borrow her sewing machine. I haven't been able to fix mine. It was nice to spend some time with them, since they were leaving for San Diego the next day. You stood against the screen door in the dining room watching as I played with Grandma's kitties, Sammie and Sugar. Sammie was her usually friendly self.

Sugar, the look-but-don't-touch-me cat, actually put up with some hugs and let me scratch him under his chin.

May 4

This morning while you were in your walker, you rolled into the dining/entry area. I moved my work onto the dining table so you could play there for a while. You rolled, this way and that, across the vinyl flooring. If there had been a speed limit, you would have come close to breaking it.

You were propelling your walker around at a slow run. When you were at the end of the dining room area, I called to you. When I had your attention, I raised my arm. I threw it out away from me to one side, and said "Go-o-o-o Tiffi!" You started up and ran across the floor to the other end of the dining/entry area. It was cute and so funny.

At 10:30 am, we were in Dr. Kelley's office for your nine month well-baby check up. Your height and weight were in the ninety-fifth percentile and are in good proportion to each other. You were in perfect health and you didn't have any fluid in your ears. Dr. Kelley, again, commented on how sweet and cooperative you were. He said we were very fortunate to have such a delightful, happy, and sociable baby. He predicted a nice life for you: fun in school, lots of friends, and that you would be a well-adjusted adult. Don't you just love him? He knows a special little person when he sees one. Of course, I'm not at all biased in my opinion!

After leaving the Doctor's office, we went to the mall. This weekend the mall was featuring "A Children's Faire." We picked up some pictures and surveyed the displays. There were a lot of preschools represented. They were demonstrating things for young visitors to do. There were also children's camps and alternative teaching schools exhibiting. I looked into the different programs while you watched all of the young children and babies. You had a grand time!

When we finished at the mall we drove to Barbara's. I had to work this afternoon, so today was your first late-night stay with her. You were very happy when I left. When I called Barbara, later from work, she told me you cried a little after I left. She also told me that you cried when either of her dogs looked at you or said anything. (She has an eight-pound miniature collie and a labrador retriever puppy.) The dogs talked to you through Barbara's sliding glass door. You didn't seem to like that. That was funny because you loved talking to Teaki and Libra through our sliding glass door, and they are both labradors.

I picked you up after work. You slept almost all of the way home. When we pulled into the driveway, you woke up. You weren't able to get back to sleep without a bottle. After your bottle, you went right to sleep. You didn't wake up at all during the rest of the night. This was getting easier for both of us each day.

I neglected to tell you, that your second upper tooth came through a bit farther today, and with your usual ease. You had some diarrhea, a stuffy nose, some occasional gum pain, lasting only a few seconds but very little irritability.

Now you have two whole upper teeth—your right central incisor and today your right lateral incisor. I can see where your left central incisor is about to come through. I'm finally getting to the point where I can tell what's happening in there. That's a big change from your first tooth.

May 5

Today, you stayed with Winnie while I was at work. Her daughter, Stacey, was home and played with you. Winnie told me that everyone who saw you said how cute you were. I guess not everyone is blessed with such a sweet and sociable baby, though I think all babies are natural charmers, each in their own special way.

May 6

These days, you want to spend more and more time standing up. Frequently, you're just barely holding onto any-thing—just balancing. If you're not crawling, eating, or in-volved in playing with something or someone, you're looking for something to stand next to.

Your little huggies are continually becoming tighter and more deliberate. You are also giving more loves and "pre-kis-ses." A "pre-kiss" being when you put your head or face against mine, hold my head and coo, chortle, or talk to me with your mouth open against my face. It's precious and heartwarming; it makes me feel absolutely **wonderful!**

May 7

Playing peek-a-boo chase with you is the order of the day on the days that I work. Today was no exception. We play while you are crawling or in your walker. It has even begun to evolve into a game of hide-and-seek, with you being the seeker. You love it!

After your morning nap we went to visit Loretta, the Cottonwood librarian. I joined the newly-formed Parent's League in our little community and am working on the "Save the Library Committee." I'm meeting with Loretta, representing the Parents League, to learn her feelings on what we can do, to keep our county from closing our small commnunity's library on July 31. Loretta has lived in Cottonwood since she was four years old. She is a three-time grandmother now.

The county has cut our library's budget every year for many years. There is nothing much left to cut except to close it completely. We won't sit back and allow that to happen.

If our library closed, the children of the area would have to travel seventeen miles for books and reference materials for school assignments.That is the distance from Cottonwood proper to the Redding main library. Many people live a number of miles outside of town, making that distance even greater. If the schools ended up compensating by decreasing the needs for research materials for assignments and /or significantly decreasing the challenge of the assignments, the children's education would suffer drastically.

May 9

This morning you said, "oh-oh (uh-ooh)" many times. You've tried to say that for a while. Until today, you weren't able to make the second, "oh" sound. You would say "uh-uhhhh." Today, it was perfectly clear and you obviously liked the way it sounded; I'll have to tell Winnie about it.

You spent part of the day with Winnie. I've had an intestinal flu problem the last few days, and last night I developed a sore throat. I wanted you to stay with Winnie so I could get some rest today, and hopefully keep this problem from getting any worse. We really can't afford for me to miss any work because of it.

When I went to pick you up, Winnie told me that you said, "uh-oh" whenever you dropped something or fell when trying to walk. I think it was your first real word. It isn't just a single syllable repeated like "dah-dah-dah" or "mah-mah-mah" or "mah-mah-nah". This is a definite word! Congratulations!

Winnie also said that, in the last few days, you have been standing practically on your own. You may have your hand on something, but more for security than balance. You are fast approaching the threshold of **walking!**

The shopping cart pad with the seat-belt, that I had ordered, came in the mail yesterday. Now I can take you on our bi-weekly shopping trips without worrying about you standing up in the shopping cart, or leaning too far forward and falling out.

After leaving Winnie's we left for your first big shopping trip. You had a terrific time at the grocery store. You were quite self-entertaining. You looked at all of the product containers, tugging at everything that I put into the cart.

The organizational challenge of the day, where to put the purse, the shopping list, and the coupons, things I have to check frequently, and in a place where you can't grab and tear them. And where or how do I arrange the breakables and smashables where you can't reach them and drop them on the floor?

Then, of course, there are the hundreds of things wrapped in that "evil, windpipe-blocking plastic!" Plastic, when and if removed and put into your mouth, could interfere with or completely block your breathing. I can't put everything out of reach. It just isn't possible. Besides, you need something to explore. The two toys I had tied to your seat-belt for your entertainment paled in the presence of millions and billions of new, colorful and exciting things on every aisle.

Why am I even worrying about how you did at the market? I was the one doing all of the adjusting. You already knew what to do; drink in all of the colors in with your eyes and touch or grab anything that didn't touch you first; or get out of the way fast enough.

You ended up playing with, by design, I might add a bag of noodles, a block of cheese, a pair of socks, and a bag of frozen vegetables, all of which were wrapped in the very tough plastic—much too tough for you to be able to tear apart. Hence, you still needed to be constantly monitored as to what was going into your mouth.

Since I was battling a sore throat, I picked up a can of soda to sip on as we shopped. There was no mistake that you were doing at least as much shopping as I was. I had done a very good job of keeping my oⴓen soda out of reach—so far. As the far end of the shopping cart became over-burdened with "dangerous cargo," I had to relocate my soda.

Two minutes after I relocated the soda, you reached for something as I was checking for a box of "older baby" nipples. Your reach caused something to move, which caused the soda can to move. You guessed it, the soda spilled. There you were with soda on your lap, under your lap, over a lot of the groceries, and cascading into my purse. I had cleverly placed my purse directly under the seat where you were sitting so you couldn't reach it. The rest of the soda found it's way to the floor.

You knew you had caused something to happen, but you weren't really certain what it was. You had cold, talking (fizzing) stuff all over you and it was dripping all around. You looked at the "soda-fall" and then looked at me with very uncertain eyes, bewildered and wondering if you should cry.

I wanted to laugh. It was really a funny scene. But you looked so uncertain that I bent over to give you some hugs first. I was sure you were tired and ready for something to eat and a nap.

After the hugs, I laughed and called you "cola-bottom." Then we went to ask a checker for something to clean up our mess. After the hugs and my laughing, you smiled, giggled and started playing with the drips of soda that fell from the groceries beside you.

When it was our turn at the check-out counter, you started to cry. You cry every time we get to the check-out counter. There's just something you do not like about sitting next to an electronic cash register.

I picked you up out of the cart, gave you some hugs and set you on the little check-writing platform, soggy bottom and all. You leaned against me and gave me some very sweet loves while we waited. All in all, I would say that your first big trip to the grocery store was a success.

May 10

This morning, you started cruising! You walked along the edge of the coffee table and reached for the sofa—too far. You sat down and crawled to the stereo. You pulled yourself up to the stereo, played with it for a minute or two, then you cruised from the stereo to an end table, then from the end table to the sofa. You side-stepped on tippy-toe to reach the sofa. The steps you took were mostly on your toes.

I'll have to look into that toe walking. I'm not sure if that is the usual, or **one** of the usual "starting methods" of early walking. I haven't run across anything in my reading, to date, about beginning walking styles. I'll check with Dr. Kelley's office when the weekend is over. It was delightful to watch you cruising along the furniture. It's one of the things I've been looking forward to.

We've both discovered that you can reach higher. You're now reaching the second shelf from the bottom in the pantry. I had already set the bottom shelf up with Tiffi things. Now I need to relocate certain things on the next shelf, until I can get Daddy to hang the pantry door.

Also, when you were in your walker this morning, you reached up onto the dining room table and removed your empty Easter basket from the edge—time to rearrange the dining room table. I've been keeping our photo album work there.

We went into town to pick up another photo album and some of your professional pictures. They were beautiful, as I knew they would be. Naturally, we bought more pictures than were included in the package offer. Who could help it? There were so many great poses. How could I pass up a picture of you in a miniature peacock-backed chair, or with a parasol, or sitting on a miniature park bench? I couldn't and I didn't.

We also went toy shopping. You needed a shape-sorting toy that was less complicated than the one you have. I had previously narrowed the choices down to three candidates from the twelve I had seen. We needed to go look for those three and make a decision.

I decided on the three-shape (circle, triangle, square) toy with "teddy bear headed shapes" and assorted playground-type equipment, exhibiting the different shaped holes. It offered you six different ways to recognize three shapes, using visual reward, sound, and motion. I felt you'd like it. I even liked it.

Home again; you had a great day out. Lots of "little people" to talk to and look at. You had a wonderful time socializing.

You enjoyed playing with your new shape toy. You weren't getting the right shape in the right hole very often, but you were having a great time. The toy was rated for ages one to three. You're not quite ten months old yet, but it seemed well suited to your interests and abilities. I think you'll find it fun and challenging without being frustrating.

May 11

You're getting better at working with your new shape toy. You enjoy it, even when not using it quite as intended. You put the bears on the appropriate shape specific slides,but upside down! What the heck, it works. It's hard to argue with success.

You've had a lot of difficulty getting to sleep these last two days, both at naptime and bedtime. I am not sure why. You felt fine when you were awake. Could it be because you are on the threshold of walking? Could you worry about something like that? Would you **worry** about something like that? Maybe it has something to do with teething. I'm not sure.

You cry and whimper whenever I put you down for sleep. I've tried waiting up to fifteen minutes before going back into your room, but you're still upset. It isn't a mad cry or a scream. It doesn't sound like frustration. It's more of a lost, forlorn cry.

Tonight, it took from 7:30 pm until 9:00 pm to get you to sleep. Most of that time was spent rocking and walking. I couldn't help but wonder if this was going to become a habit. I didn't feel it was manipulation. It seemed as though something just wasn't right or safe in the world right now, at least from your point of view. You needed extra security to get through whatever it was. So we'll just supply your needs and see what happens.

You awoke shortly after 1:00 am and weren't able to get yourself back to sleep. I went in to see you and was greeted with an enormous hug and "Mah-mah!" I checked your diaper, nothing noteworthy. I walked around the room and the hallway with you for about fifteen minutes. You relaxed and started dropping off to sleep. A couple of minutes later, I put you down. Once I had put you down, you started to cry, then wail after I left the room. I waited a few minutes—no change.

I fixed a bottle, thinking maybe a full, warm tummy would help you get to sleep. You took part of the bottle and fell asleep.

I held you for a while, but as soon as I put you down, you cried. I waited a few minutes. This had to be getting confusing for you, but what could I do?

I went back into your room and took you out of the crib. I walked you and rocked you for about thirty minutes, then offered you the rest of the bottle. After we walked for another thirty minutes or so, and you were "sound asleep." I put you down again and you immediately woke up. You started to cry as I left the room. Haven't I said this before!?! Your protest only lasted about thirty seconds before you fell asleep. At the tone, the time will be 4:00 am exactly.

May 12

Mother's Day. My first Mother's Day.

At 6:30 am you were awake, happy and rested. I wish I could say the same for me. I don't rejuvenate that quickly.

We visited with Grandma Ani-Poo and Popie today. They just got back from San Diego and were certainly glad to see you.

Grandma Ani-Poo needed some cornstarch from the store. I went to the store so that she and Popie could have a little time alone with you. You cried when I left.

You were also crying when I returned. Grandma Ani-Poo said you cried for a few minutes after I left, then played happily. But once you heard me get out of the car and walk up the gravel driveway, you started to cry again. As I walked up to the door from the outside you were headed for the door from the inside.

When I opened the door, you let out a little "uuuuh" and crawled faster toward me. Then you sat up and stretched out your arms. You were so sweet. I wonder if it is separation anxiety that has been haunting you for the last few days. Separation anxiety is the difficulty children experience when apart from their mother; a situation that occurs at different points in a child's development. I think you are realizing that

I am separate from you and my leaving frightens you, because you aren't certain if I'll return. That is a big order of logic for such a little one; but I want you to know, Tiffany, I will return.

When we arrived home this afternoon, from Grandma Ani-Poo's, you started to play with your new shape sorter. You were doing very well with the circle and triangle shapes. You learn quickly. Of course, that wasn't such a surprise, you're a very bright little girl.

Your Daddy and I exchanged "parents day" cards for Mother's Day. We've been exchanging "parents day" cards since we were married. We have always had animals in our home, and considered ourselves the "parents" of our pets. But this is the first year we've had a "man-cub" to parent. "Man-cub" was the term Rudyard Kipling used to refer to the young, human, boy in his work *The Jungle Book* .

I must admit, I felt like last year was my first real Mother's Day. During the time I was pregnant with you, I always felt like I was a bonafied mother. This time next year I bet you'll be able to say, "Happy Mother's Day," or maybe "Happy Mommy Day."

May 13

The body peachfuzz on your little self has fully developed. You now have a very fine, nearly invisible downy fuzz all over your body. You also have fine, slightly longer hair on the first knuckle area of each finger and thumb.

May 14

Today I took some "after Mother's Day" cards to the nurses who cared for us when you were born. I also took one to my gynecologist's office, to thank him and his staff for all of their support and compassion.

May 15

Today, you said, "Wow!" in a soft gentle voice. I do have to admit, that you have had some coaching during the last couple of days. This was also a day full of "bah-bah;" the Tiffi version of bye-bye. Maybe we can get you to say "bye-bye" soon. You will wave about half of the time when Daddy, Grandma Ani-Poo, Popie or I say, "Bye-bye," and, occasionally, if someone else says, "Bye-bye."

You, actually, have two bye-bye waves. One is waving your arm at the elbow, while waving your hand. The other "method" is moving your fingers up and down in a hand-only wave. Both are adorable. You sometimes do the hand-only wave when you're taking your bottle and watching us. That might actually be a "Hi" wave.

I've noticed you imitating more sounds over the last few days and talking to yourself as you play. You make many compound sounds (non-similar syllables) and have been playing patta-cake for longer periods.

May 16

You now have the circle shape of your shape sorter down pat. You can insert it into the circle-shaped holes. You do this eight or more times in a row. You are also better at lining up the triangle shape more often. The square shape completely eludes you at this point.

May 19

Mommy had a terrible weekend at work, and I still can't seem to get rid of this sore throat. Now you seem to have a tummy flu. Poohey! I thought that a day at home, just you and me, was in order. With no errand running outside of the house and no housecleaning. Just a stay at home day together to do nothing.

May 20

Today, we went to the uptown mall to shop for Irene's baby shower. Irene is one the nurses who works in the intensive care unit at Hilltop Hospital. We won't be able to go to the shower. It's tomorrow and I have to work. I'll take the gift to work and finish wrapping it on my break. One of the other nurses will take it to the shower for me.

We stopped at Beth's on our way home to show her the pictures we had taken in the studios last month. We had promised her a picture and I wanted to let her chose the one she wanted. We had a wonderful visit.

May 24

You spent part of the day with Grandma Ani-Poo and Popie while I did the grocery shopping and cleaned the house. As soon as you came home this afternoon, you headed straight for the pantry to play. You knocked one six-pack of soda off of another six-pack. You then picked up the six-pack and moved it somewhere else—strong baby. You just sat there on the floor redecorating the pantry with two soda six-packs. Before you were done "pumping six-packs," one pack was in the kitchen and the other was in the dining room. If anyone had told me that you were strong enough to lift a six-pack with one hand

I wouldn't have believed them. I know better now. But who's going to believe me!?!

Later on in your pantry play, you reached up to the second shelf from the bottom. You gripped it and pulled yourself up. And I mean up and off of the floor. Both of your feet were two to three inches off of the floor! I was shocked at this further display of strength; you are really something. Have you already decided to start training for some future women's power-lifting event in the Olympics!?!

Before you went to bed, you played with one of your little play-people and a jello mold. You put the little person in the mold and then took the little person out. In and out. In and out. You did this practically non-stop for forty minutes.

May 25

Today, I could really feel your two left upper incisors. They were actually teeth today, not just sharp points.

You have now entered the realm of "raspberries." You purse your lips and squeeze small amounts of air through them. You sound like a leaky tire; it's silly, but cute. And you said, "wow" again this morning. I love it. It's such a dear little sound.

May 26

We went to Oroville today to see your Aunt Lori. Lori's mother, brother and sister-in-law live in Oroville. She came up with her new fiance, Chad, to introduce him to her family. I qualified as part of her family; we have known each other for fourteen years. We had a marvelous visit. Chad was very nice.

May 27

Daddy gave you your morning bottle after you two had played for awhile. Then you crawled into the master bedroom looking for new things to play with and found me. Daddy wasn't far behind you. He put a plastic lid on your head. You laughed when it fell off. Daddy put it back on your head a couple of times. One time, it stayed on for quite a while despite your movements. You could feel it up there; you rolled your eyes toward the top of your head, as if your were looking for it. It was so funny!

May 28

When you were about half-way through eating your breakfast cereal, you rolled your eyes up toward your forehead and sighed. I had no idea what prompted that. It looked very out of character for a baby; more in character for an adult.

This morning, you successfully put the lid on an empty yogurt cup. You've done that, occasionally over the last few days with the nipple cap to your bottle. You get smarter every day.

June

June 1

Today's stats are: 21 pounds 14 ounces.

We have developed a new morning routine. We have added the master bedroom and bathroom to our routine morning explorations. Each morning, we have a game of chase or follow the leader into the master bedroom. We go over to my nightstand, with you in the lead, and play with what ever is there—an empty mug, a magazine, or a cardboard box, or container of lip balm.

Then it's off to the bathroom to play with the bathroom door. You sit up, push the door away, then pull it toward you. You move your feet out of the door's path and push it on past you in the other direction. You find this immensely entertaining. You look toward the top of that enormous thing that you can manipulate with such ease. It must give you a terrific sense of power to move such towering objects with such little effort.

"It's a bird—It's a plane—! No, it's Diaper Dyna Girl! She moves towering doors with a single touch. Lifts soda six-packs with a single hand. She crawls across the floor faster than a speeding adult."

She can't protect the world from marauding extra-terrestrials, but it's a lot more fun with Diaper Dyna Girl around.

June 2

You are now putting the nipple caps on your bottle regularly. You try putting lids on the top, or sometimes, the bottom of different containers to see if they will fit. If it does fit, you snap it into place and then remove it many times. You also know that if there is writing on the lid, it goes on the outside! It's so much fun to watch you learn.

June 3

After finishing your first bottle of the day, you turned yourself over onto your tummy from your back. Later, after your "brunch" solids, you had a bottle while I dressed for work. You turned over from your back to your tummy before you were a quarter of the way through your bottle. You were quite impressed with yourself. A minute later, your excitement diminished, once you discovered that you weren't getting anything out of the bottle, when you're sitting over it; and it was standing upright. You sucked and sucked—but nothing.

You looked a bit "put-out" that your bottle behaved that way. I turned you onto your back and "plugged you in.." You finished the bottle after going through the premature turning over routine one more time. Once you had finished your bottle you turned onto your side and sat up. I believe, it is safe to say, you have truly conquered going from back to tummy—finally; that was a tough one for you.

June 4

When I picked you up from Winnie's last night, she said you had turned yourself over onto your tummy anytime she put you on your back. You turned yourself over at will, but it did take some effort. You threw your legs up into the air, then over to one side. But you didn't always include your arms in the move, let alone move them at the same time. It wasn't the most efficient maneuver, but it was certainly entertaining. Once you're proficient, it probably won't be as much fun to watch.

You no longer sleep on your tummy all of the time; you also sleep on your side occasionally, or on your back. Now when I go to check on you when you're sleeping, or pick you up at Winnie's, I'm never certain which aspect of your little "ism" will be presented to me. You've attained quite a repertoire of sleeping positions.

Sometimes you look like a "delta jet"—lying on your tummy with arms along either side at about a thirty degree angle, both legs out-stretched. Then there's the "dive-bomber" position—on your tummy with arms along your sides, and both legs tucked under your tummy. There's the "swashbuck-ler" or "fencing position" where you're on your tummy with your head to one side, one arm is outstretched behind your head, or with your elbow bent and your hand touching your head or neck. The hand on the facial side is stretched out and level with your shoulder. The "Sphinx" position is you on your tummy with everything tucked under you.

My favorite is the heart-tugging "aaaaww" where you're on your tummy with arms and legs in assorted positions, but thumb in your mouth or near your mouth in a "standby" mode. Then there's the "I'm a big girl now—almost" where you lie on your side with arms and legs in assorted positions for balance. Next we have the "perfect sleeper"-lying on your back, arms and legs totally relaxed in assorted positions. (You remind me of the perfect sleeper mattress advertisement.)

And the last, but not least of your sleeping position reper-toire, is the "double reverse twist"—arms to one side, legs probably started out being tucked under you, but your bottom must have fallen over at some point, leaving the legs pointed in the opposite direction from the arms. Whenever you are in this position the angle of your head always seems to add to the appearance of complete discomfort. It's difficult to look at. It makes you appear "broken." I have a hard time understanding how could you possibly be comfortable. If I left you that way, wouldn't you wake up full of "kinks" and feeling cranky!?!

All I have to do is to try my "supposed unnoticeable" repositioning of you, and you invariably wake up. A few times, you have gone back to sleep after a number of heavy eye-blinkings with wrinkled eyebrows. But most of the time, you wake up completely and need a full course of walking around while you lean on or look over my shoulder. One time, I had to fix a bottle for you before you could get back to sleep again.

Your Grandma Ani-Poo has told me many times, "Don't try to make her comfortable, it will only wake her up." She was right. She had already gone through the very same thing with me, thirty years ago.

I thought I could be imperceptible in my efforts of repositioning you. I wasn't. Funny, how we always think we know better or can do so much better than our parents did. For some reason, first-time mothers, or first-time any endeavor persons, feel they must "reinvent the wheel."

I knew nothing about babies when I started out. I still feel that I know pathetically little. Despite all of the books and magazines I've read, continue to read, and the "on-the-job training" I've attained over the past ten-plus months, there are some areas of baby care that I flatter myself with the idea that I am an evolving professional. All of this understood, I still felt I knew better about some things. I'm sure that I'm not the only one who's felt that way. It isn't all egocentric.

Actually, I feel it is a good quality if it can be kept in perspective. We try things that are supposed to be common knowledge. We attempt things, before untried, with our babies because we care. We want to do the best we can by them. Many times it isn't any better than what has gone on before, but sometimes it is. It's all a part of change and growth in ourselves as people to try new ideas instead of just accepting old ones. Enough philosophy.

June 6

Today you went to your second baby shower. It was for Irene. The earlier shower for her was cancelled because Irene was ill. The party was held at Betty's house, another nurse from work. Betty recently left work as a nurse at the hospital to start a children's day care business. Her small clients, the nurses from the hospital, and their children were all at the shower. There were ten children there, including you. All of the children were well behaved, and the party went very smoothly.

Grandma Ani-Poo and Popie brought dinner up to the ranch for us tonight to celebrate our wedding anniversary. Your Daddy and I have been married for nine years.

After dinner Daddy put you on your Model T. You sat on it for a few minutes and beeped the horn. Then you dismounted all by yourself! Dancing was next on your program. I imagine you had choreographed your part of the evening as entertainment for our celebration—a Lilliputian floor show. You danced to the music on the radio. You've introduced a lot more hip-swiveling to your dancing. It used to be mostly upper torso and head wiggling. Now everything gets into the act. You are so delightful.

June 8

Statistics: 22 pounds 4 ounces.

You are increasing your gusto toward taking unassisted walking steps. It is now a real effort to keep up with you to see that you stay upright. You can really pick 'em up and put 'em down!

It was a hot day today. I gave you a cool bath, as I did frequently last summer when it was hot. Last summer, you detested a cool bath. Of course, at that point in your life, you weren't completely convinced that any bath, cool or warm, was at all necessary. This summer is a very different story; you loved this cool bath. You played and talked and sang the whole time. Well, not really all of the time. You still get upset sometimes when I lay you down to wash your belly button and bottom. This was one of those times. You quickly forgot your disenchantment once you became interested in a tub toy.

June 9

This morning, you headed into the dining room to play. You stayed there while I fixed your breakfast. When I walked into the dining room with your breakfast, you were standing at a dining chair next to the high-chair. When I moved toward you to put the high-chair tray in place, you raised both your arms up, in preparation for being picked up without being asked. Such a smart little girl.

After breakfast, we gathered our gear for your first trip to the lake. We took a picnic lunch. Grandma Ani-Poo and Popie were there, as were their friend, Brent, and my friend, Vicky. You guessed it, Vicky's another nurse from work.

Daddy had put the camper on the truck the night before, so today marked the maiden voyage (first trip) for the truck/ camper combination. The overhang of the camper kept the cab of the truck cool, and gave us the option of a cool place to take you in case the sun or heat of the day proved to be too much for you, without cutting the outing short.

It was a beautiful day. There were lots of colorfully rigged small catamaran boats sailing about. Speaking of color, you were sporting a bit of color, a tan, despite the sunblock.

The lake water was barely warm enough for you to try it out. I walked a few steps out into the lake, from the man-made beach, with you in my arms. I squatted down and perched you on my thigh with your feet dangling, as you faced the shore. I let you watch the shallow water lap against the beach for a while before I attempted touching your feet to the water.

You were intrigued with the movement of the water, at first. But, in very short order, you were less than impressed. You began to cry. Your feet hadn't touched the water yet. I was thinking to myself, "Okay, 1—2—touch." I hadn't made it past two, before you started to cry. I went ahead and touched your feet to the water as Popie took a picture of you. I thought you might decide you liked it once you tried it; I was wrong.

Most of the pictures we have of you show you smiling or sporting other pleasant expressions. The picture Popie took toady was bound to be an exception. Just watch, Tiffany, this will probably turn out to be one of our favorites. Some day when you're a young woman and a special boyfriend of yours comes to visit, we might be looking through some photo albums and your Dad or I will say, "Here is one of our favorite pictures of Tiffi." You'll probably blush and say, "Oh Mommmm," and try to cover the fact that you're embarrassed.

Well, sweet Tiffany, I know how that feels. I wouldn't do it to embarrass you on purpose. I do think that all parents embarrass their children, unintentionally, when they recount a certain event, special phrase, or picture of something they find precious and disarming. But the child perceives it as immature or baby-like. It's been that way for eons!

This was the longest that you had stayed outside in the sun, essentially non-stop. We didn't have a tree or an umbrella. I tried to be your shade tree all of the time, but you needed to be able to move around. You had a hat and we'd made a make-shift cabana for you. Next time, we'll bring a large umbrella.

When we arrived home, I set up a cool bath for you. You were getting to be an old hand at the cool bath experience. After your bath, we played in the family room. You stood up by your toy basket, then let go of it and tried to balance yourself unassisted. That lasted almost ten seconds.

A short time later, you were using my knee to stand up with. You bent down to pick up something, then stood up again with your knees slightly bent and your bottom pushed slightly out behind you. You let go of my knee and tried standing alone while holding a lid in one hand. You weren't able to stand up very long. You purposefully moved to sit down. You squatted down—alone—all the way down, and gently perched yourself on the floor without flopping down. And you were still holding the yogurt cup lid in your hand. Such balance!

June 10

I don't think I've told you how much you enjoy your new play mirror. You've had it for about ten days now. It's about four inches across and has fabulous reflective clarity for a non-breakable baby mirror. You can see yourself clearly at almost any distance. It is also the largest "holdable" model I could find. You look into it; smile, laugh, and chortle. Much of the time you bring the mirror right up to your face and kiss the baby you see. If the mirror is laying on the carpet, you lean over it and do front-end-only push ups to get closer to or kiss the baby.

We had a mini-milestone today. You have long enjoyed "unpacking" your diaper bag, my purse, and our "malling bag."

You remove everything inside—one by one. Occasionally, you put one or two things back in.

Today, after you finished unpacking your diaper bag, you completely repacked it—and then some. You added one of my shoes, a margarine tub, and one of Daddy's tennis shoes. You went through the whole routine twice.

While playing in the family room on the floor. you crawled over to your "Model T". You pulled up to the side of it. Once you stood up you started to push it along in front of you—sideways. I aligned you up at the back, handlebar in hand, and you started pushing. You were off! Unfortunately your car didn't want to go straight. I had to steer it for you, but you provided all of the power. We went all the way from the outside edge of the family room, into the hall around the kitchen desk, and down the hall to the big wood-stove. You were delighted with your achievement!

You have added complexities to your talkies. This has been evolving, over the last couple of weeks. You carry on full-fledged conversations with Daddy, Mildieu kitty, the puppies, your favorite toys, and with me. Of course, all of these conversations are in "babyese." You know what you're talking about. Some of the time I do, too, as I believe Mildieu does.

You and Mildieu are becoming close again. You talk to her a great deal, and she often truly listens. Your small voice is cheerful and musical. You are growing so rapidly and beautiful-ly; you grow more beautiful each week.

June 11

When I picked you up from your crib this morning, I checked your gums in the area of your right lower cuspid to see if it had started to break through yet. It hadn't. That area of your gum is thinning out but it still has a way to go before the tooth breaks through. Evidently, the stuffy nose and loose stools, you've had since the night before last, weren't heralding the debut of another tooth, and I thought I was getting good at this.

While we were playing, I noticed a white spot in the area of your left upper cuspid. I quickly looked again to see if it was a bit of milk curd or a new tooth. It was a new tooth! My budding expertise was reconfirmed. Yeah, Mom!

You are so cute crawling about playing with the doors to each room. You crawl up to a door, set yourself in it's arc of motion and move it, slowly, back and forth, back and forth. Then you try to swing it closed. It stops when it hits your foot. What do you do? You tried it again. It stopped again. Then you moved your foot out of the way and push the door closed. Once you "trained" that door it was time to move onto the next one. This time, when you wanted to swing the door closed, you moved your foot out of it's path automatically. Next trick!?!

When you crawl, sometimes it's at a basic baby pace, other times you "really move," sounding like a herd of horses running through the house. Whatever your speed phase is, you stop every two to three feet and pivot around to see if anyone is coming with you. I guess exploring is more fun when you have someone to share it with. Besides, there's just no telling

what kind of mischief a parent can get into, if there isn't a baby
there to keep an eye on things!

Dropping things over the side while sitting in your high-
chair seems to have evolved into your own research on the
study of "relative gravity." If you are no longer hungry, or
weren't to begin with, you will drop or launch your Lilliputian
silverware over the side as a statement.

When you eat, you drop spoons over the side and ignore
the action until they hit the floor. You then study their point
of impact. Or you drop the object over the side and study it
with great interest as it falls. Then you look at the spoon on
the floor or me and say, "Uh-oh!". The last research method I
noticed was to watch the spoon hit the floor, and continue to
watch it and watch it, as if you were wondering why it didn't
come back up.

I suppose your perception of gravity, if you do indeed even
have one, is that gravity is only useful when you were interested
in studying it. Otherwise, it should cease, for varying lengths of
time, so as to not interfere with your play or when you were
studying something else.

June 12

You woke up with a cough this morning; I woke up with a
headcold and sore throat. Daddy woke up with a headcold, too.
That was some fast "bug"; because we were all fine yesterday.
Your cough was very light, and I hoped it wouldn't go beyond
that. Daddy and I both felt terrible. I hope your cold doesn't
reroute itself in you and cause another ear infection.

June 13

That cuspid tooth is growing out fast. Faster, by far than any of your previous teeth. I wonder where the second tooth is, as you usually push your teeth through in pairs. If both didn't come through on the same day, the second was never more than two days behind the first. So far, I haven't see the other half of this team.

Your cough sounded congested this morning. Your forehead thermometer strip read 100 degrees. I gave you some baby acetomeniphen. You were still your sunny little self, although maybe a little quieter overall. And you ate a little less. You always do bear close watching to determine the severity of your illness because you continue to laugh, play, giggle, grin, and explore even when you're sick.

Your best indicator, so far, has been that you cry when you wake up in the morning, or after a nap, instead of playing and talking to yourself for a while. You didn't wake up crying this morning, but you didn't play either. You merely made a fuss noise, sort of a cross between a grunt and a groan. We'll just watch and wait.

The small flat pillow, that I lean you against when you take your bottle by yourself, is usually on the floor in the family room. Today was no exception. You were crawling about to find different toys to play with, when you crawled over to your pillow, laid down on it and gave it a hug. A bit later, you did the same thing. This time, however, you stayed on it for a couple of minutes and sucked your thumb. I think somebody was a little tired.

Here you were in the middle of a cold and you're still forging ahead. You passed another milestone today; you stood alone for thirty seconds. That's much longer than ever before and you were fully aware of what you were doing. Before the afternoon was over, you had stood alone three times for about thirty seconds each time. On your first solo, you pulled yourself up via my knee as I sat on the floor. You balanced yourself with one hand, smiled, then let go and **stood** there, totally unassisted. You really concentrated on what you were doing. Your eyebrows moved through varying stages of wrinkled patterns, and you pursed your lips and your chin as you worked to maintain your standing position.

When I looked down at your feet, I saw even more activity. Your toes were curled into a grip on the carpet. Sometimes, they relaxed slightly, followed almost immediately by an even tighter carpet grip. The rest of your foot wasn't exactly idle, either. Your foot would rotated outward, then rotated in a bit, then out again. When your toes relaxed your heels simultaneously pressed deeper into the carpet.

Such dynamics! And all of this going on while your body was apparently well centered over your feet. All the while, your feet worked feverishly to keep you that way. So many sophisticated fine adjustments. There were at least fifty adjustments made in that thirty seconds, and all of it under your conscious control. Pretty spectacular, if you ask me. I just wish I could have seen what your legs were doing, but you had long pants on.

Your second solo was in the guest room when you pushed yourself up from the floor. All of the accompanying fancy footwork was there, but your face found time to smile a broad Tiffi smile right in the middle of your efforts.

I was so happy for you. You were very obviously just as delighted with your new conquest as I was, if not more so! New frontiers will be yours very soon. Soon we'll be saying, "It's a jet—It's a beam of laser light—No! It's Super Tiff!"

Your third solo took place at the coffee table in the family room. By that time, you were an old pro. You simply stood there. You even picked a small toy up off of the coffee table without much adjustment needed. You dropped the toy. Then bursting with confidence, you banged both hands on the coffee table with increasing arm movement. Up and down, up and down, until—Oops!—Cushhh! Down you went, right onto your diaper. I think that's what diapers are really for—bumpers.

The trouble is many babies need them on their head, too until they learn how to fall on their bottom. You were looking straight ahead when you lost your balance. I watched you land. Your facial expression conveyed, "Humph. Foiled again." I quickly looked away before you looked at me, so I could pretend I didn't notice your fall from glory. After a second or so, I looked back to you, smiled and reached to give you a hug. You smiled and reached for me. Mission accomplished—maybe.

June 14

You seemed to feel better today, but you were still congested. I didn't want to chance taking you to Winnie's today and prolonging or complicating your cold. So I stayed home from work to be with you. As we played on the floor, you started a segment of making your favorite smacking noise.

You smacked your lips ending up with your mouth wide open.

I mimicked your smacks. Then I started touching my fingers to my lips each time I smacked.

After four times, you touched your finger to my lips when I smacked.

It was so sweet.

A little bit later, I smacked my lips and then touched them to yours and said, "Kiss." I did that three times. The next time I smacked, you smiled, leaned against me, put your open mouth to my lips, and said, "M-m-m-m." Your lovely kiss gave me a warm glow all over and brought tears to my eyes.

A bit later while we played by the nightstands in the master bedroom, you reached for the book laying there. Knowing how you liked to dissect magazines and catalogues, I removed it from your "clutches." I pointed to it and said, "Book." I repeated it a few times.

One time you pointed to the book and said "Tuh?"

I said, "Yes, book," with a smile.
You then pointed to a large plastic glass on the nightstand. You pointed at it, then looked at me as if to say, "And what's that?" I said, "Glass."
You pointed at it again.
I said "Glass!"
You responded with a smile and a chortle.
You might like to know that the book, on the nightstand you were interested in, was a journal kept by a father throughout his daughter's first year of life. The name of the book was *Good Morning Merry Sunshine.* I'm going to purchase a second copy which I will save for you. I imagine you will enjoy reading it at about the same time I give you this journal. I am certainly enjoying it. I think what excites me most about it, is that it was written by a father. It's fabulous learning a father's point of view.
You pulled yourself up to the nightstand with a mug in one hand this time. You stood, unassisted, examining the mug and lightly tapping it against the nightstand, delighting in the noise it made. While you were still standing alone, you picked something else up with your other hand. There you were standing alone like a "pro" with something in each hand, examining one and tapping the other. You stood there unassisted for well over a minute. A good thirty seconds of that time was spent with an object in each hand, before you finally lost your balance and made a "two-point landing," while still holding your current treasures.
After you tired of playing at my nightstand, you crawled around to Daddy's nightstand where the telephone was. You picked up the receiver and dropped it on the carpet, then picked it up from the floor and hung it over your shoulder. Then you started to concentrate on the phone cord, that lively, coiling, bouncing cord. You put the receiver back on the phone; picked it up; hung it up; picked it up; hung it up. I had never realized there were so many different ways to hang up a phone: receiver side up, receiver side down, the over the dial traverse

mode, the ever-popular "I don't want any more calls today" on the floor mode, and the "certain conversation editorial mode," of putting the receiver in the waste basket.

After you demonstrated all of the ways one could hang up a phone, you picked up the receiver, hooked it over your shoulder and started to dial. I disconnected the phone. I didn't want you to dial Lady Di by accident. I did let you pretend dial. After reconnecting the phone, I dialed Grandma Ani-Poo. I held the receiver to your ear so you could hear the touch tones, the ringing and Grandma Ani-Poo or Popie when they answered the phone. You loved the tones and the ringing. At first you looked at the receiver as you heard the tones. Once it started ringing, you looked at me and smiled or laughed with each ring, accompanied by a bright expression of discovery and delight. After the second ring, I started playing peak-a-boo with you so you would be laughing when the phone was answered. After the third ring, Grandma Ani-Poo picked up the phone. I let her listen to you for a few seconds, then said, "Hi" and took over the conversation. I told her what we had been doing and that she had just received her first phone call from her first grandchild. She was impressed and delighted.

After we talked to Grandma, we practiced picking up the phone and saying, "Hello."

I would pick it up and say, "Hello. Oh, you want to speak with Tiffany. She's right here. Tiffany, it's for you," then hold the receiver to your head.

You put your head against the receiver, at a slight tilt, smiled with a bright look in your eye and looked around. Sometimes you said, "Hah ahh."

I believe that's Tiffi-talk for "hello." We had a great time. It was fun watching you respond to our pretend conversations.

June 15

This morning you woke up crying again. Your temperature was 101.5 degrees. That, in conjunction with your behavior last night denoting uncomfortable ears, made me think you were developing another ear infection. After your bottle, you fell asleep again. While you were asleep, called Dr. Kelley's office. His exchange answered. He was off-call to his associate this weekend. I called his associate; Dr. Williams' for an appointment. They had an opening this morning. Dr. Williams' office is in Redding, not far from Dr. Kelley's office. I ran around and got myself ready for work, then packed your things for Winnie's.

I had to waken you, from what turned out to be a "cheap nap" of forty minutes, and we were off to the Doctor's office. The Doctor said you had an infection in each ear. Poor Tiffany. At least they weren't as bad as the first time, we caught it early. He asked us what had worked last time, then prescribed the same antibiotics.

After leaving the Doctor's office, we went to pick up a drive-thru lunch and took it over to the park to picnic in the shade. You ate a very good lunch, then I gave you your first dose of antibiotics. I knew you'd be feeling much better by this time tomorrow. After our picnic, I took you to Winnie's, then drove back to Redding for work.

June 16

Father's Day

You woke up singing and talking this morning. Hurray! It's so wonderful to hear you wake up happy again. I knew you'd feel better quickly with the antibiotics. While you were playing. you opened a plastic container that had a one-half turn screw-on top. I had put something inside the container for you to rattle. Up until today you did just that. But this morning, you opened it, dropped the contents (a plastic funnel), and played with the funnel for a few minutes. Then you dropped the funnel, picked up the lid and the container and tried to put the lid back on. After a couple of attempts, you did it. You managed to get that screw lid latched on by a combination of a slight turn and snapping it on. You did the same maneuver to get it off. You were deeply involved in your activity. No smiles, no laughs, just pure concentration. You worked with that lid for almost ten minutes.

I baked a triple chocolate cake today for Daddy and Popie, in honor of Father's Day. You managed to escape our watch, as Daddy and I talked in the kitchen, and you reached up and touched the back of the stove. You let out a wail and started to cry, then said, "Mamma." Poor Tiffany, that was hot! I touched the oven wall to see how hot it was. It was hot enough to act as a very good lesson, but not hot enough to damage anything besides your comfort. A sad experience; but, I hope, a valuable one.

You stayed with Daddy when I went to work. I was sure you and Daddy would have a nice Father's Day together.

June 17

Timeline: NASA launched the eighteenth space shuttle mission on the shuttle "Discovery" for seven days of scientific studies.

As you crawled around this morning, you paused whenever you reached a beam of sunlight touching the carpet or flooring. You reached out to touch it as if you expected it to be three-dimensional. You did seem to notice that those spots were warmer. After playing with the sun spots, you worked your way into the kitchen to the vinyl flooring. You were wearing long pajama bottoms. Your legs moved almost effortlessly, as your knees glided along smoothly, because of the friction-free effect of your pajamas on the flooring. Every so often, you looked underneath yourself at your knees gliding along with you. You looked mildly perplexed. I imagined you were thinking, "Hmmm, I wonder how it is they know what to do, when sometimes it seems that I haven't told them what to do?" We did some singing and dancing after lunch. We had the radio on and I started to dance and sing to one of my favorite songs. You copied, or tried to copy, my movements. When you heard a song that you liked, you sang too—"Dah-dah-dah." Most of the time when I hum songs to you, I hum "Dah-dum, dah-dah". Maybe that's why you did your singing in the key of "dah."

Later in the morning, you feel asleep as I held you. As I watched you sleep, I remembered that this time last year I was anticipating your birth, and praying that you would be healthy. Now here you are a beautiful, healthy, and delightful little person, just short of being eleven months old. So much has changed since this time last year. Your Daddy and I have gone from wondering what our baby will be like, how we will be as parents and what kinds of things we'll do together, to knowing your personality, reading your little body language to know how you're feeling, getting some kind of understanding about ourselves as parents, as well as enjoying playing improvised games with you to just watch you play and explore. It's so delightfully entertaining, so consuming, to watch someone discover all of the things in the world.

It seems like the time has gone by so quickly until I think of what I was doing, thinking and feeling then. Then it seems like a lifetime ago. Come to think of it, it is a lifetime ago; your lifetime.

I had just started the dishwasher after lunch, when you heard the machine churning and making swishing noises. You wriggled into the kitchen to look at it. You pulled yourself up to it and tried to turn the large "cycle display knob," but it wouldn't budge. It had a mind of it's own, but so did you. You side-stepped over to the cycle selection buttons and started pushing them. I didn't scold you because the dishwasher, though new to us in these last few days, is used and the buttons don't work. It goes full cycle whatever you do; so a little button pushing wouldn't hurt this appliance.

As I was changing your diaper before leaving for work, you put both hands against your head and made an "uncomfortable fuss" noise. I wondered if you have a headache or another ear infection. The day after you started taking the antibiotics you seemed to feel better, but today, something wasn't right. You were tired, but only took a brief, thirty minute morning nap. You had been fussy most of the morning. You even cried when I put you in your high-chair to eat. This was very unlike you. You didn't have a fever. I'm not sure if your ears have started bothering you again, if your little insides are upset, or if you're just having a crummy day.

Everybody has bad days when things just seem crummy. I'll ask Winnie to keep a particular eye on your mood today. I hoped you would have a nice full afternoon nap and things would look better to you. I hate to see my little sweetie feeling rotten.

When we arrived at Winnie's, you made it known you were ready to eat. I had given you your solid lunch, what you would take of it, but didn't have time to give you your bottle before we left. I had planned to set you up with it once you were settled at Winnie's.

When I set you on the floor next to your diaper bag, you leaned into the bag and pulled out a bottle, then tried very hard to pull the cap off of the nipple. Who's hungry? As soon as I took the cap off, you started right in while sitting up! You didn't get much that way, so I laid you down and you happily vacuumed up the liquid portion of your lunch.

June 18

This morning, while we were playing in the family room, you crawled over to your teddy bear. You told him a short story while you touched him. Then you gave him a big lovely hug, hugging him while swaying from side to side. He was upside down during your hug, but he didn't seem to mind.

Later in the morning, you were in the kitchen trying to "set" the dishwasher for me. Thank you for your help, Tiffany.

At lunch, I handed you some spoons to play with while I fed you, per usual. Instead of your usual spoon play, you held them like drumsticks and you used them like drumsticks. You drummed out a gentle rhythm on your high-chair tray. We were both impressed with your results. You are such fun.

June 20

Tiffi history was made today! I took the crib bumpers out of your crib. You had started to show an interest in climbing onto the couch, so I thought I had better take the bumpers out of your crib before you started using them to climb out of your crib.

Later, when I put you down for your nap, it felt funny to see you from across the room as I left. Before today, all I could see, as I left the room, were your little eyes peeking over the crib bumpers, as you watched me leave. Now, I could see all of you. You looked surprised that you could see me, as you watched me leave.

When I was dancing in front of you today, you started dancing right along with me. I started singing with the radio. You tossed your head about and said "Dah-dah-dah." We

danced and sang to a lot of songs. You do something new and interesting or in a different fashion almost every day. You're amazing!

June 21

Happy eleven month birthday. We celebrated by taking you to your first county fair. You had a wonderful time. You were much more intrigued with the multitudes of children there than with the pomp and glitter. You were very well behaved while we were there. Before we left, I wanted you to be able to see the rides, especially the merry-go-round. Again, you were more interested in watching the other children. I believe you saw your first visit to the fair as a success.

June 22

This morning, you crawled across the family room toward the steps, all two of them, that lead down into the living room. I started toward you, to help you practice going down the stairs backwards. As I arrived at the stairs, you very studiously turned yourself around. You effectively, if not smoothly, went down both stairs backwards. I hadn't even gotten myself into a backwards position before you were half-way finished. You knew that you had done something special, because once you were in the living room, you sat up with your legs folded and put a hand on each inner thigh, with your elbows turned out. Looking very sophisticated and very accomplished, you wrinkled your nose and giggled at me. What a baby!

After you had relished your conquest of the steps and had tired of exploring the living room, you went back up the steps to the family room. A minute later, you tried the stairs to the living room again, but you wanted to go down frontwards so I turned you around, and we went down together—backwards.

I guess the going down backwards of your own volition is going to be hit and miss for at least a while.

After lunch, we went to sign up for your first swimming class! Classes start Monday and will be four days a week for two weeks! I hope you enjoy them.

June 23

I tried your swimsuit on this morning, but it was too small. I bought it on sale a few months ago thinking I was getting it large enough for summer, but I was wrong. I had bought another one at the same time that was too large, large enough to wear over a diaper, or so I thought—it fit you perfectly, without a diaper. I took a couple of pictures of you in it, and of course we had to model it for Daddy. He won't be here tomorrow to see you in it before your class.

June 24

When I put you down this morning for your nap, you lay there quietly as if you would go to sleep. About ten minutes later, you started singing and talking to yourself. I enjoyed your rendition but didn't disturb you. I thought you would either go back to napping or would just entertain yourself for a while. Either way, I felt it was best to leave you alone and just enjoy your music. You talked and sang for almost fifteen minutes, then you started to cry. Not your usual, "I've-had-enough-of-being-alone cry," but a "something's-not-right cry." I went to your room to pick you up. Instead of just seeing a little face that was happy to see me, I saw a little face with pookie on it. Under that little face was a diaperless bottom. Under the bottom were legs covered in pookie. Your diaper contents had been dissected into many small parts, some of which had been smeared by foot or hand over the sheet. You had one foot toe deep in the middle of your diaper. What a mess. I didn't even mention the crib rails. Mess, mess, mess. It was a first, but not one you'd find a space for in any baby book, I had heard about this "milestone" from other mothers of toddlers.

I guess it was only a matter of time before this "milestone." I use cloth diapers with velcro closures during the day. Since you can undo the velcro closures on your "tennies" and mine, I should have known it wouldn't be long before you realized that your day diapers had the same velcro stuff on them.

Apparently, whatever delight you found in discovering the malleable state of pookie was short-lived, no doubt the reason for your strange cry. There was much too much stuff there for a mere **box** of diaper-wipes. This was a job for "tub-bath". There was just enough time to bathe you, put on your swimsuit and mine, and leave for your swim class.

Before leaving for class I put a diaper on over your suit to prevent any accidental piddle on your carseat, since it was a twenty minute drive to class. Our class consisted of six other babies, three with their Moms. Only one, Jerome, was younger than you. Jerome was seven months old. Another boy was seventeen months old. The rest were in their second year. There was only one other girl, Jessica, age two and one-half.

I put waterproof sunblock on your little body before we went to sit at the pool's edge. Everyone was happy sitting on the edge of the pool but one—guess who? Her initials were T.C.(Tiffany Carissa.) That's right, my darling, after watching all of that undulating blue stuff for about fifteen seconds, you started to cry. I held you snugly, my arms wrapped around you as you sat between my legs at the pool's edge.

After sitting for less than a minute, I began drizzling pool water over your feet. You started to cry again, (You had stopped.) I sloshed water over your feet, you cried. No screaming, just crying. Poor baby, you just didn't like or understand what was going on. After being bathed in a little vinyl tub only slightly larger than yourself, and not seeing any large body of water except one lake trip, that pool must have looked like an ocean.

Everyone else was in the pool. I kept you on the side for another minute. You soon stopped crying and watched my hand slosh water over your feet, which I had continued to do even while you cried. I enlarged my motions to involve your whole leg. You then reached down to touch the water. It splashed against your hand. At the first instant you looked concerned, then you giggled. You put your hand into the pool again, no smile but again a giggle. I took you into the pool— Guess who cried again?

I was sorry that you didn't understand, but it was important that you be exposed to water, to learn about it and how to be safer in it. You won't be truly water-safe, but what you can learn here could, at your age, "buy you some time" in an accident. You would know how to kick and hold onto the side, and hopefully how to hold your breath.

You cried almost the whole time we were in the water. You clung to me tightly. You stopped crying occasionally, but you were never happy. I just held you tightly and cruised through the water, waltzing with you and humming to you. You eventually relaxed, slightly. But when I tried to relax my firm grip, you became frightened again. Later, I tried a very secure, one hand grip; you weren't fooled, only scared. So we just cruised and waltzed again but that was a lot better than you did your first time at the lake. We'll work on getting you accustomed to being in and near the water for now. We can save the other stuff for a little later, another class, if necessary. Hopefully, in a few days, you will see this as fun, not as an ordeal to wait out.

June 25

Mommy had an absolutely awful shift at work last night. There were a lot of critical and unstable patients in the coronary care unit and not enough staff for them. Everyone was late getting off work. When I arrived at Winnie's to pick you up, I was greeted with your sweet little sleepy smile. It made the anguish of the work shift easier to leave behind. Whenever I pick you up at Winnie's you automatically present me with a sweet and sleepy smile even though you aren't awake, just temporarily aroused.

I believe you must be a truly happy little soul. You must be deeply secure and at peace with the world to have an unconscious smile like that. You are an especially sweet and dear little person. I think getting that little smile makes it easier for Winnie to get out of bed, let me in, and scoop you out of the playpen in the middle of the night. I often hear her say, "Awe," and give a soft little chuckle as she brings you out to me.

After swim class, and hopefully after a nap, we'll leave for your Doctor's appointment to have your ears rechecked from your last ear infection.

Swim class started out the same as yesterday. However, after we had been in the water about fifteen minutes you to started to enjoy it. You reached your hand out to touch the water. After a couple of minutes, I changed my grip on you from a wrap-around hold to a very snug grip of one hand at each under-arm, with my elbows held firmly against your lower back. I hoped you would feel just as secure, but you cried. After another minute or so when I tried that grip again, you were more comfortable with it. You didn't cry. What you did say was more of a medium pitched moan.

Another few minutes, passed. I gradually made my hold on you lighter and lighter across your back, while still holding your underarms very firmly. In about five minutes I was holding you only at your underarms. It had happened so gradually that you weren't upset. I started moving through the water backwards instead of sideways. I picked up speed gradually and pulled you along with your legs behind you.

As soon as I started backwards and your upper body wasn't directly over your hips, your bouyant bottom bobbed right up to the surface. I was so tickled by the sight, that I couldn't help but laugh. You laughed, too, not unusual for you, but a rare item at swim class. You were usually very serious when we were there—no smiles, very few laughs or giggles. You were all concentration, observation and business. Did I forget to say tolerance?

You were happy floating about "a la" Mom for the remainder of the class. I even heard a couple of more giggles.

I just realized something today. Whenever your swim teacher addressed me, it wasn't as Vivianne, but as "Tiffany's Mommy." Something told me I was going to be known as "Tiffany's Mom" for the next twenty years to your teachers, your friends, and the parents of your friends. I could see why teachers would do that. They have to learn the names of all of their students, which, in itself, could be quite an undertaking. If they were to try to remember the Moms' names also, it would be too much. I must agree, that I would much rather they spend their energy on instruction than remembering the Moms' first names. Here's to my new identity—"Tiffany's Mom."

You had a very good day at class. You seemed to convey, however, that "the jury was still out" on this venture. We'll stick with it and I'm sure you'll grow to enjoy the water.

After class, we were off to Redding; the uptown mall to exchange your swimsuit for a larger size. I hoped they would have the same style in a larger size; it was so cute.

The store didn't have the same style in your size, darn. We did find another cute one though. We stopped to visit with two little girls in the mall for a while. You all had a fabulous conversation "in code," of course.Then it was off to your Doctor's appointment.

Your appointment with Dr. Kelley was very positive—perfectly clear eardrums, no infection or fluid. He asked how you'd been feeling. I told him that you didn't seem ill, that there was no evidence of teething, but you just hadn't been yourself for the last four or so days. You whined many times when I took something from you, even though I asked for it in our usual "please" and "thank you" style. You seemed to become frustrated with attempts at different tasks and you weren't sleeping well. You'd awaken one or more times crying quietly or grumbling during the night almost as if you were having a nightmare. The Doctor checked your gums for teeth, looked at your throat again and palpated your abdomen. Nothing notable. He said to give you a couple of more days to see how you did and, as always, to call if we had any questions or new concerns.

I don't think that swimming class is the problem even though you are so serious there. The problem started before class began. If it was only a single day, I would chalk it up to "one of those days." Everyone has frumpy days; and you have a lot fewer than most folks.

Possible revelation: Work has been crummy for almost a week. I've been getting home late and unable to get to sleep for quite a while. I wake up a few times during the night, disturbed, wondering if I forgot to do something, chart something or report something to the next shift. Maybe, that's why you haven't been yourself lately, because I haven't been myself lately. You could be feeling the stress and fatigue, even though we have been playing as much and doing our usual morning routine of games and exploring.

When you were brand new, I was especially cognizant of how my moods would effect you. I seemed to have lost some of my sensitivity for that. Well, if you'll take some naps, I'll try to lie down for forty-five minutes everyday before I start getting ready for work and the babysitter. I can also rest during your whole morning nap on the days I'm off. Hopefully these steps will get us back "on track."

June 26

We have to miss class today, because the insect exterminator is coming and he didn't know exactly when he'd get here. I asked Arlene if we could use her pool tonight for a while. She said that would be fine. I hated for you to miss a day in the water after you had shown some positive response at class yesterday.

Grandma Ani-Poo and Popie will take you to their house for a while, so that once the "bug-man" leaves, I can clean the floors, vacuum the carpets, wash the cabinets, slider doors, screens, etc. of any insecticide residue. I had already spoken with Dr. Kelley and the Poison Control office on what I needed to do considering we had a wee-one in the house.who touches everything and puts almost anything into her mouth.

Four hours and a kinky back later, the house was done except for the sliding and screen doors in the master bedroom and family room. What a job. I'm going to get a real work out doing this every month for twelve months when they spray the house for insects. I hope it controls the rats, mice, or whatever it is habitating in our bedroom ceiling or wall. The noise those little "whatever they ares" make is loud enough to keep your Daddy and I from getting to sleep.

When Grandma Ani-Poo and Popie brought you home, they told me about your playing the piano in the "buff," and something about your memory. When you arrived at their house after going out to breakfast with them, they took you over near the sliding glass door so you could look out at the orchard. The sliding glass door was about twenty feet away from their piano which was in the "saloon" and on the other side of the couch. The point being, you couldn't see the piano from where you were and they said you hadn't looked at the piano when you came in.

You played by the sliding glass door for a couple of minutes with Grandma Ani-Poo as she took off your clothes and diaper, to air your little back rash and "beat the heat." You suddenly dropped the toy you were playing with, crawled around the couch and headed for the piano. You had remembered the piano from the last time you were there; it must have made quite an impression on you.

Once you had made your way over to the piano, you pulled yourself up to it and stretched you hands up to play it. Grandma Ani-Poo said you were extremely impressed with your composition. How precious you must have looked. I wish I could have seen that. Grandma Ani-Poo did take some pictures, so I will get to see those.

After an early dinner, I got you ready for swimming practice at Arlene's. When I took your diaper off I noticed you had a new rash in your groin area and among your "privates." It looked different than what was on your back. The raised areas seemed larger in diameter. A dip in the pool should feel good on that.

At the pool you cried, per usual, when you dangled your feet in the water and when we first went into the water. I wanted to cry, too; that water was cold. You really didn't seem to mind the temperature, it was just getting into the water that flustered you.

We waltzed around. You let me hold you by your underarms after a few minutes. We, finally, got Daddy to dive in and he played peek-a-boo with you. You loved that. You splashed and played in the water with your hands, and had a nice time. We had to get out after about fifteen minutes when you started to shiver. We wrapped you up, said, "goodbye," to Arlene and went home. You were too tired after your swim for me to do much with your rash, so I put a very thin layer of ointment on it when I toweled you off and dressed you for bed.

You were tired, but unable to go to sleep. There had been too much excitement during the day. Thirty minutes later, you were "down for the count." Good night, sweet Tiffany.

June 27

You had a wonderful time at swim class today. You didn't cry when we dangled your feet in the water, or when we stepped into the water. You let me hold you by your underarms as I pulled you through the water. Our teacher moved your legs when I gave the command to kick. You aren't much of a kicker. That's something we'll have to work on.

We practiced "sitting" jumps off of the side of the pool. I sat you on the pool edge and said, "Ready, set, go!" I liked that sequence better than "1, 2, 3." You were supposed to come to me in the water, on the word "go." When I said, "Ready, set," I had my hands close to you; when I said, "Go," I grabbed you by your underarms and pulled you into the water, without getting your head underwater, of course. By the end of the class you were coming to me on "Go." You really enjoyed it. You laughed and giggled a lot during class. That made me feel good, because I knew you were truly relaxed; you were being yourself.

Another thing you learned was how to reach for and hold onto the side of the pool. The second time we tried it, you not only took hold of the side, but you supported yourself! Of course, I had only moved my hand one inch away from you, in case you relaxed your grip. You didn't grip with such vigor every time or even most of the time, but you did reach for and hold the side almost every time. I was impressed. What a marvelous class you had today.

You are back to your old rarely fussy and usually sunny self today. I'm not sure what is happening inside of you; if it is physiological or emotional. Maybe it's just a stage of growing up. My reading resources say that when babies are on the threshold of a milestone, i.e., sitting up or walking, they can be irritable, have difficulty sleeping through the night, etc. I wonder if that might be the reason, but five days later there were no particular milestones, and no new teeth. I guess this period of time will have to remain one of life's mysteries.

Early this afternoon, as we played in your room, you stood up by your changing table/dresser holding onto one of the drawer knobs. You "walked" from one end of your dresser to the other end holding on to the drawer knob pull, and with your eye on the dirty clothes hamper. I say walked because, although you were holding onto something, it was with only one hand.

When I saw you walking along with a one-hand support and nicely balanced, the strangest feeling came over me. It was as if I was watching my baby walk for the first time, because the hand that you were supporting yourself with was obstructed from my vision most of the time. Even though I knew that source of support was there, everything about the way in which you were moving gave me the illusion that you were walking on your own. The feeling was incredible. I can't even begin to describe it. I sincerely want to convey the flavor of what my feelings were, but I just can't find the right words—I can't even find the not-so-right words.

June 28

Your rash was still there this morning. I called Dr. Kelley, and, fortunately, his office gave us a 10:30 am appointment. I got our gear together and off we went. I was dressed for swim class underneath my clothes and had your swim gear ready, in case we were through in time, and Dr. Kelley didn't see any reason to avoid swimming.

The Doctor said it was a yeast infection, over your back and your groin. Yeast loves moist places. The only reason I could understand it attacking your back, as it had, would be due to your perspiring a great deal in your car seat in this hot summer weather. You didn't get it last summer, but you didn't spend nearly as much time in the car then. Dr. Kelley said there was no reason to avoid swimming.

We made it in time for class and you had a wonderful time. You smiled and laughed and enjoyed the water. You even did some strong kicking. I hope we get a chance to practice kicking this weekend.

I have noticed lately that you spend more time playing near me. You do still crawl off wanting to explore other areas, but you seem to play nearby more often, and for longer periods of time. Sometimes, you'll crawl back to me if I don't follow right behind you.

It's incredible to think about where I was emotionally this time last year. I was amazed at how social strangers were toward me; asking when my baby was due; if it was my first; how I felt about my pregnancy; whether I had been very uncomfortable. I wasn't so surprised at these questions and interests coming from those probably eligible for the title of Grandma and Grandpa, but I was really impressed by the number of young men who asked, and who relayed stories of their parenting or their wife's labor if they had children of their own. When I say young, I'm including teenagers. I was nearly shocked to hear males in their teens and early twenties inquiring about my pregnancy. I thought they would be afraid to stand near me, let alone speak to me out of the fear that they might "catch it," or that someone would think we were a couple.

June 30

I'm sorry that we didn't get a chance to go swimming this weekend. Just too many hard and late nights at work. I sure hope you don't lose your new "kick" skill.

July

July 1

It's your second week of swim class. Grandma Ani-Poo and Popie came to your class today to watch and take some pictures. You had a great class. Your kicking has improved. You kick more often, and stronger for longer periods of time. You're very good at the sit dives and you start on "Go" by leaning toward me until you break contact with the deck of the pool as I catch you in my hands. You also did a lot of laughing and giggling. Grandma Ani-Poo and Popie enjoyed watching you.

Grandma Ani-Poo and Popie went home after our class. When you and I arrived home, it was time for lunch. While I was fixing your lunch, you played with your little push-top merry-go-round. You have become intrigued with it lately and knew you could activate it yourself. You are so delightfully pleased with your talent that it's fun just to watch you "make it work." You activated it again and again.

After lunch, I put you down for a nap. It turned out to be a cheap (short) nap. At least, you did get a little rest. Mom, on the other hand wasn't as lucky.

After your nap, we went to visit Nancy and her new baby, Nicholas. Nicholas is happy, healthy and does all of the usual little baby things; wriggle, grin, drool, make sweet little grunting noises and take naps every couple of hours. He must have read his "How to be a Baby" book, unlike a certain little girl I know

265

who rarely took a nap during the day, at that age, let alone every couple of hours.

Nancy will be starting back to work next week, and isn't looking forward to leaving her little sweetie. We know how that feels, don't we? It was fun watching you watch Nicholas. It reminded me of when April was intrigued with you when you were three months old. She wanted to reach out, touch you and find out what you were all about. Her movements were unpredictable and often jerky and it scared me, though I tried to not over react. I knew that Nancy must be feeling the same way now that you want to know what Nicholas is all about. You were slow and gentle with your movements, but still you were unpredictable and that really unnerves a new Mom.

When we left Nancy's, we went to the uptown mall. I checked the shoe stores that were having sales hoping to find a good buy on baby shoes. I wanted to buy them one size too large and have them for when you started walking. I found a nice pair of sandals. I also found some tennies with tiger stripes on the top and pawprint treads. Would you believe they just happened to have them two sizes too large, and that you now own a pair for when they will fit you? What can I say, I just couldn't help myself. They may not make them when you do grow into them. They were Nikes, so they were good shoes. How's that for "rationalization"?

July 2

You hold me so much tighter when you hug me these days. I love it. Sometimes when I'm holding you, you will suddenly give me a big bear-hug. Today, you gave your teddy, your pink panther and your pillow each some "loveys." You are so sweet. Something that continues to touch me deeply, every time it happens, is when you smile your sweet sleepy baby smile on the nights I pick you up at Winnie's after work.

July 3

News flash: "Tiffany Does Nice Sit Dives Today;" film at eleven. Tiffany was making headlines. Not really, but you are enjoying your classes now and showing intermittent improvement in your kicking.

Let it be known, my dear, that today was the day you discovered your belly-button. You were cruising the cabinets of the kitchen in the buff. You were in the buff to help air your bottom rash. At one point you looked down to the floor to locate something you had dropped, when **there it was** protruding out there beyond your tummy—your belly-button!

You were spellbound!

Where did this come from? What was it? How long had it been there?

Usually hidden in a diaper, or buried in baby fat during a bath, there it was making it's discovery debut. You pushed at it; it didn't move away. You tugged at it; it didn't come off.

"Did it possess special powers or was it connected to me? Hmmm, very interesting," I guessed you wondered.

Did you also wonder if it would wear off?

July 4

No swim class today, because of the holiday. Instead, you went to your first country-style Fourth of July picnic.

We only stayed at the picnic for three hours. You were well behaved, but it didn't feel right keeping you there longer; the area we sat in lost its shade early in the afternoon. You had a nice time. It was the first time that some of our neighbors had met you!

Last year, they sort of saw you but couldn't meet you; I was still pregnant. I remembered thinking that the best part of last year's picnic was getting sprayed with the overspray from the water barrel fight. Last year, it was very hot, one hundred and twelve degrees. Since July third of last year was your estimated time of arrival, there were many questions from our friends and neighbors. "Where is that baby?" many inquired.

I answered that you weren't done cooking yet, and that you would come when you were ready.

All I was interested in was having a healthy baby. As far as your sex or your estimated time of arrival—anything was fine with me. I was ready for you if you were two weeks early, or two weeks late. You would come when you were good and ready. Who could argue with you putting your arrival off a bit? It was hot out there and you were in your comfortable climate-controlled cubby hole.

July 5

This was the last day of swim class. You didn't do quite as well with your kicking or your sit dives today, but you hadn't taken a nap either. We can practice occasionally at Arlene's pool until the third session of lessons.

I decided to skip the next session, because I just couldn't keep up the pace of coming Monday through Friday for six weeks straight. Numerous things were hopelessly behind and piled up at home after just two weeks. With work as busy as it has been, it was going to be very slow getting caught up.

We do need to go to another class this summer, if at all possible, to work on your kicking and holding your breath. Since you now enjoy the water, but don't know how to move in it or hold your breath, we are actually in a more dangerous position than if you were afraid of the water.

It's amusing how much more flamboyantly you play in your bath water since you started your second week of swim class. Now you kick the water around, and energetically splash the surface of the water with your hand. You swing your arms back and forth through the water or splash with your toys. Now, when you get a bath, so does the rest of the breakfast counter, the kitchen floor, and, of course, good 'ole soggy Mom. You've become an accomplished diaper dissecting professional. I've finally come to the conclusion that we have to use disposable diapers during your morning nap. They weren't as easy to open as velcro. Or better yet, I'll put a pair of shorts on you before you go down for your nap so the velcro isn't as easily reached.

July 6

This afternoon, while we were playing in your room, I had the urge to see you sit in your little red chair. You hadn't been in it since those pictures we took just before Christmas. Now that you were standing alone for such long periods of time, I just had a feeling you would be able to sit up in your chair fairly well.

I put the chair in front of me, let you inspect it a while, then picked you up and placed you on it. You looked uncertain about it, for about one second, then you glowed with pleasure. A huge broad smile evolved across your face as you sat there unassisted. You looked so precious. You smiled at me, then carefully looked down toward your feet, then looked somewhat carefully to the side. You hardly moved a muscle, otherwise. You didn't try to turn around or get out of the chair at all. You just sat there. You sat there for almost two minutes, without a falter, until I picked you up and gave you a big squeeze. The look of delight in your eyes was so endearing. I was happy that you felt so good about your accomplishment.

Then I watched as you played with your chair. You cruised around it, crawled around it, and patted it on the seat. You seemed to be trying to sit in it, but no matter how many times you "walked" around it, you never seemed to be facing in the right direction to sit down. It was delightful to watch. I finally put you in the chair again. You sat there on your Lilliputian throne beaming with pride.

After a few more "sits," you tried to get up on your own. There wasn't much to grab onto so you decided to lean forward onto your knees. As you did, the chair came with you. You were wearing shorts, so it just stuck to your legs. I sat you on the chair a few more times; you thought it was marvelous entertainment.

I scooped you and your little red chair up and took you to the family room to show Daddy. You still had that beam of accomplishment.

July 7

You dance frequently now, even while you walk. You toss your head up and down, pick up your arm, raise it above your head and pause before you bring it down to advance a "step" as you sing. It is delightful to watch; you enjoy life so completely. You are such a pleasure.

This morning, I managed to catch a picture of you while you were sitting in your chair. You were enjoying sitting there, but you didn't have the same glow of achievement that you had yesterday.

July 8

I love you so much, Tiffany. You are such a precious little person. I have loved you since I first held you. I really feel I already loved you, even when you were growing inside of me. I wanted to do all of the right things during my pregnancy. I didn't drink wine or have caffeine for the four months before I became pregnant. So when you were born, I felt I had already loved you for a long time, but in a different way.

It's difficult to explain, but once I felt you and held you

when you were born, my love had a new and different feel to it. That feeling has happened again. Over the last week or so, I feel as though my love for you has multiplied instead of just increasing as it had been doing. A continuing, incredibly greater feeling of love for you has been going on for many days now. It is an almost consuming feeling. I'm not aware of anything in particular that might have brought it on. I have no reason or explanation, but its presence is unmistakable.

There are some new things going on with you. You have been shaking your head "No" when you finish eating. When I offer you more, even if I offer it a few times, you shake your head "No." You are definitely saying you are through! Today, when I offered you more, you rolled your eyes upward while shaking your head.

July 9

This morning while in the family room, you crawled over to the two steps leading into the sunken living room. I crawled over to watch how you approached the steps. I usually hustle over to the steps and crawl down backwards to set an example for you, then help you down as you need it. This time, I thought I'd give you a chance to try and approach it yourself without prompting. It's only two steps; they and the floor below are carpeted. There isn't any furniture in the way. This would be the place to make any mistakes to learn from.

You approached the steps and turned yourself around so that you faced the steps. You gracefully went down the first step in perfect backwards form. I was excited but kept your accolade to a quiet but cheerful, "Very good, Tiffany. Well done, Sweetie." I didn't want to completely distract you from your efforts. As I was finishing my comment, you sized up the next step.

Something inside you called for a brief intermission. You stopped and just sat on the step for about half a minute. Then you sized up the step again. For a while there, I thought you were going to take the next step down sideways, but you righted yourself on the step again. I had a sinking feeling when you sat straight up on the step, and mentally debated grabbing you, I had the feeling you were going to do something to make yourself fall. You did. You pushed a bit at the step with your feet, pushing yourself right off of the step. You landed on your back and head and rolled to one side. I felt sick. I had let you fall down the step, even though it was only one little step with a fall to a carpeted floor. It made me feel sick and awful.

You looked up at me. I knew my face was full of hurt. You started to cry, but you made only one little pre-cry sound, stopped and crawled off to play—no big deal. Since you didn't cry and didn't feel hurt, I wondered if that was a learning experience on how not to go down stairs. Time would tell.

July 10

You slept through the night without waking up. This morning, as we changed your clothes to go to town you, helped me take off your short-sleeved pajama top. I unsnapped the back and took off the left sleeve. Then you grabbed the right sleeve, which had fallen to your elbow, and pulled it off. I complimented you on your efforts; you smiled and laughed.

On our way to town, I was singing with the radio, as usual, but today I had help. Before we were half-way to Cottonwood you sang with me and "danced" in your carseat. You sang along with me almost all the way to Redding. It was so precious. I wanted to pull over and give you a great big hug.

We had a lot to do in town today. First, we saw Daddy at his new job and met his bosses. They were very nice and

seemed to enjoy meeting us. I think they are "baby people."
After Daddy took us for a tour us through the showroom he
took us out for a salad lunch.

After lunch, we stopped at the post office, went to the
uptown mall to pick up some pictures, stopped at the post
office, and then exchanged the microphone we bought the
other day, at the electronics store because it didn't fit our
equipment. I needed a microphone to record your sweet voice.

After leaving the uptown mall, we headed to the downtown
mall to our favorite card shop, to buy a special birthday card
for Jason, Beth's son. His birthday is very close to yours. He
loves balloons, so we picked up a card with a whole cluster of
balloons on the front.

Then we went to see if we could find my friend Peggy at
work. Peggy was one of my favorite patients. She had been in
my unit at Hilltop Hospital during my pregnancy. I had
written to her a couple of times, but I hadn't seen her since she
left the hospital; consequently, she had never seen you. Peggy
was at work. There weren't any customers there at the time,
so we had a nice visit. She thought you were gorgeous. I can't
imagine why? It was so nice to see her again. She's such a
sweet lady. She was surprised to hear about your swimming
classes. She gave us an invitation to visit her at her home. She
also said her daughter, Laura, who moved from Cottonwood to
central California, was coming up in August and, that maybe
we could all get together for a barbecue while Laura was in
town.

After we visited with Peggy, we went over to Cheryl's house
to see April and Randy; they had just gotten up from their nap.
We weren't able to stay long, just an hour, but it did gave you
a chance to play with April. We left to meet Daddy at home.
He was going to watch you while I attended the Cottonwood
Parents league meeting.

You didn't get a nap today, so I am sure you'll sleep well
tonight. Good night, sweet Tiffany. I'm sure you'll be asleep by
the time I get back home. I love you.

July 12

This morning, during your breakfast, you tried so hard to say something—a **word.** You made at least thirty different noises trying to get that word—that "something" said. You used your mouth, your face, your eyes, your eyebrows, your head,and your arms in your efforts. You knit your eyebrows down, then raised them tight, hold your arms up and bent them in toward your body at the elbow, with your forearms away from each other and your palms turned toward the ceiling. Such effort. Your arms seemed to say, "I am trying so hard, why won't it come out?

After a few minutes of all this effort, you began to cry in frustration. I'm sorry your word wouldn't come out, sweetheart. It will, and sooner than either of us might imagine.

You've been shaking your head "no" and often saying, "Uh-uh" after you've been eating a while. There is no question about it, those actions and sounds definitely means you are finished eating. Trying to get you to eat more leads to more energetic head shaking, grumbling and throwing of spoons onto the floor. How nice that you are able to communicate your needs and communicate when your needs have been met. I think many people tend to feed their young ones too much. I'm not an exception.

I finally captured some Tiffi talk on tape, audio cassette. You didn't say many of the complex things you are capable of, but I will catch those a bit later. Your baby vocabulary, speaking vocabulary, has increased and become more complex these last two weeks, but especially in this last week. It seemed as though you were saying complete short thoughts—phrases, not just one or two words.

July 13

This morning, you and I played "turn your head peek-a-boo"—turning your face away and back, instead of hiding it behind something. It seemed like an intellectual milestone to me—an abstract concept!?!
As we played you would point to me occasionally.
I would point to myself and say, "Mamma," then point to you and say, "Baby—Baby Tiffany."
After a few rounds of Momma-baby; when I said, "baby," you said, "Blah-bah!"
Sounded close enough to "baby" to me!
You can work your tongue around into all sorts of shapes. It seems to be increasing your interest in trying to talk, not to mention the number of sounds you are able to make now. Your tongue activity is definitely tied into your talking efforts.
Rolling your eyes upward has become one of your favorite expressions, when you're done eating and I try to give you a couple of more spoonfuls, or when you're playing and pretending to be exasperated. You are so much fun to watch and play with.

July 14

While playing with my nose this morning, you noticed my headband. I was wearing a wide blue band to keep the hair out of my eyes and face.
You pulled at it and it stretched. When you let go, it gently snapped back into place. You were fascinated. You pulled at it again, and it came down over my forehead. Then you pulled it off, down to my neck. Now you could really play with it.
I put it back in position and you started all over again. After a while I took it off and put it around your neck.
You tried to get it off.
I took it off and handed it to you.
You tried to put it back on over your head. Then you

275

grabbed either end raising it over your head and pulled it down draping the band over your head, where it finally snuggled in around your head.

July 15

This morning, you woke up permeating the hallways with, "Bah! Bah!" You were hungry and were asking for breakfast; asking for room service, no less.

After breakfast, we went into the family room to play. You started walking with the "kitty" walker that Cheryl had loaned to you, and you did it on your own. What was different about today was that when you ran into an obstacle you picked up the walker or turned it around, so you could continue walking with it in another direction. You did this a number of times. It was exciting to watch.

You just took your first step! You were standing at the couch. I brought your kitty walker over near you, three feet away from the couch. You looked at the walker, then let go of the couch. With your concentration fully directed at the walker, you took a healthy step toward it, totally unsupported! Your gaze was still locked on the walker. You rocked around on your little feet a bit, reestablished your balance, and took another healthy step; another waver then a little step, and you were there! You'd done it! You walked somewhere. I could barely believe my eyes. I was so proud of you.

You were very impressed with yourself. After all of the wondering about when you would take your first steps, I guess I thought you would do a drum-roll first to herald the event. But I didn't hear a drum-roll; it just quietly, happily happened. Congratulations, Tiffany, it's **toddler** time!

July 16

We were playing on my bed this morning. You crawled over the marshmallow mountains (pillow stacks) and crawled toward the headboard to see what you could discover. You found a haircomb with a fabric flower on it.

I pointed to it and said "flower."

You pointed to it and said, "Dowaper!"

I took that to mean flower and bathed you in praise for your picking up on the word so quickly.

Late in the morning, we drove to Dairyville, a forty-five minute ride, with Grandma Ani-Poo and Popie, to visit Fred and Connie at their new home. They had invited us over to swim in their pool. It was a great pool for kids—three and one half feet deep everywhere. It made cruising through the water with you for kicking practice very easy. You did a lot of great kicking. Overall you did rather well on your sit dives, and extremely well at holding onto the side and supporting your own weight. That was good; it has been eleven days since your last swimming "workout."

When we were through swimming, I put your jogging outfit on to prevent a chill. I put you down on the deck and pointed you toward the sliding glass door where Connie's kitten was watching us. You took a couple of crawl steps towards the glass door then stopped. You looked very puzzled. I walked past you to the slider to encourage you to come over to me and the kitten. You took a few more steps then stopped again. This time partly puzzled, partly amused, you kept looking at the decking. I hit at the decking directly under you. You looked surprised, and amused then you smiled, giggled, and hit at the decking yourself, then smiled and laughed again. I figured out what was distracting you and capturing your interest. It was the movement, the vibration of the redwood decking as you moved across it. It must have felt like crawling over a xylophone. You enjoyed having the decking "twang" under you or me, as long as I was next to you. But you were reluctant to crawl across it without an escort. I guess the xylophone didn't feel secure enough to allow you to venture away from Mom. After you finally made it over to the sliding glass door, you visited with the kitten through the door for a few minutes before we left.

Tiffany, I was so excited about your first steps yesterday, that I forgot to tell you about something. When you and I were playing at my nightstand in the bedroom there was a mug on the nightstand that had different woodland and jungle animals painted all the way around it. You pointed to the mug's handle.

I said "cup." (It seemed like an easier word to say than mug.) I chose an animal that began with one of your favorite letters (sounds) "B." It was a bunny. I pointed to the bunny and said, "Bunny."

You pointed to the bunny and said, "Bah-nah!"

I pointed at the bunny again and said, "Bunny."

You pointed to the bunny, actually putting your finger on the picture that time and said, "Bun-nyib!"

Wow! You said, "Bunny." I was so excited. I tried it a few more times. No more "bun-nyib" just "bah-nah." Then I asked, "Where is the bunny?" You pointed right to it. A couple of hours later, you still knew which one was the bunny! You are such a bright little girl.

July 17

Today at breakfast, you were using your fork to "spoon" at your cereal. You put your fork in, pushed it across the bowl, pulled it out and tapped it on the side. When I feed you, I tap your spoon on the side to remove the excess cereal. I was sure that you were mimicking my routine—precursor to the self-feed, I believe. Before today, you have been "stabbing" at your food; but your actions today were more organized.

When I picked you up at Winnie's after work, she told me that you had taken two steps for her on a couple of occasions. Look out world, it won't be long before Tiffany breaks loose into a full gallop.

July 18

This morning, you started a game of peek-a-boo at the guest room door. This game of peek-a-boo had a new twist. Instead of hiding behind the door jamb and then popping out to say "peek-a-boo," you just turned your head way around to the right, then turned it back quickly, looked at me and giggled. I said, "Peek-a-boo, Tiffi." You laughed. Then you slowly turned your head to the right again, paused, then again quickly turned your smiling face directly at me. This was definitely a new form of peek-a-boo.

The Redding television station called today They wanted to film some of our Parent's League campaign members picking up cans from one of the preschools. The cans had been collected for use in our "Save Our Libraries" campaign. They would be labeled and used for collecting donations at participating locations. The television coverage would also promote our volunteer meeting at the main library tomorrow, for the initial can distribution. They wanted us at the preschool at 1:30 pm. I took you to Winnie's early, since I wouldn't have time to go back Winnie's and get to work on time after the filming.

The reporters decided to film only the children as they carried the cans out to the station wagon and put them on the tailgate. All three of the children the reporters chose to use handled themselves beautifully. One of the children chosen rarely spoke at school or at home. The school members wondered how he would handle the situation, and if he would talk at all. He was great. He spoke clearly and answered all the interviewers questions. The news interviewer was very considerate in talking with the children first, about things that interested them, and familiarizing them with the camera before actually filming them.

July 19

Today was kick-off day, for the meeting of our campaign volunteers, to start distributing the donation cans to the local merchants for the "Save Our Libraries" fund-raising drive.

Again, I had to take you to Winnie's for the afternoon. We sure haven't been able to play together much these last few days. The initial efforts of organizing a campaign are usually the hardest. I won't get to see much of you tomorrow, either. Sunday, the day after tomorrow, will be a different story. Sunday will be your day, all day. Sunday also happens to be your FIRST BIRTHDAY!!!

Mommy was on television tonight, for a few seconds; the local television station had also filmed our campaign kick-off. They showed some footage of the kick-off with a very concise, but informative story describing our efforts.

You and I arrived home from Winnie's minutes before the local news aired. Part of the footage aired included a nine month old baby sitting on a library table playing with one of the donation cans. He was charming, a definite asset. That scene made a very strong statement.

July 20

This morning, you and Daddy were in the family room. I was in the kitchen packing your bag for Winnie's. You climbed up onto the couch all by yourself. Daddy saw you starting up and caught my attention so I could watch you. You were so proud of yourself.

Once you were on the couch, you immediately wanted to get down. You did so very smoothly, and backwards to boot! Then it was back onto the couch. This time, you reached over the couch to the kitchen desk to see what you could get a hold of.

You found a bunch of goodies, just as I was moving them out of harms way. I left a few "Mommy approved grabbies" within your reach. One of them was an ostrich feather from the Gentle Jungle. The "Jungle" is a working ranch for trained exotic animals used in movies and television. I took my exotic animal training there and worked there for a little over a year.

You enjoyed playing with that feather. Unfortunately, I couldn't get a picture of you with it. You proudly waved your plume around and talked with it—in depth, on some secret subject. It was delightful to witness. It was as though the feather was a new friend. It was new, pretty, fun, and didn't talk back or say, "No." What a great buddy.

Daddy and I have been invited to go rafting on the Sacramento River. It will be a half-day trip, with members of Grandma Ani-Poo and Popie's motorcycle club and their families. There will be a pot-luck dinner afterwards at one member's house. He lives on the river in Anderson. Neither of us have ever been river rafting before. We were really excited about it. Daddy and I took you to Winnie's house by 10:00 am.

We had a fabulous time rafting and at the pot luck. The company was grand and the weather perfect. What fun! I hope we will be invited, again, next year.

We picked you up at Winnie's at 8:00 pm. You had gone to bed at 7:30 pm. What a dirty trick to be woken up just after you'd fallen asleep. I sure am looking forward to your birthday party tomorrow. It will be our first full day together in days.

I've missed our play time together. We've been able to play some, but nothing compared to what we had become accustomed to. Sweet dreams, Tiffany. Tomorrow will be a big day for all of us. I hope you enjoy your day. Even if you aren't fully aware of what the party represents; the celebration, the decorations, and the presents should be colorful, and fun for you. I went to bed, but couldn't get to sleep. My mind was filled with the realization that on this day one year ago you had not yet been born. We were working on it. Boy, did we work on it!

You arrived seventeen days after your due date of July third. Daddy and I were sure of your due date. Since we were sure of the date, and letting you sit in there too much longer could have led to problems during your delivery. If, after a few more days the placenta had broken down beyond a certain point, you might not have been able to tolerate a vaginal delivery. Dr. Smith knew how important is was to me to have a "natural," non-medicated birth. So that morning we went to the hospital for Dr. Smith to induce labor. He started with the least amount of intervention and worked his way up, and was willing to stop the intervention if my own body processes took over. He was also willing to give each intervention enough of a chance to progress the labor, without moving to the next intervention too quickly. That was my main concern; having a cesarean because of medical inertia—not necessity. Obviously, if I truly needed a cesarean, I would have had no complaint about it.

It was 8:00 am, when we arrived at the hospital. Once we were finally on the third floor in the Labor and Delivery area, we discovered that the only alternative birthing room they had was available! I was really happy about that; they had just finished shampooing the carpet from the last birth.

I changed into my hospital gown. The external fetal monitor was attached to my abdomen, to measure the contractions' intensity, duration, and your babies heart rate. The external fetal monitor indicated a "happy heart," in other words, good heart rate variability. Your father and I were in great spirits, eager and wondering when you would make your debut. If you were born sometime that day, your birthday would share the date of the first manned moon landing. It was also the day I started training at the Gentle Jungle four years ago.

Your father was looking at a magazine and I was reviewing my books on stages of labor—coming attractions.

At 9:00 am, an IV was started for the upcoming Pitocin drip. At 10:00 am, the Pitocin drip was started.

By 8:00 pm, there hadn't been any progress of labor, despite all of that Pitocin. We'd been to the bathroom, frequently; had walked many laps up and down the halls, and I was still only at one to two centimeters dilatation, (I had accomplished that before I came in), and not yet to—1 station (a locator of labor position in relation to the cervix). Dr. Smith walked into the room. He said it was time to rupture the membranes since there hadn't been any progress for ten hours.

I had expected an absolute deluge of fluid when the membranes were ruptured, but there wasn't much. Dr. Adams said that further indicated that our due date was correct and that you were indeed overdue. When a pregnancy goes beyond full-term, the fetus begins to absorb, or process the amnionic fluid within the membranes (birth sac).

By 8:00 am, July 21, it had been a full twenty-four hours since we arrived at the hospital and I was still sitting at three centimeters dilatations and 0 to 1+ station. Your Daddy guessed that you were going to be a girl, because you were late and playing hard to get.

Girl or boy, time would tell. I couldn't wait to see you; hold you. I knew your Daddy was just as eager. Labor was laborious. The Pitocin seemed to cause more double and multi-peaked contractions than single ones.

Hey! We must have been getting somewhere—the contractions were two to three minutes apart, not to mention the two or more peaks per contraction.

I had a lot of back pain. No one had said so yet, but I bet that you were "sunny side up"(unborn child facing front of mother instead of facing toward back) and that this was the infamous "back labor."

At the tone, the time, was 5:00 pm, exactly. Beeeeeep! Thirty-three hours had passed since we started. I was at eight centimeters, barely effacing and you were at 1+ station. At eight centimeters dilatation, Dr. Smith could feel the positioning of your head. Yes, you were occiput posterior (sunny side up). You were also very large. Dr. Smith said you were too big to come out safely, vaginally, in your present position. He gave us an hour or so to persuade you to turn around. We tried to persuade you to turn, by trying different positions and more walking around. If you didn't turn around, we would have had to have a cesarean (Heavy sigh)!

I did high-knee marches up and down the halls; hung over a stack of two bean-bag chairs in various positions while coughing, deep breathing, manipulating my abdomen, anything to reposition you. You did do some turning, I wasn't sure how much.

When I felt you turn, I stayed in that position for a while

before slowly getting off of the bean-bags. But as soon as I changed positions, I felt you move back to your previous position. After many rounds of this, the continued pain in my back told me the net result was zero. When Dr. Smith examined me there had been no change.

By "sixish" pm, the Pitocin had been off for more than an hour. I should have made a formal announcement to my uterus! The contractions continued to have multiple peaks. Evidently, my uterus had just had it after the many hours of Pitocin.

I imagined you were pretty tired of it all, too. Those long, five and nine minute, contractions must have been hard. Heaven only knows what **you** thought of that twenty minute monster contraction! Your heart didn't drop with any of the contractions. It did hit the two hundred twenty beats per minute mark toward the end of that twenty minute contraction. That scared me. Dr. Smith said it wasn't anything to worry about, but it did worry me.

Mom was "maxed out"! That twenty minute contraction really did me in. I didn't ever want to go through another twenty minute wonder again.

I'd had enough. I wanted my baby, in my arms, not in my abdomen. Between your large size and my cervix refusing to fully open, I was ready to have the cesarean. Dr. Smith came back in to say that he was scheduling an operating room.

It wouldn't be long before we would get to see and hold you! I could hardly wait. Knowing that you would be in my arms soon gave me a new source of energy.

They just announced a trauma alert over the public address system. Hilltop was a regional trauma center; it handled automobile and train accidents, water skiing injuries, etc. Trauma alerts are part of the system to alert all departments of an incoming trauma; to announce how long before the trauma would arrive, so all departments involved would be prepared at the time of arrival. It could be a long time before we went to surgery, depending on what surgery the incoming trauma required. My newly arrived energy was immediately stolen from me at the thought of hours of delay.

Our nurse told us that the trauma was a compound fracture of an arm. That didn't sound worth a trauma alert to me, there had to be more to it than that. Dr. Smith called to find out how long before we could have the on-call surgery team. The emergency room seemed to think it would be quite a while before the trauma patient went upstairs to the operating room, and that his surgery would be quite long.

Dr. Smith was calling in the second on-call surgery team so we wouldn't have to wait until the trauma was resolved. "Thank you Dr. Smith." It had been a rough day-and-a-half; I wouldn't have done well waiting too much longer. My mental faculties were drawing thin.

Terrific—another trauma alert was just announced for five minutes. There went the second surgical team. I sure hoped it didn't turn out to be something extensive like a five hour head surgery. I truly didn't think I could last that long. Dr. Smith walked into my room, he knew we had also heard the second trauma alert. He said it wouldn't be a long wait. He had just called in a third team, constituting an emergency cesarean. He also said he was going down to the surgery department; that if he was down there stomping around, things would happen faster. "Thank you again, Dr. Smith."

I hoped it would be real soon. It was incredible how much harder the contractions were to handle when I knew they weren't going to bring me a baby. Once I had submitted to the decision for surgery, every contraction afterward seemed overwhelming and unfair. I realized once I put this on paper, that I wasn't being rational. But, at the time, I truly believed the contractions should stop, after the decision to have the cesarean was made. Obviously, the reasoning of a highly fatigued mind and body. Remember, that was after thirty-four hours of labor and twenty hours of Pitocin drip-enhanced contractions.

I tried to focus on the thought of just how long you'd last—seventy to eighty-plus years! The long effort didn't seem quite as spectacular when I thought about how long we'd both derive pleasure from it!

Fathers weren't allowed into the operating room for surgical deliveries unless they had attended a class on cesarean delivery (Mom's attended also.) People usually only take such classes when their Doctor knew they were going to have a cesarean delivery.

I knew I'd need your Daddy to be there with me even more, if for some reason I required a cesarean, so I wanted us to take that class. Daddy didn't think it made much sense to take the classes since we didn't expect a cesarean, but I kept prompting him to **please** go. I looked on it as an insurance policy, feeling if we had it we wouldn't need it.

So many deliveries end up as cesarean these days. I just wasn't willing to take the chance of it happening to us, and your Daddy not being allowed to attend your delivery because it happened in the operating room.

We worked hard to get into a class in the face of cancelled and rescheduled classes. I tried every feasible hospital. Being a rural area and only four hospitals within a thirty mile radius, it was difficult. We finally connected with a class.

At 7:45 pm we were on our way to surgery. We had worked at "birthing" for 34 hours by the time I received the epidural anesthesia.

We just couldn't do this birth in the usual fashion. I was very sorry that we had to do it this way. We had tried everything, and given each step plenty of time. Forcing a vaginal birth under the prevailing circumstances could very probably have resulted in a true emergency cesarean, if you were to get "stuck" half-way out, being such a sizable critter. If the delivery room had been set up as a surgical suite, we could have tried, but that situation didn't exist at Hilltop.

You were soon to be part of our family and the world. Being

delivered from your warm, "automatic" uterine environment into the "cold" world is supposed to rather traumatic. You would have to breathe for yourself, demand feeding when hungry, and hope Mom and Dad would keep you warm, but not too warm. Everyone alive has been born, but nobody remembers it. If it was indeed traumatic, the trauma had to be very short-lived and rapidly forgotten. I was born myself, thirty years ago, but I certainly don't remember a thing about it.

Considering all of the squeezing you'd been through that last day and a half, I bet you were eager to get out of that squeeze bag, even if it was climate controlled.

Dr. Smith had a colleague assist him, and Dr. Lin was our Anesthesiologist. Of course, you and I were there. And thanks to taking the cesarean classes, your Daddy was there too, sitting next to my head. We very eagerly awaited your debut! Daddy watched the whole surgery. I didn't have the least bit of desire to watch, not when it was happening to my own body.

No sooner had Dr. Smith grabbed your head and started to pull you out, than you let out a great cry, and kept on crying. I was right, you couldn't wait to get out of that tight spot, out into the world where you could move around without everything pushing back at you. Dr. Smith announced that we had a beautiful, **not-so-little** girl.

The Doctors and nurses tried to guess how much you weighed. You were even bigger than Dr. Smith had anticipated at his last exam. Daddy guessed ten and one-half pounds. You were still crying as they took you over to the corner of the operating room to dry you off.

At some point during my recounting of your birth I fell asleep. I wasn't sure where the part of it I thought through ended and the portion I had dreamed through started, but I did finally drift off to sleep with my thoughts.

July 21

Happy First Birthday

This morning after breakfast, you walked a couple of steps toward the dishwasher. Daddy saw it, too. It was the first time he had seen you take any steps. A few minutes later, you went over to the couch, climbed onto it and reached for the ostrich feather on the kitchen desk. You swished it about, intrigued with the floating motion of the tips of the feathers. Daddy swished it near your face; you grinned, turned your face away, and made a funny wrinkled face expression. You carried the feather with you on and off the couch many times. Swishing, dragging, dropping it, and picking it up again; Tiffi and her feather friend.

I neglected to mention something. For the last week, you have been raising yourself up on all fours in spider-fashion in the middle of the floor. With your bottom up in the air, you look through your legs across the room, upside down. You have been tickled by this inverted view of the world. You do it many times a day, just for the fun of it. It was adorable to watch.

Grandma Ani-Poo and Popie arrived while Daddy was feeding you lunch. You waved at them through the dining room window as they walked toward the house. Once you finished lunch, you talked to and waved at the puppies while Popie played with them. Grandma Ani-Poo and I were finishing the fruit salad for your birthday party. I wanted to start a tradition of serving fruit salad in a watermelon bowl instead of having a birthday cake, at least for the first few years. A small sweet treat was fine, but none of us really needed to eat cake. The salad bowl would have a candle in the middle shaped like a number one. You would get a cupcake with icing, just to see what you would do with it.

Party time! I handed you a small package I had wrapped loosely for you to open by yourself. I started it for you, with just a break in the paper, something for you to get a hold of.

You had no trouble getting to the little prize inside. It was a little birthday bear key chain, complete with uncut colored aluminum keys—your very own real keys, not "baby" plastic keys.

You opened a couple of other packages on your own—those that couldn't be damaged by possible over-energetic baby handling. Grandma Ani-Poo and Popie bought a small portable wading pool for you. They brought it in unwrapped, and leaned it against a large box. You were completely taken with it. You climbed into it and tried to climb up and over the other side.

You seemed to enjoy the crepe paper and streamer decorations I had put up over the breakfast bar and in the dining room. Everyone was wearing party hats, including you. After opening presents and playing, it was time to eat. I put some fresh cream cheese frosting on your cupcake, and put a single candle in it. We all presented it to you as we sang "Happy Birthday." You tried to blow out your candle with a pursed-lip leaky balloon noise. I blew the candle out for you, before you tried to grab for it.

That cupcake was your first "sweet" that wasn't a fruit. It seemed you deserved a shot at a real goodie on your birthday. I do have to admit, I hoped you wouldn't be too excited about it.

You grabbed the cupcake. The icing was wonderful; you squished it between your fingers a few times, then finally licked some of it off. You were interested in it, but more for it's squishy quality than it's taste. You had a lot more fun playing with it than eating it, which didn't hurt my feelings at all.

After a few minutes, I turned it over as you hadn't yet discovered there was cake underneath the squishy stuff. You poked at it, but didn't eat any. I pulled off a few small bits and offered them to you. You ate one of the bits, but wouldn't take anymore. You just played with it. There were definite advantages to having the party fare after a meal.

Grandma Ani-Poo and Popie left shortly after the "cake." It was getting close to nap time for you. You'd had a very exciting afternoon.

After your nap, you were ready to go again. You came out to play with your new toys. At one point, you stopped playing amongst your new treasures and carried your birthday bear key chain over to the couch. You climbed onto the couch, positioned yourself in standard "big person" fashion, leaning against the back of the couch with both arms stretched away from your sides. It's such a shame that you are such a tense child (ha ha).

It was early to bed for our little "yearling." You'd had quite an exciting day. I was glad that you enjoyed your first birthday.

Today's activities were quite different from this day last year. You were busy trying to be born, and I was working hard to help you accomplish that. It was easy to see why they call birthing "labor."

You woke up as Daddy and I were finishing dinner. You weren't able to get back to sleep easily. I went to pick you up while Daddy cleaned up the table for me. I looked at the clock as I walked toward your room. It read 7:45 pm, thirty-five minutes before you were born this day last year. I was in the operating room at that time.

I wondered if there were any thoughts in your young mind about where you were and what you were doing this time last year, if somewhere inside of you, you knew that this was the evening of your birth.

When I picked you up, you leaned on my shoulder and hugged me tightly. I walked around your room with you. I talked to you, hugged you, and kissed you. You drifted off to sleep in a few minutes.

I put you into your crib, after a few more minutes of huggies, then went into the family room where Daddy was. We watched one of our favorite television shows and recounted the highlights of the day. At nine o'clock we went to bed. I don't really remember what happened on the television show. I had been thinking about what we were doing this time last year, especially around 8:20 pm, the time you were born; how much had happened; how incredibly different you were now; and how fast you'd grown.

A little after 9:30 pm you woke up again, crying and uncomfortable. I didn't wait to see if you could get yourself back to sleep. I wanted to be with you. Tonight was special. I gathered you up into my arms. Since you hadn't taken much of your dinner bottle, I fixed one for you. I fed you in the rocking chair as we shared some huggies. You took most of the bottle, gazing tenderly into my eyes, just as you had done when you were younger. I cradled you and talked to you about the first time I saw you, the first time I held you, and about the first time Daddy fed you, shortly after your birth.

At 9:30 pm, one year ago today, you were in the hospital nursery with Daddy. I was about halfway through my time in the recovery room. Frank, my recovery room nurse would periodically ask me to wiggle my toes. I remember what a spooky feeling it was to try. Everything from my chest down felt as though it weighed two or three tons, as if it didn't really belong to the rest of my body.

When I tried to wiggle my toes, it felt like I was trying to lift a piano with them. I couldn't tell if they were moving. Frank assured me that they were. I wondered if this was how a person who was newly paralysed felt—a seemingly unresponsive body with limbs that don't feel or behave like they belong to the rest of your body. The sensation was frightening, even though I knew the origin and that it was temporary. How consuming and overwhelming it must be for someone who didn't know if it was going to be temporary or permanent—unbelievable.

Back to the present. I stayed with you long after you fell asleep on my shoulder. I wanted to hold you tonight during the time you were born one year ago today, and until the time that I was first able to hold and marvel at you.

My emotions were running so strong tonight. It's difficult to describe the intensity. I found myself crying as different memories came to mind. The tears and the feelings weren't sad, they were more of awe and amazement.

I love you, sweet Tiffany, more than you could ever hope to know and understand. I don't even **completely** understand it myself. Good night, dear, sweet creature of God. I will see you in the morning, when you are ready to tackle a bright new day.

July 22

This morning you decided that since you were no longer an infant, it was time to get on with toddler things; actually, I guess "waddler" would be more accurate, since you weren't really walking yet.

You were ready to start with "more mature" activities such as climbing. You tried to climb at least half of the things you came across: your wading pool; the couch, as usual; and the study pillow next to my nightstand in the bedroom.

When you finished your before nap bottle, you offered it to me as you usually do. But today's was a limited offer. You gave it to me, then after a few seconds you took it away. You did this a few times; a new twist.

After your nap, we headed out for the first day of your second "semester" of swimming classes. When we arrived, we found that they had to cancel the class this session, not enough people had signed up. Darn! The pool director did say that we could use one corner of the shallow end while the other swimming class was in session.

We practiced putting your head underwater. It didn't require much space in the pool, and we hadn't tried it yet. I tried putting your face underwater a few times. I used the same cueing we used in the swimming classes we had just finished taking. I would say, "Ready—set—go," and gradually lowered your face to the water at a very shallow angle. On the word "go" I blew into your mouth from a few inches away, to prevent water from getting into your airway, as I reluctantly lowered your face into the water. You did get a small amount of water in your mouth, but you didn't cough or cry.

I was very ambivalent about this particular exercise. Dr. Kelley didn't think it was a good idea either, when we asked him about it; as you could take in too much pool water. You didn't seem at all upset with the exercise, but you weren't closing your mouth all of the way. You did close it a couple of times, but opened it again just before your mouth was in the water. I stopped the exercise once you had taken a total of three swallows of the water. I couldn't really expect that you would know what to do the first day we tried it. I was over-anxious about the whole exercise. I felt I should do the exercise; I wanted you to know how to close your mouth to keep water from getting into it. But I was so uncertain about my feelings, that I decided it best to wait until I was more resolved.

Your kicking wasn't very good today. You were probably preoccupied with wondering what Mommy was so concerned about. You did enjoy being in the water tremendously, as usual. As we drove home, you had a finger in each ear and tilted your head frequently. It must have felt funny from having water in both ears.

Daddy picked you up after his work today. He said you were really tired, and went to bed at 7:30 pm. Maybe you went to bed early because you're older now; you know, more mature. over the hill at age 366 days.

July 23

This morning you entertained yourself so beautifully. You spent a great deal of time playing with the toys and the things near your playpen and toy box. You amused yourself with talking and playing for almost forty minutes.

You also shocked me this morning by heading right up the spiral staircase when you crawled down the hall, instead of heading into the master bedroom. I stayed right behind you and let you climb while I watched. I stopped you at the fifth step and insisted that you come back down.

Going down stairs wasn't yet part of your programming. I had to direct you into coming back down, as I manipulated your little body through the motions of climbing down the stairs backwards.

Once we came down three of the five steps, you stopped trying to go right back up; you helped with the motions of coming down the last two steps. I couldn't move away from you at all. These steps weren't made of wood or fully carpeted. The steps had a carpeted insert on top, but were made of metal with open space between each step. In other words you could fall through the steps. Each step was wedge-shaped, to make a spiral case. They were a lot harder for you to navigate than your basic rectangular steps.

As soon as you were back on the floor, you were ready to go up again. I only let you go up three steps this time. Then we came back down.

What a frightening experience. My heart was in my throat when I saw you head for those stairs. My imagination raced through mental images of what could have happened to you had you done it unobserved! As you can tell by now, we did not have a security gate at the base of the staircase. You can be certain there will be one there tomorrow.

July 24

This morning, before we left to buy a security gate for the staircase, you stood up from all fours in the middle of the floor, and you did it very smoothly. You'd never stood up that easily before! Right after your accomplishment, we left for town.

We went to a discount department warehouse for the security gate. At the warehouse you fill out an order form based on what they have in their catalog, give the order to a clerk, then someone "pulls" your order from the warehouse, stock while you wait.

When I started to fill out the order form, you decided you wanted to have it. I pulled out a form for you, and another of the tiny pencils they provided for writing. You started to draw on my order sheet with your pencil, with the correct end of the pencil, no less! How about that! Our little Tiffany drawing purposefully with the business end of a pencil, at the ripe old age of twelve months!

I pulled out another order sheet and started to write on it. You followed suit. As you were designing your order, I completed mine. By the time I had finished my order form, you were drawing on a page in the catalog. No problem, each page had a plastic sleeve covering.

When Daddy came home from work, I told him about your writing efforts and about your standing up so easily in the middle of the floor today. He said that you stood up smoothly the other day, after he picked you up from Winnie's. He didn't say anything because he thought you had done it before. Daddy sees another first! How nice that everyone is getting in on the "firsts."

July 25

You woke up before Daddy had to leave for work today. He had some morning hugs, while I fixed your cereal and bottle. Daddy put you into your high-chair and he told me that the other night when he was giving you dinner that you not only "spooned" at it, but that you "fed" some to him. More "baby-type sharing." I think it's precious.

Daddy tried to get you to feed him this morning so I could witness it, but you weren't giving command performances today. I was sure, I would get to see it soon.

After breakfast, we practiced reading. As we looked at picture books, you pointed to the picture of a cat.

You said, "Kaah." Then you pointed to the picture of a dog and said, "Dah."

I asked, "Where is the kitty?"

You pointed to the cat. Then you pointed to the picture of the duck and said, "Dah."

Oh well, I'm still impressed. You can pick out a kitty a mile away!

You helped "feed" me some lunch today. It was so sweet. Your movements were very gentle and fairly smooth. Even though you would miss my mouth occasionally, you never did thrust at my mouth. Your movements were touchingly gentle.

You are definitely fascinated with tooth-brushing. If you are within sight of me when I begin to brush my teeth, you stop what you are doing, and come over to the sink to watch. You even come if you can't see me, but hear "tooth-brushing noises."

You hold onto the edge of the sink counter, stand on your tip-toes and watch intently. You look at me, then at my reflection in the mirror. I don't know exactly what you find so fascinating—the sound, the movements, or the foaming toothpaste.

I have capitalized on the fact that you love watching this. I gave you your own "toothbrush" so that you could brush when I did. Hopefully, that will be the basis for forming a very good habit. Wouldn't it be great if you really enjoyed brushing your teeth, and didn't have to be coerced into it? You might avoid having any cavities. Well, I can dream, can't I?

July 26

Timeline: This day last year was the first day you woke up in your new home. How fast the time passes.

Lately, you have been singing glorious little songs with much more complex, tongue moving sounds. Your tongue movements are more purposeful and coordinated, and has made for some fabulous talkies. I love it!

You tried to ride your little, wheeled horse toy today. You only went backwards, but you didn't care. It was all fun to you. It's interesting how backwards is the easiest to accomplish.

July 27

You can push your wheeled horse forward. You still like going backwards, but you mostly went forward today. You got a kick out of pushing him along by his saddle handle when you weren't riding him. You could make more "clippity clops" that way. The horse has a built-in noise maker that makes more noise the faster the horse moved.

July 28

You have a teaching toy that has pictures of different farm animals on it. You are supposed to point the dial to a picture, pull the string and listen to the sound that animal makes. You have watched me do this many times, so you can listen to the sounds. Today, you turned the pointer to the farmer and tried to pull the string; but weren't able to pull the string without help. So you selected a picture, then requested help to pull it.

You knew what to do, you just lacked the strength. The fact that you learn by imitation demonstrates itself more and more frequently, and more profoundly as your knowledge, experimenting and attention span increase.

July 31

As we watched the morning news, we learned that there will be a "blue moon" tonight. I hadn't realized that there really was such a thing. I thought it was just a songwriter's romantic notion.

A blue moon is when two full moons occur within the same month. The second full moon is called the blue moon. This didn't happen very often. Hence, the saying, once in a blue moon. Tonight will be the first blue moon since you were born. Happy blue moon, Tiffany.

At the hospital, we often notice that we are much busier during a full moon—more paramedic calls, more people coming into the emergency room, and more hospital admissions. It will be interesting to see if a blue moon demonstrates any extra impact.

While you were playing in the pantry today, you stacked some of your baby food jars into a tower three jars high. I believe, from my child development readings that stacks of two were the norm for your present age! You made another three-jar tower, then you were off to new experiences.

You have more accomplishments to your credit today. You used the "reins" on your little riding horse more purposefully. You pulled him along by the rein handle or moved it out of the way if you didn't want to hold it as you rode. Sometimes you tried to pull the handle up through his neck when you sat on him.

August

August 1

Your Mommy was in today's newspaper in an interview article describing the efforts of the Cottonwood Parents' League's "Save Our Libraries" campaign, to stop the planned closure of so many of our county's branch libraries.

Blue moon report: Tonight's shift at work was wilder than our usual full moon fare. We had two full heart attack calls for our Paramedic unit; a young man fell off of the Shasta Dam, fortunately he wasn't badly hurt; and there were more auto accidents than usual. Interesting.

I recall a study, that I believe was done in Chicago, indicating an increased number of crimes during the full moon. It might be interesting to see information relating to the differences between full moons and blue moons.

August 2

This morning, while we were at the uptown mall, we had an early lunch at the deli. When I was finished my lunch, I fed your fruit to you as you sat in your stroller. You smiled and reached your arms up toward me. I bent down to wipe your face, and give you a kiss. You were faster and kissed me first. I smiled and my eyes teared. I said, "Thank you, sweet Tiffany." Then I started teasing you with a napkin as if I were cleaning a horrendous mess from your face. When I leaned farther down to touch my nose to yours, you reached up with your arms, held my shoulder and gave me another kiss. You are so dear. I was deeply touched by these tender displays. You have such a warm, loving, and gentle personality. There were two young men sitting in a booth across the aisle from us in the little deli. I overheard one of them say to the other, "That was really sweet."

You wave "bye-bye" regularly now. It's so cute. When you see someone leaving, you wave "bye-bye" and try to say "bye-bye." You even wave "Hi" and say "ll-lo" for hello, just as you do when you pick up your play telephone. You have, only recently, become consistent with something that I understand as hello. Always something new.

This afternoon, we went out to an early dinner with Grandma Ani-Poo and Popie. After eating, we all went to the grocery store. There I let you walk around the store with Daddy and I each holding a hand. You worked very hard at moving your feet properly. You did well when you concentrated on what you were doing. But once you became interested in your surroundings, your footwork got all messed up. Your left foot would try to take two steps sometimes before letting the right foot have a turn, or your right foot tried to go over and walk on the left side, just to see what it was like over there.

It was the first time you and I had someone with us so that you could practice walking with two hands to hold. I really enjoyed walking with you. I felt very proud to be walking alongside my sweet and lovely baby girl.

I saved the sweetest thing for last. This morning, when we were playing on the floor in the family room, you leaned up to my face and gave me a real kiss. It was so precious; completely unsolicited. A minute later, you did it again. I was totally disarmed by your tenderness.

August 4

Today, we went out to lunch with Daddy. You were already hungry when we arrived. You leaned back in the clip-to-the table baby seat to have your bottle. When you finished your bottle, I gave you a cracker broken into a few pieces. You ate all of it. I broke up another cracker for you. You, very thoughtfully, offered part of it to Daddy. He leaned forward to accept it. He took it in his mouth and closed his lips around it. You smiled and looked very pleased.

But when Daddy kept the cracker and didn't offer it back to you, a couple of seconds later, the smile gradually fell from your face, leaving a genuinely hurt expression. You looked at him with disillusion. Then you looked at me the same way, as if to say, "He took my cracker and didn't give it back. I didn't think he would really eat it. He wasn't supposed to eat it. That's not how the game goes."

Such a pitiful expression. You were genuinely hurt. We didn't dare laugh, but we couldn't help but find it funny. Daddy thought he was playing the game just right. As it turned out, he had thwarted the main ingredient—pretend.

Afterward, Daddy went grocery shopping with us. You were very well behaved in the store . It sure was a lot easier having someone else along to help keep certain damageables out of your reach, a real challenge with the new shallower grocery carts.

Daddy pushed you in the cart while I "retrieved of the goods." It was a long process, as we hadn't shopped in this particular market before, not to mention the place was positively huge. You reached out and gave Daddy a hug every so often.

August 5

This morning, you had a very nice encounter with Mildieu. She was sitting in the little wicker chair in the family room.

You went over to the chair and talked to her with your hands very close to her. You didn't make any quick movements around her face; most considerate of you. You were very close, but knew not to intrude too far.

Mildieu accepted these overtures very graciously and continued to do so even after it had lasted a few minutes. She did finally start to look as though it were an effort. Her face showed, "Well, should I stay and wait this out, or should I excuse myself and take off?" I allowed Mildieu to exercise her self-restraint for a few more seconds. Then I moved you from the chair and interested you in something else. As you played, I thanked Mildieu kitty for her kind and gentle patience.

Grandma Ani-Poo came up to play with you for awhile. She arrived just as you were finishing your morning nap. I thought I'd wash my hair, since Grandma was there, in case you woke up before I finished.

You woke up just as I started to dry my hair. Grandma went into your room to get you. You greeted her with a big hug. She was happy and touched. You reached up to her and when she responded with reaching for you, you gave her a huge hug. Grandma Ani-Poo was in heaven.

The last few days, you have been waking up happier, talking to yourself profusely, the way you used to. You do have some trouble getting off to a nap, but the turmoil is short-lived. Sometimes, you just talk and entertain yourself for ten to twenty minutes without going to sleep. At least that gives you a little private time, time free from supervision and from faces that take on a concerned, worried, or even panicked expression when you approach, touch, pick up, or mouth something.

Grandma Ani-Poo walked you around in the hallway. You went long distances, guided by only one hand. Later, you tried walking around in the dining room on your knees. Not crawling, but walking on your knees.

You have acquired a new skill over the last few days. You used to grab your pillow, position it and lie on your side on one arm. Now you ease yourself down to lying on your back with only one arm —occasionally, by pure balance and no supporting arm, with a relatively soft landing. Look, Mom, no hands!" Another development—you have been resisting taking your bottle lying down. You work at taking your bottle sitting up. You have become very good at it, too. You suck out whatever air might be left and then work on sucking in the milk. Lately you prefer this over tilting the bottle upward. You also resist taking your bottles in the rocker, something you had enjoyed so much before your nap and bedtime. Changing preferences are all part of growing up, I suppose.

After your bath this afternoon, you tried your hand at dressing yourself. You took a pair of pants out of your diaper bag and put them against your tummy, so they would look like were actually wearing them. I thought that was very smart. On another attempt, you tried to get your foot in one of the legs, but couldn't quite do it.

Once you were dressed, you were off to explore the kitchen. You came across a paper sack lying on the floor. It must have looked like clothing to you, you tried to put it on. First, you put it on over your tummy. Then, you tried to put it on like a pair of pants. There was a hole, more than big enough to get both of your legs into, but you couldn't get your leg through the end. They just don't make "clothes" the way they used to.

This evening before dinner, I felt like brushing my teeth. Sure enough, you showed your usual interest as I started to brush. I handed your new toothbrush to you and you actually brushed your teeth, or should I say gums.

August 6

I called the zookeeper of a small California zoo today to
see if their facility would be interested in acquiring Basette,
my tiger friend. Her owners have to sell their business.
Basette is allowed to live on the business property, because it
is outside the city limits. She can't live on their home property,
because their home is within the city limits. The bottom line
is that Basette needs a new home. It isn't easy to find a new
home for a tiger, so I wanted to help them find possibilities.

I had a headache this morning. No big deal. I took some
aspirin, but the headache continued to get stronger anyway.
By the time I had to leave for work, it was extremely uncomfortable. I took another dose of aspirin, and had an after lunch
snack, to see if more food would help.

At work, I requested to sit at the cardiac monitors, because
my headache continued to get worse, and walking around
made it more intense. It came to a point, where I could barely
turn my head to either side. It was a profoundly painful effort
just to lean forward in my chair to push the buttons that
generated the printouts of the patient's heart rhythms. As
time passed, it became hard to focus on the rhythm strips to
write the necessary information on them.

The pain continued to accelerate to the point where I just
couldn't function any longer. I had to request to leave. I
couldn't possibly drive, so I called Daddy, told him what was
happening, and that I needed him to come pick me up. It was
9:30 pm. I asked him to call Arlene; to have her or one of her
daughters come to the house to sit with you while Daddy came
after me.

I don't know why I was having this nearly intolerable
explosive pain in my head. Some of my peers suggested it could
be a migraine headache. I had never had one before. They say

migraines are "the worst" headaches. This was without a doubt, the worst. Surely, a good nights sleep would cure it.

August 7

My "worst" headache was even worse this morning. Last night; I didn't think it could possibly become any more painful. It felt like a perpetually mushrooming wave of explosions. Any time I tried to turn my head, change my position, or heaven forbid, have to sneeze, the level, of what felt like internal nuclear fission escalated dramatically.

Our family Doctor, Dr. Jacobs.was nice enough to give me an appointment on a moment's notice this morning. We took you to Winnie's. Then Daddy took me to Dr. Jacobs, who felt certain I had meningitis. Meningitis is an infection, an inflammation of one of the layers of tissue that surround the brain and spinal cord. Dr. Jacobs wasn't sure which type, or of the severity. He asked us to meet him at the emergency room where he would take a sample of my spinal fluid for analysis.

Shortly after we arrived in the emergency room, Dr. Jacobs preformed the lumbar puncture to obtain the sample of spinal fluid for testing.

The sample of fluid he took wasn't conclusive regarding whether the meningitis was viral or bacterial. The bacterial version was treatable with antibiotics. The viral (virus) version wouldn't respond to antibiotics. Just as with a flu, you can't kill a virus with antibiotics; you rest in bed and drink plenty of fluids (and hurt). Sound familiar? In this case, you also treated the pain.

Dr. Jacobs admitted me into the hospital. He put me on the appropriate antibiotics, in case the infection was bacterial. Tomorrow morning, he will do another lumbar puncture to determine which version of infection it was.

Even though the viral version is not treatable, it would be the lesser of the two evils for us, as far as you were concerned.

Bacterial meningitis could be devastating for you, if you were to get it. The viral form would not be so grim.

I missed my little Tiffany. I was afraid of what the Doctor might find. I didn't want anything bad to happen to you. The fears were hard to handle in the midst of the incredible pain. They gave me morphine for the pain. I would welcome any degree of relief. I just wanted the nurses to give me the medication, turn off the lights, and leave me alone. I needed to escape the pain, at least some of it.

It will be a few days before I will get to see you again. Be healthy, and enjoy the "one-on-one" time with your Daddy, in the meantime.

August 8

The results of the second lumbar puncture were conclusive; the meningitis was viral.

The pain during the day today was horribly difficult, the evening was a little better. The morphine took away almost half of the pain. I wished it would take all of it, but half was still a welcome relief.

Daddy told me you took a lot of steps at Winnie's today.

August 9

The morphine took care of all of the pain, so we switched to a synthetic narcotic tablet. It only took care of about half of the pain, but I could take it home with me. I couldn't take the IV morphine home. Since the pain was the only thing they could treat at the hospital, the meningitis being viral, I pushed to be discharged. I could be in pain at home. I couldn't afford to stay in the hospital if I didn't absolutely have to, no matter how run down I was. I was still paying the hospital, in installments, for your delivery last year.

I talked with Dr. Jacobs and Dr. Kelley, this morning, about what types of precautions and how much contact I would be allowed to have with you. The answer: limit close contact, wear a face mask during close contact, no kissing and no big huggies.

How awful. But, of course, we'll stick to it. We don't want to do anything to increase your chance of getting this nasty bug. Dr. Jacobs discharged me from the hospital at about 2:30 pm. Daddy took me home, tucked me in, and then drove back to Winnie's to get you.

August 10

You clung to Daddy when he took you to Winnie's today. You didn't want to leave him again. This made the fifth day in a row that you had spent the whole day at Winnie's. My poor baby must be confused and scared. You hadn't seen your Mommy for three days. You've only seen Daddy for a few minutes in the morning, and a few minutes before bed, for the last four days. That was just too much. I asked Daddy to go back and get you at 2:30 pm.

August 11

Grandma Ani-Poo and Popie came over this afternoon. They had just arrived back in town from a short trip. They didn't know that I was sick until they arrived today. Once you arrived home from Winnie's, you had a great time playing with Grandma Ani-Poo and Popie. You were so hungry for **family**, and so confused by all of the separation.

You took a lot of steps on your own, just for Grandma Ani-Poo and Popie. You obviously felt better. I could hear you talking and laughing from the bedroom. It was so nice to hear all of those little "Tiffi noises" in the house. I **really** missed that. You said, "Ooooh" to Grandma. You also had some nice talks with Mildieu.

August 13

You walked five feet today all by yourself. You nodded your head "yes" a few times over the last couple of days, purposefully, though not necessarily appropriately.

August 14

Today, you fed yourself a spoonful of vegetables. The spoon was right side up, too. And you said, "ti-er" (tiger) for the first time.

August 15

So far, you showed no sign of flu, fever, vomiting or any of the other problems we were told to watch for. Thank goodness!

Grandma Ani-Poo and Popie came over today to let you play in your wading pool. You frequently walked two or more feet, unsupported!

August 16

You were fussy, off and on, today. In the evening, you felt hot. Your temperature was 103.5 degrees. You vomited twice, once was the acetomeniphen I had given you. You were having frequent loose stools. I was scared.

I called Dr. Kelley who said it only sounded like an intestinal flu; that it was common for the same virus that causes meningitis to manifest itself differently in a baby. Wonderful!

We could easily live with that. I hated for you to have the flu. But, far better the flu than the meningitis.

August 17

You walked all the way across the living room today, even though you had a temperature of 103.0 degrees. By early afternoon, you were tired and fussy from the fever. Who wouldn't be?

Mommy's pain medicine now takes care of all of the head pain, so I am a little more mobile. I actually got out of bed for more than an hour at a time today. Now that my head isn't constantly "exploding" every time I moved, I noticed how "just plain sick" I really feel.

August 18

Today, your temperature was 100.5, you're having less diarrhea, and are feeling more like yourself.

August 19

Grandma Ani-Poo and Popie took you to their house today. You went for a walk in their pecan orchard. You kept walking over into your Grand-Uncle Jack's walnut orchard, the property next to Grandma Ani-Poo and Popie's.

During your bath, there today, you helped by trying to wash your hands and feet. After your bath, you tried to put your shoes on by yourself. You have always been **quite** good at taking them off. Now, you were trying your hand at putting them on.

August 20

No fever today. Terrific! You went back to Grandma's. I haven't been very good company the last two weeks, being so sick. I couldn't spend more than a little bit of time with you even when I wanted to. Grandma Ani-Poo and Popie were much more entertaining and I needed the rest. So for now, this worked out best for everybody.

When you came home tonight, you were so endearing. You wouldn't take "no" for an answer when you gave me a long tight hug. You waved "hi" and "bye-bye" every time I entered or left the room. You were so sweet. I'll be glad when we could get back to huggies and lovies, as usual.

August 23

The last couple of days, you have fed yourself many spoonfuls of food. Most of the time, the spoon was right side up! You also mimiced the melody of words that you weren't able to say. If someone said, "Hello, Tiffi," you would mimic the inflections of the phrase using whatever syllables suited your fancy. The syllables were different, but the sound, and the cadence were the same.

Today was Mommy's two week follow-up appointment. Dr. Jacobs told me to get more rest, because my lab test results needed to be better and my blood pressure was too high. High blood pressure is very unusual for me. My blood pressure usually borders on being too low. He scheduled a follow-up appointment for two weeks from today.

August 24

You now take us by the hand, actually the thumb or finger and lead us. This usually means you want to go for a walk, or to go up and down the two carpeted steps to the "sunken" living room. You are so precious.

August 25

This was "animal day" for you. You spent most of the day with or talking to Teaki, Libra and Mildieu. You said, "hello" to the dogs through the sliding glass door. If Libra saw you, she would slowly, quietly walk up to the door and kiss you through the glass.

Twice, you spotted Mildieu during your play, said, "hello" and walked over to pet her. You didn't stay long. You just talked and petted for a couple of minutes and went on your way. I'm sure that was the perfect visit as far as Mildieu was concerned.

Epilogue

When I look back at these entries, I realize, again, their importance. As I read them, I remember. I am able to relive the true flavor of the events, and I am surprised at how much I would have forgotten without this record. When you were three months old, I read through the journal to date, and found some things I had completely forgotten. Those experiences were less than three months in the past. I had considered some of them experiences I thought I would never forget. I would never want to have let the hundreds of special moments fade to a soft blur. This ongoing letter to you, Tiffany, was not easy to keep. But I was committed to doing so. It was very important to me that you have this journal. Few people know so many of the things that happened to them and around them during their first years of life—a time of which few people have a functioning recall. I want you to have that knowledge, an insight into a very special time. Thank you, Tiffany, for blessing us with your precious and unconditional love and your happy and gentle manner. You are a treasure and I truly Love You.

Secrets of Successful Journaling

What you need to keep a journal

1. Purchase a "u-fill-em-up" blank book.
2. Keep a book mark in your journaling book.
3. Keep a pen clipped to your journaling book.
4. Record in your journaling book everyday.

Blank books come in many different sizes from pocket-size to large sketch books. Lined blank books are, of course, the easiest to use. But if you have artistic abilities, you may want to consider a sketch book for combining writing with your artwork. There are also a wide variety of styles and covers available—plain, fabric and illustrated.

To save time, choose a bookmark and keep it in your journaling book to mark your current page. This will save you time when you go to your book to journal. If you want to get fancy, stitch a ribbon onto the binding, at the back edge of the pages, to use as your bookmark.

Keeping a pen with the book will prevent you from having to locate one each day when you are ready to journal. You may want to slip it between the spine, or edge of the book and the bound pages themselves—depending on how the book is bound. You could also clip it to the cover, or secure it with a rubberband.

How you can keep a journal

Optimally, you should choose one place and one time of day to do your writing. Use that same place every day for your writing. This place could be in your kitchen, in your bedroom, favorite chair, under your favorite tree or in the employee lounge where you work. Preferably, it is a quiet place where you can think.

The benefit, of using the same place every day, is when you go to that place regularly to do your writing, you come to associate it with writing. Within a short time, you should be able to program yourself to write when in that area or chair.

The same is true for writing at the same time of day—be it in the morning, in the evening after a meal, or before bed. If you write at the same time each day you will, as with writing in the same place, program yourself to write at that time of day. The two of these steps used together will prove to be a very powerful method in aiding your flow of thoughts.

The next best thing is to keep the pen clipped to the journaling book, as mentioned, and mentally commit yourself to maintaining it for two weeks. Writing in it every day, at whatever place you can and at whatever time you can, each day is a good start. If you tell yourself you don't have the time—**make** the time!

Research studies tell us that it takes seven days of repeating a task, seven days in a row, to develop a habit. Committing to journaling for two weeks will give you a solid base for a new habit. At the end of that two weeks commit to it for another two weeks, and stick to it. By that time, you will have a semi-automatic habit to journal, even if you are doing it at different places and different times each day.

Unfortunately, most of us have heavy demands on our time—we work, go to school, or have more than one child in the family—and can't always manage to write in the same place or at the same time. Most people are just too busy these days to manage that.

Anyone who has raised children knows that time is a precious resource. I committed myself to "making" the time to write. Whether the time was during a nap, while Tiffany amused herself playing, or as she or our cat, Mildieu, sat on my lap "helping" me write, I wrote. You too can do it; but you must commit to it in the beginning, and stick to your commitment for the two week period to build a solid habit base. You can do it if you want to.

If you falter in your commitment in the first two weeks, don't give up. Give yourself another chance and try again, this time with a stronger commitment to journaling every day for the two weeks.

Remember to write what you feel. Don't worry about your spelling or your grammar—it isn't going to be graded! Just write. If you make it too hard on yourself in the beginning, you will be less likely to stay with it. Be easy on yourself. Enjoy yourself. Congratulate yourself on what you are trying to. Develop your habit first, then you can pay more attention to your literary skills.

Remember to get **something**, anything, down on paper to start with. It's staring at a blank page that stops people from writing. Simply write. You can edit later. You can't write (create) and edit at the same time. Let your thoughts flow through your pen or pencil. Once you begin to write, the thoughts and the feelings will come.

Bibliography

Caplan, Frank and Theresa A. Caplan. *The First Twelve Months of Life.* New York: Bantam Books, 1984.

Korte, Diana and Roberta Scaer. *A Good Birth, A Safe Birth.* New York: Bantam Books, 1984.

Simkin, Penny, R.P.T.; Janet Whalley, R.N., B.S.N.; and Ann Keppler, R.N. M.N. *Pregnancy Childbirth and the Newborn, A Complete Guide for Expectant Parents.* Minnesota: Meadowbrook Press, 1984.

The Merck Manual. New Jersey: Merck Sharp and Dohme Research Laboratories. 1984.

O r d e r   B l a n k

Tender Moments makes an excellent gift book for mothers, grandmothers, child educators, students of child development, and people who enjoy children.

Please, send me _____ copies of *Tender Moments Diary of a First-time Mother* @ **$12.95** per copy.

For 3 or more copies, $9.70 each (a 25% discount per copy).

Telephone Orders: 1-800-548-4556. Have your Mastercard, Visa, or American Express card ready.

Postal Orders: Pacific Coast Publishers, 710 Silver Spur Road, Suite 126-F, Rolling Hills Estates, CA 90274-3695 U.S.A. Make checks payable to: Pacific Coast Publishers

Name: _____

Address: _____

City/State: _____ Zip: _____

Californians, please, add 6.25 % sales tax.

Shipping: $1.65 for first book, and 75 cents for each additional book.

☐ I can't wait 3-4 weeks for my order via book rate. Here is $4.15 per book for air mail shipping.

☐ Please, send me a FREE copy of *Secrets of Successful Journaling*. I am enclosing a self-addressed, stamped envelope.

—— Attention Schools, Businesses and Organizations ——

Tender Moments is available at quantity discounts with bulk purchases for fund-raisers, education, business, or sales promotional use.

Order Blank

Tender Moments makes an excellent gift book for mothers, grandmothers, child educators, students of child development, and people who enjoy children.

Please, send me ____ copies of *Tender Moments Diary of a First-time Mother* @ $12.95 per copy.

For 3 or more copies, $9.70 each (a 25% discount per copy).

Telephone Orders: 1-800-548-4556. Have your Mastercard, Visa, or American Express card ready.

Postal Orders: Pacific Coast Publishers, 710 Silver Spur Road, Suite 126-F, Rolling Hills Estates, CA 90274-3695 U.S.A.
Make checks payable to: Pacific Coast Publishers

Name: _____

Address: _____

City/State: _____ Zip: _____

Californians, please, add 6.25 % sales tax.

Shipping: $1.65 for first book, and 75 cents for each additional book.

☐ I can't wait 3-4 weeks for my order via book rate. Here is
  $4.15 per book for air mail shipping.
☐ Please, send me a FREE copy of *Secrets of Successful Journaling*. I
  am enclosing a self-addressed, stamped envelope.

—— Attention Schools, Businesses and Organizations ——
Tender Moments is available at quantity discounts with bulk purchases for fund-raisers, education, business, or sales promotional use.